Deleuze and History

Deleuze Connections

"It is not the elements or the sets which define the multiplicity. What defines it is the AND, as something which has its place between the elements or between the sets. AND, AND, AND – stammering.'

Gilles Deleuze and Claire Parnet, *Dialogues*

General Editor
Ian Buchanan

Editorial Advisory Board
Keith Ansell-Pearson
Rosi Braidotti
Claire Colebrook
Tom Conley
Gregg Lambert
Adrian Parr
Paul Patton
Patricia Pisters

Titles Available in the Series
Ian Buchanan and Claire Colebrook (eds), *Deleuze and Feminist Theory*
Ian Buchanan and John Marks (eds), *Deleuze and Literature*
Mark Bonta and John Protevi (eds), *Deleuze and Geophilosophy*
Ian Buchanan and Marcel Swiboda (eds), *Deleuze and Music*
Ian Buchanan and Gregg Lambert (eds), *Deleuze and Space*
Martin Fuglsang and Bent Meier Sørensen (eds), *Deleuze and the Social*
Ian Buchanan and Adrian Parr (eds), *Deleuze and the Contemporary World*
Constantin V. Boundas (ed.), *Deleuze and Philosophy*
Ian Buchanan and Nicholas Thoburn (eds), *Deleuze and Politics*
Chrysanthi Nigianni and Merl Storr (eds), *Deleuze and Queer Theory*
Jeffrey A. Bell and Claire Colebrook (eds), *Deleuze and History*
Laura Cull (ed.), *Deleuze and Performance*

Forthcoming Titles in the Series
Mark Poster and David Savat (eds), *Deleuze and New Technology*
Ian Buchanan and Laura Guillaume (eds), *Deleuze and the Body*
Stephen Zepke and Simon O'Sullivan (eds), *Deleuze and Contemporary Art*
Paul Patton and Simone Bignall (eds), *Deleuze and the Postcolonial*

Deleuze and History

Edited by Jeffrey A. Bell and
Claire Colebrook

Edinburgh University Press

Edinburgh University Press Ltd
22 George Square, Edinburgh

www.euppublishing.com

Typeset in 10.5/13 Sabon
by Servis Filmsetting Ltd, Stockport, Cheshire, and
printed and bound in Great Britain by
CPI Antony Rowe, Chippenham and Eastbourne

A CIP record for this book is available from the British Library

ISBN 978 0 7486 3608 2 (hardback)
ISBN 978 0 7486 3609 9 (paperback)

Contents

Introduction

Claire Colebrook

Post-structuralism, Postmodernism and Historicism

Perhaps no writer of the twentieth century has done more to intensify the experience of time as Gilles Deleuze. Drawing on the philosophy of Henri Bergson, who had already insisted that the human intellect tends to spatialise time in order to make its efficient and ready way in the world (Bergson 1931), Deleuze went even further than Bergson in calling for a thought of time in its pure state: an intuition of duration that would not impose a uniform clock time on the diverse fluxions of this creative universe. As I will argue in the conclusion of this chapter, it was Deleuze's argument in favour of intensive quantities – against Bergson's rejection of this notion in *Time and Free Will* (1910) – that led the way for Deleuze and Guattari to posit a human history beyond humanity: that is, Deleuze and Guattari produce a 'deep' history that accounts for the emergence of the human according to man's capacity to reduce all intensities to calculable quantities; this reaches its zenith in capitalism, but can also be overcome in capitalism through death. Death, for Deleuze and Guattari, will be the human being's capacity to experience the annihilation of all its coded, historicised and all too human quantities. Man, for Deleuze and Guattari, is produced in history – in narrated, managed, political and epochal time – as an animal who organises matters according to manageable quantities; time in its pure state is intuited, and becomes revolutionary, when intensities are experienced as having their own duration. (We can think, today, of the way human history is confronted with a multitude of other durations, from the slow geological time whose production of fossil fuels is now bringing 'man's' own history into crisis, to the high speeds of imaging and nano-technologies that will create non-human modes of production.) However, it is Deleuze's very inflation of the importance and distinction of time that seems to entail a critique and possible annihilation of history: any narrative, mapping or sequence that would place events in a causal order, and would try to understand relations among individuals, environments, social systems, power structures and political movements, would of necessity have to downplay the incommensurability of durations. Often, as many of the essays in this volume indicate, Deleuze and Guattari did seem to argue against the explanatory power of historicism, and in this regard we could place them within a post-Marxist and post-1968 milieu that would reject grand narratives and causal explanations in favour of *events*.

Whereas Marxism, which ranges from a vulgar economic determinism to a complex understanding of history as an interpretive horizon (Jameson 1981), ultimately must – *as Marxism* – rely on a minimal degree of historical sense, the concept of the event has been theorised in such a way as to account for a radical break or rupture with history, predictability, causation, continuity and any notion of human time as an adequate mapping of life in general. Various forms of Marxism had attempted to be post-Hegelian: attending to material conditions and non-conscious or unintentional lines of causality without presupposing an inevitable economic trajectory that would unfold from some proper human essence. Perhaps the most significant of such ventures was that of Louis Althusser, for whom the economy was determining only in 'the last instance', and for whom the subject was an effect of ideology (Althusser 1971). There could be no retrieval of man as a praxis-oriented individual from the alienation of labour and political structures; for Althusser the subject was an effect of such structures, with the structure of ideology being crucial in the experience of oneself as a seeming agent. Ideology was not an unfortunate illusion that the study of material history might erase. On the contrary, the very notion of a self who might view, comprehend and master his own historical narration was an effect of ideology. The only properly Marxist response, for Althusser, was science: an examination of economic relations that would reveal the contradictions of capitalism. The ideal would not be the liberation of humanity in its practical, social, communicative and labouring essence, but an overcoming of the lures of subjectivity as the locus of truth. Althusser was, in this regard, in tune with a much broader movement opposed both to hermeneutics (or the interpretation of history to disclose its underlying sense) and its accompanying notions of experience or 'the lived'. There was no longer any question of discerning the authentic human potentiality prior to its fall into alienation and historical causation; for the very experience of history as a human narrative was *imaginary*: there is no reason or intentionality in history, but we nevertheless live our economic (or inhuman) conditions and events as though they made sense or were in accord with some general march of human reason (Jameson 1978). Both Althusser and Fredric Jameson and, much later, Alain Badiou, would draw positively upon the work of Jacques Lacan: there is no subject of intentionality who goes through time and history and whose agency we can track. On the contrary, there is only a random and contingent series of events and it is from this sequence of the 'real' that we posit a subject who must have been their hidden or alienated cause. The subject is not the victim of history so much as the lure or illusion we posit when we create history as a meaningful and intentional sequence (Žižek 1999).

One way of understanding postmodernism or post-1968 thought is as a general retreat from history in favour of disrupted and disruptive localised claims each with their own timelines and schemas of narration. Fredric Jameson has lamented this loss of a sense of history and has aimed to retain a properly Marxist attention to narrative modes of understanding, even if such narratives are now read as socially symbolic acts that are required to order a history that is an ultimate but unrepresentable 'real'. But in many respects Marxists like Jameson and Terry Eagleton (1997), who see postmodernism as an impoverished restriction of politics to differential textual relations, are arguing a losing battle, for even if one wishes to maintain historical sense it is hard to do so in an age of globalism with its competing narratives, worldviews, timelines and increasingly inhuman scales of temporality. In the case of Jean-François Lyotard's *The Postmodern Condition* (1984), the rejection of grand narratives precludes any unified understanding of the flow of time and necessitates, instead, a regime of incommensurable phrases. In terms of historical understanding this might appear to lead to historicism, or the rejection of a unified history in favour of a series of competing historical narratives or 'petit récits', all articulating local and located viewpoints. More influential for the practice of historians was Michel Foucault's argument for an archaeology of knowledge: there can be no continuous historical narration precisely because the very notion of the narrator ('man' or 'humanity') alters and varies, as does the very experience of time and space that is narrated (Foucault 1972). Foucault referred to the 'historical a priori', indicating that history was at once a priori (and therefore not the history of 'man' or subjectivity) at the same time as the a priori was itself historical. The very relation between the 'inside' and 'outside', or thought and its exterior, is itself historically contingent (Foucault 1970). Today we may think of life as intrinsically historical, with 'man' becoming what he is through time; but this is itself an historical phenomenon, and quite different from pre-modern conceptions of a humanity that was merely one aspect of a cosmos with an essence that could only be discerned, in part and by analogy, by our finite understanding.

It was perhaps Jacques Derrida's deconstruction that has been most responsible for the perception that post-'68 French thought was a form of anti-historicism, idealism, textualism or overly individualist attention to events. Derrida's early work had, in fact, begun with a recognition of the extreme importance of *genesis*: countering any structuralist forms of historicism that would simply place one cultural paradigm after another, Derrida insisted that a truly responsible mode of thinking would have to account for the emergence of various historical totalities *and* their relation to truth, which could not be reduced to an infra-historical determination (Derrida 2003). Already in his early criticisms of phenomenology and its attempt to enclose history within the 'lived' of human sense and experience, Derrida had rejected Marxist appropriations of phenomenology. Tran Duc Thao's *Phenomenology and Dialectical Materialism* (1986) had tied Husserl's insistence on the necessity of giving an account of the genesis of formal structures, such as language and logic, with a Marxist attention to the extra-individual and economic-material conditions of emergence. Such an attention to the retrieval of origins, Derrida argued, was at once the height of philosophical responsibility at the same time as it precluded a consideration of those anarchic or untamed forces that disrupted any meaningful structure (Derrida 1978). Notoriously, Derrida would refer to such forces as '*écriture*', 'trace' or '*différance*': in order for an experienced sense to be transmitted through time it must be inscribed in some manner of formal system – ranging from a repeatable gesture to linguistic signifiers. But this would mean that any experience of the present would never be in full command of itself, for in order to live or experience a 'now' as this identifiable now I must have already marked or determined it in some way, anticipated its carrying-over into the future. Husserl had already insisted that the lived present was composed of retentions and protentions; experience is always, in part, a retaining of what has been and a projection of what will come. Derrida radicalises this manoeuvre by arguing that this process of temporal synthesis is not consciousness' own: in the narrow sense we would require something like writing or signs in order for consciousness to mark out a relation or series of times. In his later work on Marx, Derrida (1994) extended this criticism of the lived present to argue for the necessity of mourning, ghosts and spectrality at the heart of experience or spirit. We cannot simply follow Marx and see consciousness or man as having a proper human and self-commanding essence that falls into the division of labour but then retrieves its proper potential when it understands its own history. Indeed, to be faithful to the spirit of Marx and Marx's materialism, we must recognise that we inherit the past as a body of work to be read; this means that the sense or potential of the past is never fully given, for its ghosts, and possible futures, may always be re-read or re-encountered. This does not lead to an ahistorical free for all; on the contrary, it is precisely because the past remains as a spectre or ghostly present, haunting us, that 'our' future is always open. To read Marx, or the past, is to open the present to that which it does not fully command or comprehend.

In many respects, as I have already suggested, Deleuze and Guattari might be placed within this milieu of post-'68 counter-historicism, insisting on the aleatory and rupturing nature of the event. Their *A Thousand Plateaus* (as indicated by its title) refuses to posit any plane or regime that might account for the movement and nature of other durations. Not only are the plateaus of this text marked by dates that signal distinct speeds – such as the points within textual history where science discerns geological formations or when linguists take formal systems as the basis of all sense and meaning – Deleuze and Guattari also offer a direct criticism of the 'despotism of the signifier'. In addition to the experience of life undertaken by man as a speaking and gesturing animal there are also potentialities for events at the molecular level – too fast or small for the human eye – along with the slow time of evolutionary creation. The very structure of *A Thousand Plateaus* as a series of plateaus, which the authors suggest can be read in any sequence, supports a philosophy of events: whatever the seeming consistency of a plane or point of view it is always possible for a potentiality to alter the very nature of what might seem to be possible. In Deleuze's work this attention to singularities, events, the aleatory, the virtual and the *incorporeal* – as well as the imperative of counter-actualisation, or thinking of the larger range of potentials from which this actual world has been generated – appears to legitimate a philosophy of becoming *against* history. That is, even when history is an attempt to denaturalise or de-universalise the present by showing how things might have been otherwise, it tends to focus on possibility rather than potentiality, or the possible rather than the virtual. We could, for example, look back at the English Revolution and at the debates among levellers, ranters, shakers, the new model army and parliament and argue that from this range of voices a more radical form of government (perhaps communist or socialist) might have been possible (Hill 1972). Or, we could take the same historical moment, traditionally narrated in terms of agents and larger political forces, and introduce broader material forces, such as the flows of goods, bodies and matter made possible by various levels of transportation, technological development, climactic and geographic milieus and demographics (DeLanda 1997).

Focusing on possibility, or the play of various factors in any actual 'slice' of time, would demand a shift from extensive and linear explanation – one event after another in a sequence that can be narrated according to one point of view (such as the history of ideas, economic history or social history) – towards intensive and non-linear history. As intensive, time would not be a sequence of equivalent units; some times – such as a century of industrial revolution, or the last decade of the twentieth century in which research on the brain developed at an exponential rate – would witness a massively complex pace of change across a number of levels; the human body would move differently, think differently, be connected to other bodies in different ways (from literal modes of transportation to immaterial forms of imaging and communication). These intensities require non-linear models, for it may be the case that one series of becoming (such as technological development) may create a slowing down in another (so that the expansion of human efficiency machines in factory labour might lead to forms of corporeal impoverishment precluding the development of language skills), and these in turn would need to be connected to geopolitical timelines, such as the 'development' of Western consumer cultures and their increasing efficiency through the connection of their sign systems, economic modes of production and military regimes with geographic milieus, whose histories operate at different speeds and intensities. But even this attention to the range of material possibilities not accounted for by a series of human agents and conscious attentions does not account for the strong sense of the virtual, becoming and singularity that Deleuze would express in a number of texts that might appear to be at odds with the more historical and materialist focus of *A Thousand Plateaus*. We could then, as Slavoj Žižek (2004) has done, mark an opposition between the realism of Deleuze and Guattari and an idealist, otherworldly Deleuze of texts such as *The Logic of Sense* (Deleuze 1990a). It is this 'second' Deleuze who attends to 'time in its pure state', who stresses 'incorporeal events' and who favours a time of Aion (an eternal time, not spaced out into a sequence, in which any body would be both expanding and diminishing at once, for only temporally located and finite viewpoints determine relations of more or less, greater or smaller) over a time of Chronos, the clock time that is spaced out into units and can be added and subtracted into notions of more or less, before and after. Žižek's parsing of Deleuze into an idealist and materialist depending on the occasion is a mistake; for the radical nature of Deleuze's materialism lies in its capacity to account for the genesis of the virtual, the incorporeal and the eternal *in matter*. Matter itself, and not human speculation or thought, creates the virtual, the incorporeal and sense. This can be understood if we distinguish between bodies (including social bodies, political bodies, bodies of knowledge and other individuals, including sign systems, artworks and theories) and matter, which is a potentiality for the assemblage of bodies, and which is both real and virtual. As real, matter is not generated from anything else, and does not require anything else in order to 'be'; as virtual, matter has no intrinsic body or predetermined relations, and is that from which actual bodies, relations and spatio-temporal co-ordinates emerge (Deleuze and Guattari 1977: 53). In terms of history this has four consequences which can be discerned across all of Deleuze's and Deleuze and Guattari's work, but which is given explicitly in *Anti-Oedipus*, the first volume of *Capitalism and Schizophrenia*.

> We can say that social production, under determinate conditions, derives primarily from desiring production: which is to say that *Homo Natura* comes first. But we must also say, more accurately, that desiring-production is first and foremost social in nature, and tends to free itself only at the end: which is to say that *Homo historia* comes first. (Deleuze and Guattari 1977: 33)

Four Theses on History

1. It is possible and necessary to write a universal history, and to do so requires a history undertaken from the point of view of capitalism as the 'truth' or hidden logic of all previous epochs: 'it is correct to retrospectively understand all history in the light of capitalism' (Deleuze and Guattari 1977: 140).
2. There is nothing inevitable about capitalism and genuinely non-capitalist social formations have occurred. Indeed, the task of genuine historical research requires that we think beyond the seeming universality of the capitalist paradigm. In turn, thinking beyond capitalism requires a genuine historical sense: 'universal history is the history of contingencies' (Deleuze and Guattari 1977: 140).
3. Thinking can only be diminished and impoverished by focusing on conditions of emergence, on contexts, on causes and on probabilities. Great thought is untimely; it seizes upon a truth or essence that cannot be reduced to its occurrence within chronological time. If philosophy, art and science have any value it is only insofar as they transcend lived time

to grasp that which has a radically eternal reality. To write a history of art, a history of philosophy or a history of science is a domesticating act that can only diminish the force of scientific, philosophical and artistic events.

4. Real history is materialist history. Such a history is tied to capitalism precisely because capital (or the liberation of matters from formed bodies) is the tendency of matter itself. Histories of bodies – the history of men, societies, ideas, networks, artworks, or geological bodies – need to be coupled with the intuitions made possible by capitalism: matter may tend towards stratification or the formation of relatively stable bodies, but matter also has another side or concomitant tendency towards escape, a line of flight, deterritorialisation or de-actualisation. Both of these tendencies or sides of matter can be intuited in a genuinely materialist history, which for the Deleuze and Guattari of *Anti-Oedipus* is also a genuinely Marxist history.

Deleuze and Guattari are committed to all four of these claims, and yet at first glance such postulates appear to be mutually exclusive or in contradiction. At the very least they seem to be at odds with one of the ideas we might have of Deleuze and Guattari – that they are resistant to any of the grand narratives that would place the present situation of capitalism and subjectivity in some evolutionary trajectory, a trajectory that would also intimate capitalism's potential demise. It is the peculiarly complex relation among these four postulates that also enables Deleuze and Guattari to enact a new method of historiography.

To begin with, we might ask just what it is that Deleuze and Guattari are writing a history of, or what their universal history in both volumes of *Capitalism and Schizophrenia* is attempting to historicise. According to Deleuze, if we want to understand an author we need to see the problem to which they are responding. The problem of *Anti-Oedipus* is perhaps *the* problem of political theory: how is it that desiring life enslaves itself, and is not merely duped by fascism but desires fascism? Deleuze and Guattari refuse to pass too quickly, or unhistorically, to an answer. They will not simply posit a beginning in which life is complete and unfallen: a primitive communism that would then be overtaken, accidentally, by some fall into alienation or capitalism. Instead they begin from the present – from the situation of the bourgeois capitalist subject – and ask: what is life such that the present is possible?

> If the universal comes at the end – the body without organs and desiring-production – under the conditions determined by an apparently victorious capitalism, where do we find enough innocence for generating universal history? (Deleuze and Guattari 1977: 139)

This brings us directly to history or the genesis of the present and is in accord with Deleuze's entire commitment to a vitalist geneticism; one ought not to accept any already given and actualised form but should ask how such a form emerged, what that emergence can tell us about the life from which any actuality has taken shape, and how such a life – beyond its already created possibilities – might yield other potentials. History, then, should not take the terms already given, such as man, subjectivity, the polis, the speaking subject or the family, as its point of departure. Rather, history needs to account for the genesis of the subject.

On the one hand a genuinely historical account must be sensitive to the alterations, mutations, transformations and accidents that occur through time. A history that took any object – man, society, organisms, language, laws, the family, totalitarianism – as its point of departure would not be truly historical; it would have taken time as a process of genuine becoming and mapped that time according to one static unit. This problem of the genesis of actual, lived or corporeal bodies, alongside the incorporeal events that disclose that *other time* of the virtual which exists and insists to disturb clock time or spatialised time, is central to Deleuze's reading of Bergson, his books on cinema and his work (with Guattari) on language: the intellect tends to take processes of complex difference that are radically temporal (where becoming is not the change *of* some underlying stable form but an intensive process of fluxes without any resting point) and fix that differential multiplicity into a series of stable units. In terms of history this occurs when we see history as the process of interacting human agents; we take an historical result (modern man) and use that as our unit of measure. The same would apply if we took any social formation, such as the family or 'society' (as a collection of speaking rational agents) and then traced various changes *of* this unit, rather than seeing the unit itself as the result of temporal change.

On the other hand, insofar as we want to step back from any constituted unit (man, society, economies, cultures, languages) in order to trace the genesis of those 'assemblages', we need to be talking about something; Deleuze's philosophy aims at 'time in its pure state', which is time *as such* and not the temporal change *of* any object. Deleuze and Guattari's project in *Capitalism and Schizophrenia* aims to inject this radical temporality into a frozen form: the man or subject whom we take to be the agent of history is himself an event within history, and when we want to talk about that broader history beyond man we are really talking about *life*: 'Hence it is at the level of a generalised theory of flows that one is able to reply to the question: how does one come to desire strength while also desiring one's own impotence?' (Deleuze and Guattari 1977:

239). It is for this reason that Deleuze and Guattari conclude *Anti-Oedipus* with a comparison between traditional vitalisms (which posit some generative purposive force – often anthropomorphic – flowing through matter) and mechanism, in which the real is composed of nothing more than random collisions of material units (Deleuze and Guattari 1977: 284). Their path between these two possibilities depends upon a redefinition of the concept of death, which they see as dominating contemporary capitalism and which precludes us from intuiting those radical forces in capitalism that expose a genuine, virtualist, radically historical and micropolitical vitalism. To anticipate the conclusion of this chapter: death in capitalist social formations is understood as a death instinct, or the tendency of the depletion and spending of forces (Deleuze and Guattari 1977: 334). Death, or zero degree, becomes a way of mapping all social forces as abstract quantities that tend towards the ultimate spending and dissolution. Against this, Deleuze and Guattari posit the experience of death (or, as they refer to it elsewhere, becoming imperceptible, or becoming a body without organs). Here, we take any actualised force, such as the power to see, to speak, to hear, to produce, to love, and imagine its progressive diminution to degree zero; at what thresholds would we still be who we are, how much variance would we be able to bear before becoming radically other? We can consider such a contrast between the death instinct and the experience of death in light of our current historical position. Should we regard the challenges of global warming, climate change, terrorism and inhuman forces as a propulsion of man as a quantum of energy towards depletion and extinction (the death instinct)? Or should we see such forces as the challenge of the experience of death, where we would experiment and imagine what 'we' might be like if we diminished our consumptions and productions, if we reduced – perhaps to the point of non-being – all those forces that we have, until now, taken to be human, and to be the ground of man as historical agent?

Now it is often supposed that vitalism, in its positing of something as general as 'life', is a counter-historical gesture. A radical historicism would commit us to an absence of any general and universalising forms; we could not posit life in general, for we would only know life as it is given in this or that temporally located formation. Such a commitment to a radical historicism would preclude us from talking about 'man', 'human nature', 'laws of historical development', or universal history. The very notion of universal history suggests that whatever historical contingencies we may observe it is nevertheless legitimate to suggest that all differences can be explained according to some law of development.

It is here that we have to add nuance to Deleuze and Guattari's vitalism, which from their earliest statements in *Anti-Oedipus* to their final remarks in *What is Philosophy?* is defined as being situated between vitalism and mechanism in their usual senses. In contrast with a traditional vitalism that would act through matter as an organising principle and would be directed towards some end (as a mode of finalism) Deleuze and Guattari insist that the vital tendency towards difference, creativity and becoming is molecular: it is directed *not* towards the creation or maintenance of some identifiable form but is intrinsically variable, nothing other than a capacity or tendency of variation. It is the concept of the 'machine' that allows Deleuze and Guattari to formulate what they refer to as a passive vitalism: unlike mechanism which is able to explain how systems, bodies, wholes or structures are able to maintain themselves, but which cannot explain how such wholes come into being, nor how they change, vitalism is capable of explaining the formation or genesis of relatively stable forms. This is because Deleuze and Guattari begin from a notion of matter as intensive: matter is not already distributed in space, composed of discrete units that enter into relation, either contingently (mechanism) or according to some over-arching finality (organicism, in which each part is what it is only in accord with its functioning as a part). Matter, as intensity, has a tendency of *desire*: this means that it is oriented beyond itself, not to something it lacks (for that would be the desire of one thing for another), but towards other intensities or forces of desire. It is through that entering into relation of material tendencies or desires that machines are formed.

A machine is at once composed of desires, producing a space or distribution of terms through connection (which Deleuze and Guattari refer to as the first synthesis). But, as they insist throughout their entire corpus, relations are external: so there is always an excess of potentiality in any connection. A desire connects with another desire and actualises a certain relation, or machine, but could also enter into other connections and be actualised differently. This is where Deleuze and Guattari's materialist concept of the virtual allows for a 'machinic' rather than mechanist conception. On a mechanistic account matter is already extensive, already actualised, and one regards time as nothing more than the various combinations into which matter can enter: human bodies may form feudal societies here, capitalist societies there; molecules may form certain substances under these atmospheric conditions, but create different composites in a milieu devoid of oxygen or with a different magnetic field. By contrast, the strong virtual and passive vitalism of Deleuze and Guattari is intensive and differential, and does not stop at ultimate elements but insists that in the beginning are intensities and differential relations. Matter becomes substance or body when (at least) two differentials or intensities enter into relation: the eye and light (a capacity to form an organ of seeing, a capacity for waves to be visualised) are the results of a differential encounter through time that is composed of speeds and thresholds. Multicellular organisms are the result of the entering into relation of chemical capacities of single-celled organisms, with these single-celled organisms being the result of encounters between inorganic chemical capacities. Any organism is, therefore, a composition of connections – the entering into relation of material capacities – along with a series of disjunctions, such that these connections create lines of divergence: the eye and light produce a seeing machine, while other lines of encounter – such as bats and their negotiation of space through sound waves – produce different lines.

We tend to see these first two syntheses of connection and disjunction as 'global' and 'exclusive'. That is we tend to see connection as connection between or among wholes, rather than connection producing wholes. Deleuze and Guattari treat this reference to global wholes as an illegitimate transcendent use of the synthesis: connection is referred to some already existing term rather than the term being explained immanently as the result of connection (Deleuze and Guattari 1977: 46). We mistakenly see history as the relation among bodies (often human bodies), rather than as a field of connections from which bodies are composed. What a body *is* can be understood only through a micro-history, which analyses the production of powers from connections of forces. Deleuze and Guattari's criticism of capitalism in *Anti-Oedipus* is that capitalist historical analyses ultimately rely upon the already constituted aggregates of the family, whereas we should see the family as a machine composed of parts, all of which are directly political and historical. The 'father' and 'mother' are not bodies that allow us to explain the functions of breast, phallus, voice, gaze and so on; rather, it is through a political assemblage – the private practices of breast-feeding and child-rearing, with the father as office worker and wage-earner – that the production of familial persons is to be explained (Deleuze and Guattari 1977: 57). That is, it is only possible to have the white bourgeois man of reason whose organs are privatised – one enjoys art and music in the privacy of one's home, while speech is for communication among individuals, and sexuality a concern of marriage – thanks to a history that has detached organs from their social, historical and molecular field. It is not 'man' who owns an eye that sees, an ear that hears and a voice that speaks; in the beginning are functions, such as a collective visual captivation in spectacle, a primitive pulsation of the ear that urges the body to move, and a chanting of the voice in cries that send charges of desire across a body that is not yet individualised at the level of private persons (Deleuze and Guattari 1977: 211).

Deleuze and Guattari see the body of capitalist man as at once the outcome of a global use of the connective synthesis, which can only see connection among parts, not the creation of parts from the connection of intensities, and as a result of the exclusive use of the disjunctive synthesis (Deleuze and Guattari 1977: 67). One is male *or* female; one either identifies with one's father to be successfully Oedipalised or one suffers from psychosis; one is either the white Western man of reason or some relative other. What cannot be admitted, but is exposed – Deleuze and Guattari argue – in the racial and historical delirium that exists alongside capitalism, is an inclusive use of the disjunctive synthesis: 'All delirium possesses a world-historical, political, and racial content, mixing and sweeping along races, cultures, continents, and kingdoms' (Deleuze and Guattari 1977: 88). Here an individual is 'all the names of history', and this is because any body is individuated and humanised today by adopting a relation to all the intensities of which the modern family is a result (Deleuze and Guattari 1977: 21, 89). The 'father' of the family is also the tax-man, the cop, the banker and the labourer, whose function can in turn only be understood in relation to global markets and the relation between the West and its imagined others, with this field in turn being possible only through transformations of social machines from forms of primitivism and barbarism to modern familial individuals in democracies (Deleuze and Guattari 1977: 64):

> The father, the mother, and the self are at grips with, and directly coupled to, the elements of the political and historical situation – the soldier, the cop, the occupier, the collaborator, the radical, the resister, the boss, the boss's wife . . . the family is never a microcosm in the sense of an autonomous figure, even when inscribed in a larger circle that it is said to mediate and express. . . . There is always an uncle from America; a brother who went bad; an aunt who took off with a military man; a cousin out of work, bankrupt, or a victim of the Crash; an anarchist grandfather; a grandmother in the hospital, crazy or senile. . . . Families are filled with gaps, and transacted by breaks that are not familial: the Commune, the Dreyfus Affair, religion and atheism, the Spanish Civil War, the rise of fascism, Stalinism, the Vietnam war, May '68 – all these things form complexes of the unconscious, more effective than everlasting Oedipus. (Deleuze and Guattari 1977: 97)

This is why Deleuze and Guattari reverse the relation that psychoanalysis establishes between the Oedipal triangle and history. For Freud, earlier formations – such as a collection of bodies whose desire is invested in the king or despot – can be explained because the group fantasy is formed from individual desires: we desire our fathers, originally, but can be socialised to translate that into love of king and country: 'For what is the meaning of "so *that* was what *this* meant"? The crushing of the "so" onto Oedipus and castration. The sigh of relief: you see, the colonel, the instructor, the teacher, the boss, all of *this* meant *that*: Oedipus and castration, "all history in a new version"' (Deleuze and Guattari 1977: 67). For Deleuze and Guattari, all fantasy is historical, political and collective; and all fantasy is group fantasy (Deleuze and Guattari 1977: 62). A social machine begins with the assembling of bodies through intensities, and is initially polyvocal: a tribe becomes one dancing movement with the sound and rhythm of percussive refrains, the visual captivation by body-paints and scars, the spatial distribution of dance formations, and the aural enjoyment of incantations (Deleuze and Guattari 1977: 188). But there is no single code, as there is in the modern 'despotism of the signifier', where we reduce all signs and events to signs *of* a general and represented reality mediated or constructed by the man of communication (Deleuze and Guattari 1977: 206). So, in addition to the synthesis of connection (producing relation of powers across a space, or a territory) and a synthesis of disjunction (creating distinctions between one potential and another, so that one is male or female, this or that tribe), there is also the synthesis of conjunction: all these bodies and powers regarded as parts of a created whole. The illegitimate use of this synthesis of conjunction occurs when we think of this whole as pre-existent, governing and total: so, rather than seeing the great body of capital as that which occurs after bodies have been assembled into markets and productive relations, we see all social forms as explained by capitalism as an economic system. For Deleuze and Guattari capitalism as a social form is also tied to the 'despotism of the signifier', where there is (supposedly) one already actualised and undifferentiated matter, available for distribution, representation and circulation by man as communicating and labouring animal.

Deleuze and Guattari's distinction between capitalism as a virtual tendency or *created* whole existing alongside effected parts (Deleuze and Guattari 1977: 42) and capitalism as an actual body is the key to their universal history. If we see capitalism as virtual then we note that in addition to the capitalist relations we now have, say between one worker and an employer, or a unionised labour force and a group of shareholders, there is also the idea or potentiality of capitalism. This potential, witnessed today in the social political form of capitalism, is the differential: a potentiality of matter as such which has the same pertinence in historical and social analysis as it does in science and art, although it functions in different ways. Deleuze and Guattari argue that capitalism is possible as an actual social and historical form – capitalism as a social body that works to turn all its human parts into motors of production always through the differential relation between labour and capital – because of a tendency in life as such, a tendency that is discernible at the limits of all relations: 'material economic reality [is] the process of production wherein Nature = Industry, Nature = History' (Deleuze and Guattari 1977: 25). We could refer to this potential or tendency as the differential as such. That is, a relation, rather than being overcoded by a transcendent term, is nothing more than the consequence of two mutually productive powers. Life begins not with terms that enter into relation, but with relations among quantities that produce fields or territories of relatively stable terms. This tendency of life as desire or as differential can be seen in capitalism's tendency to liberate all flows and relations from any single organising body (Deleuze and Guattari 1977: 254). Capitalism removes transcendent bodies, such as the monarchy, the Church or State, allowing forces to enter into relation freely. However, even though it has removed all codes and transcendent bodies – for we no longer act for the sake of a transcendent heaven or eternal good – bodies and their powers are axiomatised: measured through one particular differential, the production of labour in relation to capital (Deleuze and Guattari 1977: 223). All production, including the production of ideas, sensations, images and even history, is what it is today through its relation to the axioms of capital. When historical research is evaluated by research councils in terms of its relevance or availability for communities of users, when we watch historical dramas to enjoy and consume a sense of the past, when we wander through Stratford-upon-Avon and pay to enter Anne Hathaway's cottage, and when we think of past epochs as composed of units such as the individual, the family and the community, then we live and move within the logic of actualised capitalism, in which all that exists are human bodies as private and familial individuals, possessed of a past that exists as so many images to be circulated, consumed and exchanged:

> The reign of images is the new way in which capitalism utilizes the schizzes and diverts the flows: composite images, images flattened onto other images, so that when this operation reaches its outcome the little ego of each person, related to its father-mother, is truly the center of the world. (Deleuze and Guattari 1977: 265)

What Deleuze and Guattari want to open up, in their history of capitalism, is the difference between capitalism as a potential for the production of desires through differential relations, and capitalism as an actual social formation that has reduced all potential differentials to relations between bodies as powers of labour and production as production of capital. So, a machinic and vitalist mode of history understands bodies as the effect of the encounter of differentials (the machine), with all individuals bearing a potential for *other* relations (the vital lines of flight that double any body, and indicate a future beyond present possibility):

> It is solely under these conditions that capital becomes the full body, the new socius or the quasi cause that appropriates all of the productive forces. We are no longer in the domain of the quantum or of the quantitas, but in that of the differential relation as a conjunction that defines the immanent social field particular to capitalism, and confers on the abstraction as such its effectively concrete value, its tendency to concretization. The abstraction has not ceased to be what it is, but it no longer appears in the simple quantity as a variable relation between independent terms; it has taken upon itself the independence, the quality of the terms and the quantity of relations. (Deleuze and Guattari 1977: 227)

Mechanism and Vitalism

Consider this in terms of history: a 'mechanist' conception of history would see interactions, encounters, changes, transitions and revolutions as nothing other than the random or chance encounter of elements. More importantly, such elements could have no intrinsic quality or tendency. One could not explain human history according to human nature, and – contra Marxism – the sequence of social and political formations could not be seen to flow from some tendency of economies or technologies towards increasing rationalisation. Certainly, one could not, as Freud was to do, see all human life as structured by an Oedipal narrative – a child's desire for a mother followed by hostility towards, and then identification, with the father – a narrative that, for Freud, could help explain 'primitive' and pre-modern investments in tribal chieftains and emperors as proto-father-figures. A mechanistic account would reject any privileged scene, essence or relation as a way of accounting for human history. It would be opposed both to an idealist form of Freudianism, in which something like the idea or 'signifier' of the phallus would act as a governing force for human relations, and to any form of materialism that posited essences in matter, such as some biological, sexual or human nature that would unfold variously through time. On the contrary, and in accord with a strict commitment to immanence, mechanism posits no force, trajectory or tendency other than that of matter, with matter being devoid of all forms of intentionality, teleology or subjectivity: that is, there is not a 'who' or a 'what' that goes through time or 'has' a history, for history is just the random and undirected production of changes.

One might pause here to see how such a mechanism would also be in accord with a certain form of Darwinism or 'epigenesis': against the notion that it is the organism or whole that maintains itself through time, Darwinism is committed to a random process of variations that produce recognisable forms through populations. What maintains 'itself' through time is not some intentionality of the organism; rather, survival is achieved statistically where some changes are 'selected' because of their relation to other elements. The eye and brain evolve not because life is oriented towards the production of an organism that would be capable of apprehending or giving sense to the world; and capitalism occurs not because it is in the nature of human life to become increasingly instrumental at the level of technology in order to arrive at some final liberation from the needs of life. Neither the human nor modern life has any necessity or meaning. History would be without a subject; history is not the journey through time of a life, for life has no being or sense other than its variation. To a certain extent Deleuze and Guattari's commitment to desiring machines is just such a refusal of both a subject of history and what they refer to as an 'active' vitalism, a vitalism in which there is some underlying activity which discloses itself through time as the agent of history. However, they are also – and precisely through the concept of the machine and the machine *as desire* – equally opposed to a mere mechanism. Their commitment to vitalism is, in contrast with organicist modes where 'life' is taken to be some form of spirit or identity directing matter, an immanently materialist vitalism. Their passive vitalism is committed to, first, a certain pre-formationism (at the level of evolution); second, a universal history with a tendency to capitalism (at the level of social history); *and* third, a commitment to the eternal (at the level of this history of ideas or history of philosophy).

We can sketch these in turn: preformationism refuses the complete mechanism of matter that would create wholes through contingent collisions. For Deleuze and Guattari matter is composed of divergent or singular potentialities. This is not a preformationism of the *organism*, whereby time is the coming to fulfilment of proper forms, but a modified path between finalism and mechanism. There is no single end or actualisation that determines a potentiality, even though every potentiality has its singular power to create different encounters, depending upon the other desires or potentials it encounters. Considered in terms of history, we might say that the French, English, Russian and American

Revolutions could have occurred differently, had other bodies and other locales come into play, but we could also say that there is something like the *Idea* of revolution, which occurs as a potentiality for all social bodies. While this Idea is never exhausted in any actual instance it gives us something like an essence: not essence as a stable form – where all revolutions would share some common core feature – but an essence of variation, where all revolutions express a power to differ: from cultural revolutions, to economic and industrial revolutions, to failed bourgeois revolutions. Deleuze and Guattari conclude *Anti-Oedipus* by referring to the 'abstract subjective essence' of life rendered evident in capitalism (Deleuze and Guattari 1977: 300); this is not man as a proper being, but a capacity for deterritorialisation – or the expansive creativity of desire made possible through the interconnection and redirection of flows of productivity, released from any privileged locus (Deleuze and Guattari 1977: 27). Historical analysis is at once an examination of variation, looking at the ways a potentiality is actualised in particular assemblages, at the same time as it intuits these singular powers, which Deleuze and Guattari name variously, but which include revolution, terror, despotism, the State, exchange, labour, race, sexuality. The point of history is to see these potentialities *beyond* their current Oedipal forms.

In *Anti-Oedipus*, one of the most important of these potentialities is race, for it is race or the distribution of bodies across space, with a reduction of multiple intensive differences to *disjunctions* (this *or* that), that opens the process of human territorialisation from which, eventually, the universal white man of reason will be coded. It is in capitalism, and with the Oedipal concept of the subject, that we posit man as a universal underlying sameness, with all history tending towards man's enlightened recognition of his own self-formation through time:

> The first things to be distributed on the body without organs are races, cultures and their gods. The fact has often been overlooked that the schizo indeed participates in history; he hallucinates and raves universal history, and proliferates the races. All delirium is racial, which does not necessarily mean racist. It is not a matter of the regions of the body without organs 'representing' races and cultures. The full body does not represent anything at all. On the contrary, the races and cultures designate regions on this body – that is, zones of intensities, fields of potentials. (Deleuze and Guattari 1977: 85)

Against that Hegelian conception of human evolution and historicism where 'man' is the destined result of all becoming, Deleuze and Guattari insist that one can write a history of the genesis of the human, looking at the ways various potentialities are actualised (such as the hand that becomes deterritorialised as a tool, and the eye that becomes split into two functions of seeing and reading) but always in relation to other matters that create variation: 'individuations are produced only within fields of forces expressly defined by intensive vibrations, and that animate cruel personages only in so far as they are induced organs, parts of desiring machines' (Deleuze and Guattari 1977: 85).

This leads to the second aspect of their passive vitalism, which is a universal history that can be read through capitalism. Here again, the key distinction is between an active and passive vitalism or, as they term it in *Anti-Oedipus*, between an immanent (legitimate) use of the syntheses and a transcendent (illegitimate) use. If we see capitalism as the proper whole towards which man as a rational animal tends, gradually freeing himself from anti-markets and norms in order to arrive at a purely formal liberalism at the end of ideology, then we have taken one of life's productions – the white bourgeois man of reason, and the capitalist social machine of markets and axioms of labour/capital – and used that to explain life in general. An external, or transcendent, form is assumed from the start. This gives a certain form to the first synthesis of connection, where men gather together to form societies, rather than seeing 'man' as the result of bodies entering into connection. The second synthesis of disjunction, which in its exclusive form demands that one is either male *or* female, socialised under Oedipus *or* psychotic, a useful labouring individual *or* inhuman, can – like the third synthesis of conjunction – be used legitimately to present capitalism as a tendency that allows for a reading of history, not in terms of man as *homo faber*, but with regard to the intensities of matter as desire (Deleuze and Guattari 1977: 309). An inclusive use of disjunction occurs in the racial and historical deliriums that subtend all desires; the father in the Oedipal triangle is merely a point through which one feels the intensity of history. So the father who is an embattled miner, a white supremacist, an arch royalist and a nationalist harking back to a golden age before immigration opens the familial field onto all the codings of history. Desire takes an an-Oedipal and directly revolutionary form when it operates by inclusive disjunction: I am British and black and female and Muslim and a feminist and . . . I am of this family and not of your kind: 'This is free disjunction; the differential positions persist in their entirety, they even take on a free quality, but they are all inhabited by a faceless and transpositional subject' (Deleuze and Guattari 1977: 77). All social machines, Deleuze and Guattari argue, occur through the repression of desiring machines. Bodies can only enter into relation through desire, but when that relation is overcoded or axiomatised certain potentialities for desire are repressed.

Consider the basic form of connection in capitalism, between man and image. In its capitalist form images are circulated through the axiomatics of labour-capital: not only do we buy images (from the designer clothes we purchase to the body-images we ingest and impose on our own selves) we also reduce all circulating matter and relations to nothing but images. We regard matter as so much undifferentiated material to be represented or signified by 'man', the meaning-bestowing animal par excellence. We even see past and future as a domain of images: history as so much narrative material or text, the future as both marketable and manageable at the level of image (both the futures market and future studies). If, however, we begin with the assumption of capitalism, man and the family as the *consequence* of syntheses of connection, disjunction and conjunction, we can then recognise both the contingency of capitalism as a social form, and its deterritorialising tendency or potential in all social machines. Two bodies enter into connection through desire, and in so doing deterritorialise – for the mouth becomes an organ of sucking, chanting, biting, grimacing or speaking depending on the other bodies and milieus it encounters. Such deterritorialisations produce new territories: the child at the breast in the family, the collected tribe, the discoursing community. A social machine creates disjunctions and in so doing precludes certain connections: you marry from this tribe or that, desire males or females, accept social order or psychosis. Capitalism is also a reterritorialisation, for it at once frees relations from external bodies – for *anything* can be an object of exchange, including religious ideas, historical images, academic prestige – while reducing all exchange or flow to the differential relation between a body's productive capacity and capital. History, ideas, politics – all of these can be exchanged, circulated and sold, but always in terms of the ultimate quantification of capital.

If, however, we were to see the deterritorialising power of capital as a potential, then we could recognise capitalism both as immanent to all social formations and as radically historical. Deleuze and Guattari's commitment to a passive, materialist and virtualist vitalism underpins their historical postulates and leads to distinct methodological imperatives. First, it is because matter is inflected or has its own tendencies to variation that we cannot reduce matter to the interaction of units or atoms. Deleuze and Guattari define matter not as substance that goes through change, but as nothing other than a capacity for change and becoming *from which* substances are formed. This is why capitalism as a universal tendency needs to be understood in two senses. In Deleuze and Guattari's sense, 'life' is a tendency towards difference, creativity, variation, becoming; *any* explanation of life that refers to a unit or measure – such as capital's quantities of labour or capital – has taken a production or effect as a cause. Life begins not as quantities *of* this or that identifiable substance, but as quantities of force which, in relation, produce identifiable or discernible qualities. Before we have capitalism's variables – so much labour power, so much capital, varying in relation to technology and efficiency – there are just desiring potentials. If there is a truth or universalism to capital it is the truth of desire.

There is a capacity or tendency in what Deleuze and Guattari refer to as 'social machines' for deterritorialisation, and this capacity is both what can create new territories or stabilities, and what can destabilise or de-form (Deleuze and Guattari 1977: 141). We see this today in its most intense form in late capitalism: capital is capable of taking any formed relation among powers, such as the nuclear family with its production of female women as 'mothers', and releasing those bodies from their coded roles – there are any number of industries today that rely on releasing desire from its familial forms, ranging from the cultural industries that market feminist and lesbian desires, to various forms of marketing directed at single women and new modes of subject formation. On the one hand, then, capital works against territorialisation and the production of stable social machines that code desire; on the other hand, *as an axiomatic*, capitalism also directs those released desires through the circulation of money. For Deleuze and Guattari we can see this tendency towards capitalism or decoding as the motor of history, for bodies enter into relation to form territories, and in so doing form relatively stable wholes, but can only do so because of a capacity for a body's desire to create itself anew through productive relations:

> If capitalism is the universal truth, it is so in the sense that makes capitalism *the negative* of all social formations. It is the thing, the unnameable, the generalized decoding of flows that reveals *a contrario* the secret of all these formations, coding the flows and even overcoding them, rather than let anything escape coding. Primitive societies are not outside history; rather, it is capitalism that is at the end of history, it is capitalism that results from a long history of contingencies and accidents, and that brings on this end. (Deleuze and Guattari 1977: 153)

Pre-capitalist social machines, such as feudalism, will at once draw upon this tendency, in allowing for markets and the flows of goods, but will also 'ward off' the tendencies of a state in general, or a single network, that would enable flows in general without restriction. And just as capitalism, as the free flow and exchange of bodies, always contributes to, but is not fully actualised in, pre-modern societies, so capitalism has its 'archaisms'. These are those aspects – such as the signifier – which hark back to earlier social machines (Deleuze and Guattari 1977: 135). Capitalism may have released the connections and relations of bodies from external or transcendent codes, such as religion or monarchy, but it reterritorialises on an immanent body. All difference and relation is reduced to the difference of signs, with man as a speaking exchanging animal who subjects himself to 'the law' of universal linguistic exchange, for were he not to do so he would fall back into the dark night of the undifferentiated, pre-Oedipal and chaotic night of the 'beyond' of Oedipus and subjectivity (Deleuze and Guattari 1977: 78).

Deleuze and Guattari use history in *Anti-Oedipus* to show that the linguistic and familial subject of modernity is the consequence of a contingent history, for there is nothing inevitable about arriving at modernity. The idea that 'we' are all constituted through a system of signs and that we live that subjection to linguistic systems through the imaginary of the Oedipus complex can only be understood with reference back to earlier modes of subjection and polyvocal regimes of signs. Before man can become an Oedipal, rational, liberal individual subjected to the law of language, there must be a formation of human bodies into productive units *and* a repression of the intense germinal influx (Deleuze and Guattari 1977: 162). Two historical 'events' are crucial here: the privatisation of organs and the coding of race. The first organ to be privatised, Deleuze and Guattari argue, is the anus: what occurs is the removal of one bodily function into a private domain, with a concomitant flow that is now lived as a meaningless waste outside that socially productive whole (Deleuze and Guattari 1977: 211). This, in turn, will allow for later flows to be privatised, such as the libido and property; with capitalism one lives one's sexuality as one's own, and regards money as a vehicle or medium through which to manage one's own desires. An historical focus, such as Deleuze and Guattari's, would argue that *there must have been* – even if it cannot be located in time – the production of something like a private sphere, created through a body's relation to flows (flows of shit, of libido, of money). Such an event would be transcendental; we can only posit from the present perspective of private man, with his own sexuality and desires, a point at which the social and collective production of this body was repressed, and displaced onto an image of bourgeois familial man (Deleuze and Guattari 1977: 91). All historical-political interventions would be *empirical*, so that, for example, one could see the ways in which the English Revolution was able to do away with the king while remaining enslaved to the norms of man as a speaking, familial and labouring individual who desires and manages his 'own' property. But such empirical histories would be coupled with a transcendental focus: what is the logic of life such that it produces local, individuated, exchanging and productive subjects? The empirical event – such as the English Revolution – can be understood only when shadowed by the transcendental event, or the posited genesis of 'man' as a being with determined interests, interests that *must have been* formed from originally impersonal, collective and revolutionary desires.

The second event at the transcendental level is the coding of race. Empirically, we write a history of 'man' as a subject functioning in socially coded, self-recognising and functioning wholes; but such a stable and identifiable human subject can be formed only through the repression of difference. Not only is there no such natural kind as 'man', or even 'the family' – such selections occur only when an array of complex, varying and radically different genetic variations are coded as belonging to certain groups or territories (Deleuze and Guattari 1977: 98). 'Man' is a consequence of territorialisation; for it is only in the assembling of bodies together that something like a kind or type can emerge. But he is also an effect of deterritorialisation; for it is through the liberation from supposedly tribal, national or racial differences that something like 'man in general' can be thought (Deleuze and Guattari 1977: 104). The 'man' of capitalism is, though, also a reterritorialisation, for modern 'man' becomes nothing other than a formal capacity for speech and labour. In this respect one race comes to function as the privileged territory for humanity in general; for it is only through the white man, marked by a face that signals speech and reason, that something like 'man' is formed. Capitalism both figures man as an exchanging, speaking and (Oedipal) sexual being, at the same time as it begins from the assumption that man has no essence other than his socio-historical existence.

History must, then, not only historicise man, but also historicise at a transcendental level those logics that create man as the basic and foundational unit. Deleuze and Guattari's history of capitalism is, therefore, an empirical history of social formations, and a transcendental universal history that accounts for the production of social machines as such. Such machines are possible only through deterritorialisation, or the capacity for formed bodies to enter into relations that bring about their deformation. Even though capitalism is a formation within history, it is the advent of capitalism that allows us to see the potential for deterritorialisation. Once despotism has been internalised (where we all subject ourselves to the law) and once the signifier appears as an internal limit (where we are all subjects because we are determined through systems of signs), we come very close to a far more radical deterritorialisation that would not be one more social machine among others. Here, we would free ourselves not only from external authorities but also from the codings that make up capitalism: could desire be something other than the desire *of* man for what he lacks? Capitalism comes close to allowing for such a desire insofar as it tends to deterritorialise human bodies, at the same time as it recodes desire in terms of the family. The importance of history lies in the proximity and distance of capitalism and revolution. On the one hand capitalism comes close to a complete liberation both from despotism and the repression of desire for some anti-productive body posited beyond life. On the other hand, it is because capital installs despotism *within life* that it is also especially pernicious.

The 'man' of capitalism, the man who has no being other than his capacity to enter into relations of labour and capital, is at once an effect of coding (he just *is* this conjunction of flows of labour and capital) at the same time as he is the historic result of racial processes. For a body can become a human organism only through its relation to other machines: an organism takes on a social function by connecting with other working and producing bodies, by a collective investment of organs – a body is its capacity to hunt, to kill, to feed, to inflict pain, to give birth, and so on. All of these organising capacities are defined both through other bodies whose capacities are selected and through other machines that select a body's functions. A human body becomes a 'hunter' only in relation to a certain mapping of the earth and a desire for other animal bodies, becomes a chieftain in a capacity to inflict pain and consume more of what is socially produced, or becomes a father only after coupling with certain other bodies (women) who are defined as reproductive and as prohibited to others. Desire is not the desire of this or that already organised body; indeed, bodies (social bodies, human bodies, political bodies) are consequences of desire. Desire is at once directly revolutionary because it is de-forming or deterritorialising, at very same time as it is territorialising: 'desire is revolutionary in its essence' (Deleuze and Guattari 1977: 116). A territory or range of connections can only be produced if a potentiality or force extends beyond itself to produce a relation. A body is produced from powers of difference: everything from molecular life to human bodies and social systems involves relatively stable relations among powers: an organism forms and reproduces itself not only because it harbours DNA, but because that DNA was itself the result of an interaction of proteins, and this effected power will in turn interact with other powers – other genes but also non-genetic powers. Deleuze and Guattari explain this 'machinic desire' at the level of genetics, where DNA as the identity that is carried through time is the result of interactions of proteins, where organs occur as a consequence of encounters between potentials for change (the eye being the solution to the problem of light), and where organisms such as the human body are at once explicable according to an internal propensity for variation (the development of the hand as tool, voice as speech, and brain as 'screen', all acting in concert). Deleuze and Guattari redefine vitalism by focusing on the molecular, so that the living body is at once composed of machines – each organ such as the eye, ear, brain or heart is composed of its own souls and perceptions and becomes what it is in relation to other organs – at the same time as the body is formed in relation to machines; the hand develops as a tool in relation to an earth that can be tilled; the brain develops as a concept-forming machine in conjunction with a voice made possible by a lowering of the larynx and with other technical machines such as writing, sign systems, factories, cameras, canvases, buildings and so on. Such a vitalism is contrasted with mechanism because mechanism cannot recognise the capacity of life to enter into variation at the smallest level. Mechanism builds machines from static and pre-formed units, whereas Deleuze and Guattari define matter as having no quality other than a capacity to differ, and to differ in relation.

Doing History

Already in *Anti-Oedipus* Deleuze and Guattari give a definition of the body without organs that anticipates the ultimate theory of matter and stratification we find in *A Thousand Plateaus*, and this suggests that there is no real distinction between the theory of life we find in the later works and the historical narrative of *Anti-Oedipus*. What unites both accounts is a theory of matter that encompasses the virtual and desire, or the virtual *as desire*. And it is this nexus of terms – matter, desire, the real – that allows Deleuze and Guattari to remain committed both to a strong sense of history *and* to an understanding of the eternal. Matter for Deleuze and Guattari is not an already distributed and extended substance that then enters into relations and combinations. Even in *Anti-Oedipus* – before the pronouncement in *A Thousand Plateaus* that 'MONISM = PLURALISM', or that there is one matter that is given only in a multiplicity of actual events – they insist that matter is a capacity or potentiality for relations. The actual extended world that we perceive in the series of chronological time, or the world that can be given as historically narratable, is possible only because of the intense germinal influx, the potentiality for production that is necessarily limited, repressed or lived as a series of differentiated terms. It is this intensive 'spatium', or the potentiality for spaces *in time*, that a genuine history must intuit:

> It is a question of . . . identifying races, cultures, and gods with fields of intensity on the body without organs, identifying personages with states that fill these fields, and with effects that fulgurate within and traverse these fields. Whence the role of names, with a magic all their own: there is no ego that identifies with races, peoples, and persons in a theatre of representation, but proper names that identify races, peoples, and persons with regions, thresholds, or effects in a production of intensive quantities. . . . To seize an intensive real as produced in the coextension of nature and history. . . (Deleuze and Guattari 1977: 87)

In terms of history of philosophy and history of art, this led Deleuze to a certain mode of reading. A text expresses a problem, and that problem is at once thoroughly of its time and untimely. Considering the art of Francis Bacon, Deleuze argues that every painter works with the entire history of painting, and that Bacon's problem of the relation between ground and figure needs to be understood as a response to Cezanne-ism, itself a problem of the relations among colour, canvas, line and ground (Deleuze 2004). Similarly, in the history of philosophy, we need to understand Spinoza in relation to the Cartesian problem of mind and extended matter, a problem that Spinoza will reconfigure by refusing to establish a relation between two substances; instead, mind and matter become expressions of one substance (Deleuze 1990b). What Deleuze deploys here is a radically historical concept of 'stratigraphic' time (Deleuze 1994). Time is actualised in terms of a series of before and after; but time is also the potential (with each new addition to the series) to redefine the whole: so we need to see Bacon as after Cezanne, and Kant as after Hume, as well as seeing capitalism as a social machine following primitivism and despotism. Were we not to do so we would lose the sense of life as desire, as *non-linear* in its creation of itself with each new encounter, encounters that alter the very domain of the possible. There is no contradiction whatsoever in the commitment to non-linerarity alongside a strong sense of irreversible becoming. Consider, first, the case of art and philosophy: Bacon could only respond to the problem of figure and ground once the canvas and paint themselves had become the object of art's attention, and this attention to matter was possible only after a history of Christian art had been striving to present the very body of Christ, as divine matter, as directly spiritual. Kant could only pose the problem of the transcendental subject, a subject who synthesises time and space, once Hume had posed the problem of experience itself and the impossibility of having an intuition of time itself. Art and philosophy are at once responses to the past (and hence thoroughly historical), at the same time as each event *in time* reconfigures time itself. Every new painting or artwork allows us to view the entire history of painting differently: once the modernists had focused on form it became possible to perceive the purely formal features of Byzantine mosaics; once Kant had articulated the model of transcendental philosophy it became possible to read all previous philosophies in terms of the idealism/empiricism problem.

There is at once a sequence that distributes time spatially (or historically), with each work or event taking its place in a chronological order, and an eternal, 'stratigraphic' or untimely series of events in which every new occurrence opens up a potential to refigure all time. This is how we can understand capitalism. It is, as Deleuze and Guattari narrate, a form of social machine that follows on from primitivism and despotism and that also retains aspects of both these social machines as 'archaisms'. The family and its Oedipal formation are residues of prior formations. While capitalism is a social machine that operates by allowing everything to enter into, and be defined by, its capacity to be exchanged, reformed and circulated, it allows one form – the family and the speaking subject – to act as a privileged body that appears to define and control the socio-historical political whole (Deleuze and Guattari 1977: 91). All exchange and all societies appear to be subtended by familial man. But while capitalism is an event within historical time, clearly different from feudalism and primitivism, once capitalism occurs it allows for a re-reading of all history. Such a re-reading is legitimate if we distinguish capitalism as a timeless virtual potentiality from capitalism as an actual social machine. The mistake would be to take capitalism as historically actualised – as the social machine governed by the exchange of labour and capital, coded through familial man – and then read previous social machines as leading up to or reducible to man as an individual labourer. The more radical historical path is to see actual capitalism as possible only because of life's potentiality as desire. That is, there can be social machines only because bodies as desiring and producing powers enter into connection and relation. Such connections can be stable – or socially and historically individuated – only if the very productive capacities that make them possible are in some way restricted, diminished or repressed. Repression, then, is not the hiding away of secret desires or one's own private and familial fantasies; repression occurs when productive desire that is historical in its tendency to change and variation is stabilised into those wholes (such as societies or individuals) that are narrated historically (Deleuze and Guattari 1977: 120). Capitalism as an immanent virtual power, the power for the production of social and political bodies through connection, is intuitable today only with the destruction of all external and transcendent forms of coding. But just as we are now capable of witnessing desiring life itself in all its creativity and production *without* the norms of religion, the royal state or universal human nature, we also appear to have reached the end of history. For if there are no longer battles to be fought regarding transcendent norms, and if all we have is life itself with governments oriented to the maximisation and management of life without any imposed norm, then where is the motor of history to be located?

Deleuze and Guattari observe that all revolutions or historical events take the form of a return to degree zero: a sweeping away of illegitimate, external and imposed bodies in favour of the true power and right of life itself. The primitive despot could be overthrown by a king who claimed to be God's anointed, while the king could be overthrown by the collective will of the people, and even human democracy can be challenged – as it is today in any number of movements claiming to speak for the earth or embattled 'life'. Deleuze and Guattari's answer to the problem of this arrival of capitalism as the end of history, as the point in time when we appear to have arrived at nothing other than life itself, is death. Death in capitalism and its commitment to immanence has become a death instinct. All life forms are capacities or quantities of so much energy which needs to be managed, conserved, maximised and ultimately spent until it returns to zero. The death instinct is a highly organic model which governs the capitalist understanding of the individual as bio-power – as so much life ready for management, preservation and spending. This model of 'bourgeois thermodynamics' also characterises capitalism's own understanding of itself (Deleuze 1994). There are various quantities – of labour, capital and life – all entering into relation; politico-economic management becomes a question of maximising the production of these quantities, always with a sense of a resource that is limited and winding down to zero. Not only does this characterise capitalism as an axiomatic that always operates with the relation between labour and capital, it also works with a death instinct. Life is essentially submission to this system of labour and capital, a spending or depletion of force, with no possibility of a force or drive outside familial production in the Oedipal triangle (always seen as involving renunciation of real desire for the sake of social equilibrium). As we know today, even those times spent outside work – time spent viewing television, listening to one's ipod, taking leisure breaks – are areas of capitalist production and exchange. In contrast with this thermodynamic death instinct, in which it is always a question of more or less, and in which time and history are read according to an *actual* capitalism, Deleuze and Guattari argue for a different understanding of death *as experience*. Every force or intensity begins from degree zero, or a point of death or dissolution, and increases to the point of discernibility: 'The body without organs is the matter that always fills space to given degrees of intensity, and the partial objects are these degrees, these intensive parts that produce the real in space starting from matter as intensity = 0' (Deleuze and Guattari 1977: 326–7). The human organism becomes a seeing, eating, reading, speaking and producing machine at certain thresholds. But at what point, today, could these thresholds be crossed and altered? Modern art, for example, operates with the minimal intensities of sound and light, exploring the points from which systems are formed. Histories of the present can begin by exploring these thresholds of the human organism; we might need to begin asking about the formation of sympathies – at what point do we begin to feel recognition for others – and for other affects: at what point in global and demographic crises do we begin or cease to imagine a future? How can our connections with consumption and production be varied to create new sustainable forms of humanity? What can past modes of seeing, labouring, feeling or creating tell us about the variability of a humanity effected from a series of historical stratifications? It is the complexity of this type of question that yielded the peculiar form of the two volumes of *Capitalism and Schizophrenia*: Deleuze and Guattari compose histories of social forms, sign systems and organisms and place these alongside enquiries into the visual form of the face, the literary form of the novella, the role of art in becoming imperceptible, and various interspersed passages on American literature and modernist writing.

That is, rather than regard life, time and history as the mechanical rearrangement of quantities of force – so in opposition to Marxist histories that begin with an understanding of the economic in terms of markets and individuals – Deleuze and Guattari create a history that explains the genesis of individuals and their social relations, and that regards forces *not* as relations among quantities, but as the production of quantities through relations. Deleuze and Guattari use two ideas to explain this, the first of which is death as an experience rather than as a model (Deleuze and Guattari 1977: 329). If the body without organs can be understood as all the potential forces of matter *before* the production of differentiated terms and stable points, then one can – as an organised body – try to take already effected quantities to their zero degree. What would it be not to imagine oneself as man, the speaking and labouring individual possessed with so much life, and instead regard oneself as composed of forces that can be varied? One could see Deleuze and Guattari's history of primitivism, despotism and capitalism as a charting of the production of quantities from zero degree forces. Man becomes a speaking, reasoning, familial being only once desire is regarded as so much libido organised according to the mother-father-child triangle of Oedipus (Deleuze and Guattari 1977: 97). But beyond that quantification of libido within the bourgeois family, there are racial and historical intensities. And those intensities can be considered as forces, ranging from discernible quantities down to zero. Revolution occurs not with individuals in relation to capital, but with the individual's experimentation of new modes of differential beyond that of labour-capital. The *experience* of death is just this capacity to imagine any quantity in its diminution or variability, to a point of extinction or redefinition:

> it is absurd to speak of a death desire that would presumably be in qualitative opposition to a life desire. Death is not desired, there is only death that desires, by virtue of the body without organs or the immobile motor, and there is also life that desires, by virtue of the working organs. (Deleuze and Guattari 1977: 329)

The second idea governing Deleuze and Guattari's radical historicism is that of the differential calculus, where one no longer works with the relations among terms, but with the production of terms from relations. In their historical account of human social machines through time they regard individuals in the polity to be composed from racial and historical intensities. This then produces a history that is neither social history in its usual sense nor a history of macro structures and great individuals. Instead, one needs to read macro or 'molar' social formations as composed from molecular intensities. One can think, here, of the ways in which monarchical power in the English Revolution was composed from a series of investments that were racial and historical. Prior to Charles I, Elizabeth was desired and experienced as a monarch embodying the virtues of whiteness and Englishness; sexual motifs of purity also inflected national images of unity and origin. But this production of the virgin queen not only harboured the archaisms of a religious investment in the virgin Mary (which in turn resonated with pagan earth goddess myths) it also relied upon concrete micropolitical investments. Here, we do not see political machines as functioning by the imposition of images, ideology or false consciousness, because – as Deleuze and Guattari show in *A Thousand Plateaus* – the feudal machine relied on the production, for example, of knights (coupling with the horse and stirrup to produce a certain 'machine'). The social movement of the English Revolution worked directly with desire, producing images of Christ and holiness that would be distinct from the king, while also creating practices of individual reading, labour and social gathering. Intensities – of whiteness, of suffering, of spiritual fervour – composed individuals differently: one could either be a revolutionary puritan, experimenting with spiritual intensities beyond the coded forms of kingship and state, or one could, as the royalist poets, Archbishop Laud and the new model army were to do, reterritorilise those intensities on stratified power networks. Such an attention to intensities and investments is also a capitalist history, for it allows an intersection between bodies as labouring and productive of the social machine, and bodies as composed of desires and intensive investments. At what point or threshold did the desire for spirit as such, liberated from the monarchical forms and property, become recoded and reterritorialised on the body of bourgeois man and the inner authority? Such a history would attend at once to art and to the relations among bodies, and to the production of intensities and their circulation.

References

Althusser, L. (1971), *Lenin and Philosophy, and Other Essays*, trans. Ben Brewster, London: New Left Books.

Bergson, H. (1910), *Time and Free Will*, trans. Frank Pogson, London: Sonnenschein.

Bergson, H. (1931), *Creative Evolution*, trans. Arthur Mitchell, New York: Holt.

DeLanda, M. (1997), *A Thousand Years of Nonlinear History*, New York: Zone Books.

Deleuze, G. (1988), *Bergsonism*, trans. Hugh Tomlinson and Barbara Habberjam, New York: Zone Books.

Deleuze, G. (1990a), *The Logic of Sense*, trans. Mark Lester with Charles Stivale, ed. Constantin V. Boundas, New York: Columbia University Press.

Deleuze, G. (1990b), *Expressionism in Philosophy: Spinoza*, trans. Martin Joughin, New York: Zone Books.

Deleuze, G. (1993), *The Fold: Leibniz and the Baroque*, trans. Tom Conley, Minneapolis: University of Minnesota Press.

Deleuze, G. (1994), *Difference and Repetition*, trans. Paul Patton, London: Athlone Press.

Deleuze, G. (2004), *Francis Bacon: The Logic of Sensation*, trans. Daniel W. Smith, Minneapolis: University of Minnesota Press.

Deleuze, G. (2006), *Nietzsche and Philosophy*, trans. Hugh Tomlinson, New York: Columbia University Press.

Deleuze, G. and F. Guattari (1977), *Anti-Oedipus: Capitalism and Schizophrenia*, trans. Robert Hurley, Mark Seem and Helen R. Lane, Minneapolis: University of Minnesota Press, 1983.

Deleuze, G. and F. Guattari (1987), *A Thousand Plateaus: Capitalism and Schizophrenia*, trans. Brian Massumi, Minneapolis: University of Minnesota Press.

Deleuze, G. and F. Guattari (1994), *What is Philosophy?* trans. Hugh Tomlinson and Graham Burchell, New York: Columbia University Press.

Derrida, J. (1978), *Edmund Husserl's Origin of Geometry, an Introduction*, trans. John P. Leavey, Jr., Lincoln: University of Nebraska Press.

Derrida, J. (1994), *Specters of Marx: The State of the Debt, the Work of Mourning, and the New International*, trans. Peggy Kamuf, New York: Routledge.

Derrida, J. (2003), *The Problem of Genesis in Husserl's Philosophy*, trans. Marian Hobson, Chicago: University of Chicago Press.

Eagleton, T. (1997), *The Illusions of Postmodernism*, Oxford: Blackwell Publishers.

Foucault, M. (1972), *The Archaeology of Knowledge*, trans. A. M. Sheridan Smith, New York: Pantheon Books.

Foucault, M. (1970), *The Order of Things: An Archaeology of the Human Sciences*, London: Tavistock Publications.

Hill, C. (1972), *The World Turned Upside Down: Radical Ideas During the English Revolution*, London: Temple Smith.

Jameson, F. (1978), 'Imaginary and Symbolic in Lacan: Marxism, Psychoanalytic Criticism, and the Problem of Subject', *Yale French Studies*, 55–6: 338–95.

Jameson, F. (1981), *The Political Unconscious: Narrative as a Socially Symbolic Act*, Ithaca: Cornell University Press.

Lyotard, J-F. (1984), *The Postmodern Condition: A Report on Knowledge*, trans. Geoff Bennington and Brian Massumi, Minneapolis: University of Minnesota Press.

Thao, Tran Duc. (1986), *Phenomenology and Dialectical Materialism*, trans. Daniel J. Herman and Donald V. Morano, Dordrecht: Kluwer Academic Publishers.

Žižek, S. (1999), *The Ticklish Subject: The Absent Centre of Political Ontology*, London: Verso.

Žižek, S. (2004), *Organs Without Bodies: Deleuze and Consequences*, New York: Routledge.

Chapter 1

Events, Becoming and History

Paul Patton

Deleuze and Guattari appear to be ambivalent towards History and historians. *Anti-Oedipus* advocates a universalism that would retrospectively understand all history in the light of capitalism (Deleuze and Guattari 2004: 153–4). *A Thousand Plateaus* draws extensively on the work of historians of Europe and Asia as well as specialised works of economic and military history, histories of science, mathematics, technology, music, art and philosophy. On the other hand, they assert the need for a Nomadology that would be 'the opposite of a history' (Deleuze and Guattari 1987: 23). Nomadology, like so many of the other disciplines proposed in *A Thousand Plateaus* (rhizomatics, pragmatics, schizoanalysis and so on) is essentially the study of certain kinds of assemblages (State and war-machine) and the relations between them. What is the function of so much historical material in works of philosophy devoted to the description of abstract machines or assemblages?

In his 1990 interview with Antonio Negri, Deleuze comments that he had become 'more and more aware of the possibility of distinguishing between becoming and history' (Deleuze 1995: 170). By the time of his final work with Guattari, this distinction took the form of a contrast between an historical realm in which events are actualised in bodies and states of affairs and an a-historical realm of pure events, where these are the 'shadowy and secret part [of an event] that is continually subtracted from or added to its actualization' (Deleuze and Guattari 1994: 156). They drew a parallel distinction between Philosophy, understood as the practice of thought that produces concepts that express these pure events, and History: 'what History grasps of the event is its effectuation in states of affairs or in lived experience, but the event in its becoming, in its specific consistency, in its self-positing concept, escapes History' (Deleuze and Guattari 1994: 110).[1] From a normative point of view, Philosophy appears privileged by virtue of its relation to the pure event and becoming since these are the conditions of experimentation and change. History (*L'histoire*) is not experimentation but only 'the set of almost negative conditions that make possible the experimentation of something that escapes history' (Deleuze and Guattari 1994: 111).

This apparent devaluation of History at the expense of Philosophy needs to be tempered by Deleuze and Guattari's conception of the nature and task of Philosophy. Their account of its critical function relies upon historical knowledge about the circumstances under which Philosophy emerged as a specific form of thought in Ancient Greece and about the evolution of capitalism and its relationship to States. On their view, Philosophy is not representational and not directed at discovering ahistorical truths because it is a kind of practical reason undertaken in pursuit of new earths and peoples that do not yet exist. It achieves its utopian aims when the power of absolute deterritorialisation associated with its concepts is aligned with one or other form of relative deterritorialisation present in the historical milieu (Deleuze and Guattari 1994: 85–113).

However, questions remain about the distinction between becoming and history. How does it relate to other distinctions that Deleuze draws between the 'evental' realm of becoming and the corporeal realm of bodies and states of affairs? How does it relate to the differences between the virtual and the actual, between problems and solutions, between effects and causes, between the sense or meaning of propositions and the actualities they describe, between the plane of organisation and the plane of consistency on which there are no longer species or kinds of body but only body-events or haecceities? Here we encounter a difficult problem, namely how to read Deleuze's texts in relation to one another and in relation to the problems and concepts they appear to share. My approach does not take his successive books to be expressions of a single, uniform philosophy in which there is no change from one project to the next, but rather a succession of experiments in which the same issues and concepts are taken up and reworked from a different angle. Deleuze does say that he has tried, in all his books, to discover the nature of events (Deleuze 1995: 141). He does not say that he has succeeded or that he has arrived at a final theory of the nature of events. There are many indications that we should proceed with caution, taking into account the different problems from one book to the next as well as the relative constancy of some of the resources and resultant formulations.

Structure, Genesis and Sense: The Metaphysics of Pure Events

History is not a primary concern in *Difference and Repetition*, where Deleuze is more concerned with the traditional image of thought in Philosophy and its treatment of sameness and difference, recurrence and repetition. Nonetheless, an early version of the distinction between the realm of becoming and history is implicit in his discussion of the ideational synthesis of difference (Deleuze 1994: 168–221). Following Kant, he identifies the Ideas that are the ultimate objects of thought with quasi-transcendent problems that orient human thinking. His transcendental empiricism allows him to go beyond Kant and propose an open-ended list of Ideas that includes the ultimate objects of physical, biological, social, linguistic and other domains of thought. He defines these problematic Ideas as differential multiplicities or structures and suggests that they are 'of the order of events' (Deleuze 1994: 188). He also proposes that the relationship between the determinants of a problem and its solutions be understood as a relation between two series of events which develop on parallel planes, echoing without resembling one another: 'real events on the level of the engendered solutions and ideal events embedded in the conditions of the problem' (Deleuze 1994: 189). In this manner, following Geoffroy Saint-Hilaire, real organisms might be said to actualise the 'differential relations between pure anatomical elements' that make up the Idea of the organism as such. Or, following Marx, the real social relations of a given society might be said to actualise the differential relations of production that make up the social Idea (Deleuze 1994: 184–6).

Insofar as Deleuze provides here the barest outlines of a conception of history, it follows the structuralist model of Althusser and his collaborators who were, Deleuze suggests, 'profoundly correct in showing the presence of a genuine structure in *Capital* and in rejecting historicist interpretations of Marxism' (Deleuze 1994: 186). He takes the capitalist mode of production to be a differential multiplicity or structure whose virtual, internal movements determine the real events that succeed one another in historical time. For this reason, he denies that there is any difficulty in reconciling structure and genesis so long as we understand that genesis does not take place between actual things but 'between the virtual and its actualization'. In other words, the genesis of actual states of affairs takes place in a 'supra-historical' time that goes from the differential elements of an ideational structure to real things and the 'diverse real relationships that constitute at each moment the actuality of time' (Deleuze 1994: 183).[2]

Deleuze's conception of history at this point follows Althusser's suggestion that there would be different kinds of historicity corresponding to particular modes of production: a temporality of the feudal mode, a temporality of the capitalist mode of production and so on.[3] However, because capitalism is only one solution to the problem or pure event of society as such, this structural-Marxist conception of history was also obliged to account for the transition from one social structure to another. It implied a distinction between those events that express the unfolding in history of a given mode of production and those that express the transition from one mode of production to another. In a phrase that recalls the Althusserian concept of 'overdetermination', Deleuze suggests that the historical transition from one solution to another occurs by way of the 'condensation' of the singular points of a given structure into a 'sublime occasion, *Kairos*, which makes the [new] solution explode like something abrupt, brutal and revolutionary' (Deleuze 1994: 190).[4] He equates these revolutionary moments at which the pure event of society breaks through into history with the manifestation of a freedom, 'which is always hidden among the remains of the old order and the first fruits of a new' (Deleuze 1994: 193).

In *The Logic of Sense* we find the same identification of pure events with problems, and the spatio-temporal actualisation of those events with solutions, as in *Difference and Repetition*. However, the concepts do not appear in the same configuration.[5] Deleuze was more concerned here with the nature of sense or meaning, understood as the depthless surface between words and things, and its relation to the structures of signification in which it is produced, to non-sense, and to the impersonal transcendental field on which he locates the corporeal as well as the incorporeal intensities that provide the raw material and subject matter of psychoanalysis. History is not a primary concern of *The Logic of Sense* either, although the reference to Novalis's distinction between ideal Protestantism and real Lutheranism does give an historical illustration of the distinction between pure events and their actualisation in a given context (Deleuze 1990: 53).

Bearing in mind the overriding concern with language and the problematics of surface, *The Logic of Sense* still provides one of the most detailed accounts of the incorporeal realm of becoming and the pure event to be found anywhere in Deleuze. The equivalence between sense and pure (ideal) events or becomings is established at the outset, where it is also allied with a particular relation to time. Lewis Carroll's example of Alice's growing – in which her becoming taller is co-extensive with her becoming shorter, depending upon the temporal direction in which we view this event – is taken to show 'the simultaneity of a becoming whose characteristic is to elude the present' (Deleuze 1990: 1). This paradoxical simultaneity of contradictory processes provides a reason for distinguishing an historical time within which events occur (*Chronos*) from a time of the event (Aion) that remains irreducible to the former (Deleuze 1990: 5).

This conception of events and their relationship to time owes much to the Stoics, for whom events were considered to be incorporeal effects of bodily causes. It implies that the pure event of battle is something over and above the movements of men, horses and equipment on a given occasion. The pure event is expressed in these particular elements while nevertheless remaining irreducible to them. As Deleuze explains in *Dialogues*:

> The event is always produced by bodies which collide, lacerate each other or interpenetrate, the flesh and the sword. But this effect itself is not of the order of bodies, an impassive, incorporeal, impenetrable battle, which towers over its own accomplishment and dominates its effectuation. (Deleuze and Parnet 1987: 64)

The Logic of Sense offers reasons why battle functions as an exemplary event in so much of modern literature: because it can be actualised in different ways on different occasions and because, on any given occasion, different participants will grasp different levels of its actualisation. As a consequence, in any flesh and blood battle, 'the event hovers over its own field, being neutral in relation to all of its temporal actualisations, neutral and impassive in relation to the victor and the vanquished, the coward and the brave' (Deleuze 1990: 100). This conception of pure events as real but non-actual entities, expressed in the successive configurations of material bodies but irreducible to any particular set of such configurations, continues to inform the distinction between becoming and history up until Deleuze's final work. However, its precise meaning is not self-evident.

Some of the formulations employed in these early texts suggest a substantive distinction between two distinct realms of being. On this reading, pure events might be understood on the model of Platonic forms that can only be imitated but never fully realised in any actual thing, event or state of affairs. A literal reading of the event of battle hovering over its particular incarnations and participants might suggest this way of understanding the extra-corporeal realm of pure events, as might Deleuze's examples of pure events of society, atomism, organism, psychic structure, language and so on in *Difference and Repetition*. The same is true of Joë

Bousquet's remark that his wound 'existed before him' and Deleuze's suggestion that events of this kind that determine the fate of an individual life must be understood as 'not what occurs (an accident)' but rather as 'inside what occurs, the purely expressed. It signals and awaits us' (Deleuze 1990: 149). In these terms, pure events would be real and apparently transcendent objects only partially expressed in their spatio-temporal incarnations. At best, actual historical events would approximate the pure event, a part of which always remains not simply unactualised but 'indifferent to actualization, since its reality does not depend upon it. The event is immaterial, incorporeal, unlivable: pure *reserve*' (Deleuze and Guattari 1994: 156).

Of course, Deleuze's inverted Platonism and his identification of pure events with transcendental problems would imply a number of modifications to this model. Pure events are modelled on certain kinds of mathematical problem rather than, as with Plato, the pure form or Idea of a given quality: the Just as that which is only just, and so on. It follows that pure events require specification in ways that already determine the kinds of solution available. However, if we follow this line of thought through *The Logic of Sense* and its Stoic metaphysics, we encounter a whole universe of banal everyday events such as being-cut-with-a-knife, the becoming-green of trees, walking, sinning, being-eaten and so on. This way of understanding the realm of pure events seems to lead to a Meinongian universe of intentional objects in which neither their identity conditions nor their number are well defined. We might wonder how the event of being cut is related to my accident with the razor this morning, or whether there is a pure event of walking down the stairs to my apartment as well as a pure event of walking. Sometimes Deleuze's overturned Platonic world of simulacra does appear to evoke this kind of ontological madness. But is this the best way to understand the distinction between becoming and history?

There are several reasons to be wary of this quasi-Platonic model of the extra-historical realm of becoming. One has to do with the essential connection that Deleuze asserts between events and language. *The Logic of Sense* identifies the pure event with the sense or the 'expressed' in what is said and argues that it is in the very nature of events to be 'expressed or expressible' in propositions. Since what is expressed in a proposition is its sense, it follows that sense and event are two sides of the same incorporeal surface: sense is the event, '*on the condition that the event is not confused with its spatio-temporal realization in a state of affairs*' (Deleuze 1990: 22). Deleuze does not draw a distinction between two sorts of events but rather between events, which are ideal by nature, and their spatio-temporal realisation in states of affairs (Deleuze 1990: 53). In the same way, he insists that the difference between historical time and event time is not an ontological distinction between two temporal orders but a distinction between two 'readings' of time (Deleuze 1990: 61).

A further reason to question the Platonising interpretation of pure events is Deleuze's increasingly resolute hostility to transcendence in all its manifestations. This is one of the significant changes that takes place in his thinking alongside his growing commitment to the distinction between becoming and history. In *Difference and Repetition* he was happy to treat Ideas or problems as both immanent and transcendent, and to attribute to the ideal series of events 'the double property of transcendence and immanence in relation to the real' (Deleuze 1994: 169, 189). By contrast, in *What is Philosophy?*, transcendence is described as a constant temptation, one of the forms of which is 'the illusion of the eternal when it is forgotten that concepts must be created' (Deleuze and Guattari 1994: 49–50). The metaphysical reading of pure events above succumbs to precisely this temptation. That is no doubt why he is careful to specify that although the pure event might seem to be transcendent, it is 'pure immanence of what is not actualized or of what remains indifferent to actualization, since its reality does not depend upon it' (Deleuze and Guattari 1994: 156).

A final reason to be wary of the substantive understanding of the realm of pure events relates to the task of Philosophy as this is outlined in *What is Philosophy?* The purpose of creating concepts is to give linguistic expression to the pure event expressed in actual events (Deleuze and Guattari 1994: 159). But we encounter difficulties if we try to understand this process in terms of the Platonic model. For this implies that pure events must be discovered in the states of affairs that express them. Yet there appears to be a radical indeterminacy of the event in relation to the historical occurrence or, to put it another way, the state of affairs appears to underdetermine the event or events expressed in it. Controversies in history and political science are made of this. Consider the event of colonisation: did this in a particular country amount to invasion or peaceful occupation? In its purest form, is this a problem of capture of territory, peoples and resources by a technologically superior power, or is it a problem of encounter between different peoples that might have taken very different forms to those that it took historically? (Patton 2006). The question becomes even more complex when we take into account the utopian aspiration of Philosophy: its goal is not just the creation of concepts but the creation of concepts that call for new earths and new peoples. What determines which concepts will serve this purpose and therefore which events are expressed in what happens in accordance with this requirement? What determines which concepts are 'Interesting, Remarkable or Important' in the sense that they give expression to what is coming about (becoming) rather than what has already happened? (Deleuze and Guattari 1994: 82; 111).

Events Untimely and Sublime

One way to approach these questions is suggested by Deleuze's recurrent comparisons between his own approach to Philosophy and that of Nietzsche. In a 1967 interview, 'Nietzsche's Burst of Laughter', he says that Nietzsche located all his work in a dimension that was neither that of history, even dialectically understood, nor that of the eternal: 'What he calls this new dimension which operates both in time and against time is the *untimely*' (Deleuze 2004: 129). He goes on to suggest that perhaps a reason for the 'return to Nietzsche' in France around this time was the rediscovery of his concept of the untimely dimension. This was certainly true of Deleuze's own philosophy. His 1968 Preface to *Difference and Repetition* describes the task of modern Philosophy as that of over-coming 'the alternatives temporal/non-temporal, historical/eternal and particular/universal' and following Nietzsche's discovery of the untimely as a means to act on the present for the benefit, it is hoped, of a time to come (Deleuze 1994: xxi).[6] *What is Philosophy?* aligns Philosophy with the experimental function of thought apparently at the expense of History, which is concerned only with the 'almost negative conditions' that make it possible to create something new. The text repeats the same lines from Nietzsche's *Untimely Meditation* in describing the 'unhistorical vapour that has nothing to do with the eternal', but that is rather 'the becoming without which nothing would come about in history but that does not merge with history' (Deleuze and Guattari 1994: 112). What does this alignment of Philosophy with thought as experimentation and with Nietzsche's untimely tell us about the relationship of becoming and pure events to both History and history?

One response is suggested by Deleuze's remarks in 'Nietzsche's Burst of Laughter' about those moments at which the untimely and the historical coincide. He gives examples from the successful struggles for the liberation of colonised peoples carried out in Egypt and Cuba in the 1950s and Vietnam in the 1960s (Deleuze 2004: 130). The parallels between these events and the moments of transition from one historical structure to another referred to in *Difference and Repetition* are evident. They are all turning points in history after which some things will never be the same as before. Towards the end of this interview in April 1967, Deleuze laments the absence of such earth-shattering events in France. After the May uprising in Paris less than a year later, he often referred to these events in similar terms, describing this as 'of the order of a pure event' (Deleuze 2006: 233); as 'a becoming breaking through into history' (Deleuze 1995: 153); and as 'a demonstration, an irruption, of a becoming in its pure state' (Deleuze 1995: 171).[7] Events of this kind express the creative power of becoming or the untimely to transform or reinterpret historical reality. For Nietzsche, Deleuze points out, things are already interpretations, so to reinterpret is to change things: 'Politics, too, is in the business of interpretation' (Deleuze 2004: 130). It follows that in those moments where becoming breaks though into history 'there is always a coincidence of poetic acts and historical events or political actions, the glorious incarnation of something *sublime* or *untimely*' (Deleuze 2004: 130, emphasis added).

Deleuze's characterisation of these untimely events as sublime points to the necessary relationship between events and interpretation. In *The Critique of Judgment* Kant distinguished two kinds of sublime: the 'mathematical sublime', which is the feeling aroused in us by sensory experiences of natural phenomena that 'convey the idea of their infinity', and the dynamical sublime, which is produced in us by those appearances of nature's might and power that are so overwhelming that the prospect of human resistance to them is inconceivable. To these two kinds of experience of the sublime we can add a third not discussed by Kant but consistent with his overall conception of the mental faculties, namely the hermeneutical sublime. This is the experience produced by those phenomena which threaten to overwhelm not just our powers of imagination or the capacity of the human will to resist even the threat of annihilation but also our capacity to understand or identify the phenomena in question. Several commentators suggested that September 11 was an event of this kind (Battersby 2003; Derrida 2003; Kearney 2003). Derrida pointed to this dimension when he argued that, in addition to the magnitude of the forces that brought about the collapse of the towers, the suffering inflicted upon so many people and the fear and terror that this event inspired, what made this such an extraordinary and sublime event was the damage wrought upon 'the conceptual, semantic, and one could even say hermeneutic apparatus that might have allowed one to see coming, to comprehend, interpret, describe, speak of, and name "September 11"' (Derrida 2003: 93). However, he also went on to generalise this hermeneutically sublime dimension of September 11 by suggesting that every event implies the possibility of resistance to our existing means of representation. In other words, in order for there to be an event we must be able to recognise, identify, interpret or describe a given occurrence as a certain kind of event. At the same time, however, to the extent that an event is a new occurrence at a given moment in time, it must also be endowed with the potential to resist this kind of incorporation within our existing systems of recognition, interpretation and description. In this sense, he argues, every event, insofar as it is an event, carries the potential to break with the past and to inaugurate a new kind of event: 'The event is what comes and, in coming, comes to surprise me, to surprise and to suspend comprehension: the event is first of all *that which* I do not first of all comprehend. Better, the event is first of all *that* I do not comprehend' (Derrida 2003: 90).

For Derrida, it is the indeterminate and paradoxical future – the 'to come' that is the condition of there being events at all – that ensures that there is a degree of the hermeneutical sublime in every event. He understands the 'to come' as a structural future, presupposed by but irreducible to any actual future present. What Derrida refers to as the 'to come' and Foucault as the 'actual', Deleuze calls absolute deterritorialisation, becoming or the untimely. It is the pure 'event-ness' that is expressed in every event and, for that reason, immanent in history. It follows that every event raises with greater or lesser urgency the hermeneutic question 'what happened?' In this sense, as Deleuze pointed out in *The Logic of Sense*, all events are signs requiring interpretation. This enigmatic character of events might also be derived from the ambiguous relationship they have to time. On the one hand, they occur at a more or less precise moment in historical time (Chronos). On the other hand, it is difficult to pinpoint a precise moment at which a given event takes place. This is because the unactualised part, the pure event-ness of the event, belongs to a different order of time (Aion), in which it retreats and advances in two directions at once, being the perpetual object of a double question: What is going to happen? What has just happened? The agonising aspect of the pure event is that it is always and at the same time something which has just happened and something about to happen; never something which is happening. The x, with respect to which one feels that *it* just happened, is the object of the 'novella'; and the x which is always about to happen, is the object of the 'tale'. The pure event is both tale and novella, never an actuality. It is in this sense that events are *signs* (Deleuze 1990: 63).

All events are signs in the sense that they provoke the questions that History and historians seek to answer: What has happened? What is going to happen? Explanations can be given of particular events at different levels: macropolitical, micropolitical, long *durée*, short term and so on. But these are never conclusive, if only because they work within a given hermeneutical framework. Most historical events are readily assimilable within such frameworks, but every now and then something happens that we cannot assimilate or understand. The events that Deleuze calls instances of 'becoming breaking through into history' are instances of this kind. They exhibit the hermeneutical sublime in the highest degree insofar as they realise the potential to break with existing frameworks of understanding. Far from being the actualisations of a particular pre-existing event, they are eruptions of 'eventality', pure eventness or becoming: absolute deterritorialisation. On other occasions, however, we pass over such thresholds of sense almost without being aware that we have done so. For example, in societies established by colonisation, such as Australia, a succession of subtle changes to the political imaginary renders problematic the character of this foundational event. The removal of overt discrimination and the inclusion of the Aboriginal inhabitants as full members of the political community means that 'we' now have to understand what happened from the point of view of the colonised as well as the colonisers. It is no longer evident that there is a coherent, single answer to the question 'what happened?'

It is in relation to these almost imperceptible events that genealogical explanation can be most useful. Consider Nietzsche's response to the epochal event of which he was convinced that few in Europe in the late nineteenth century were even conscious, let alone aware of what it meant: the death of God.[8] In this sense, the death of God is something that has already happened, but also something that is yet to come. It raises the historical question par excellence – *what has happened?* – but also the prospective, diagnostic question: *what is going to happen? The Genealogy of Morals* sketches an answer to these questions by answering the prior question posed by the demise of European Christianity, namely, what was meant by belief in God? Nietzsche points to the peculiar opposition between good and evil and the 'inversion of the value-positing eye' that is bound up with this 'slave revolt' in morality; to the origins of bad conscience and the manner in which this was used by the priesthood in its effort to contain the worst effects of human *ressentiment*; and, finally, to the character of the ascetic ideal, by which he means the belief in a world behind the actual world that allows for a variety of forms of imaginary expression on the part of a human will to power that prefers to will nothingness than not will (Nietzsche 1994: 28). This response is an effort to comprehend both the nature and magnitude but also the meaning of this cataclysmic event. In other words, the philosophical response to historical events that we find in Nietzsche is an interpretative exercise.

Much of Foucault's work takes a similar form. He reinterprets past practices, institutions and forms of knowledge, always from the perspective of a hitherto unnoticed distance from them. His genealogies describe the discursive and non-discursive formations (*dispositifs*) from which we are separated by imperceptible fractures in the hermeneutical frameworks in which we live and experience the historical present. In this manner, he shows up the madness of incarcerating the insane, the arbitrariness and injustice of imprisoning convicts, the irrationality of making our identity as subjects depend upon our sexual behaviour. These are all examples of practices that were previously considered unproblematic or unavoidable but that we can now perceive as contingent and open to change (Foucault 1997). Deleuze argues that Foucault writes from the perspective of the *actuel* albeit in a sense closer to Nietzsche's untimely than to the ordinary French sense of this word, namely that which is current or present. He supports this reading by pointing to a passage in *The Archaeology of Knowledge* in which Foucault draws a distinction between the present (*notre actualité*) and 'the border of time that surrounds our present, overhangs it and indicates it in its otherness' in order to suggest that Foucault writes from this border between present and future (Foucault 1972: 130). Even though Foucault's text does not describe it in this way, this border region is what Deleuze means by the *actuel*. *What is Philosophy?* spells out the proximity of Deleuze's 'becoming', Nietzsche's untimely (*l'inactuel* or *l'intempestif*) and Foucault's *actuel* in suggesting that all three terms refer to 'that which is in the process of coming about': not to what we presently are or recently were, but rather to 'what we are in the process of becoming – that is to say, the Other, our becoming-other' (Deleuze and Guattari 1994: 112).[9] However, while Deleuze regularly compares Nietzsche's untimely and Foucault's *actuel* with the realm of becoming and pure eventness that is the object of his own Philosophy, he nowhere undertakes the same kind of genealogical interpretation of events. His comments on a text by Charles Péguy suggest that there is an important difference between historical responses to the question 'what happened?' and the philosophical response advocated and undertaken by Deleuze.

The Internal Dynamics of Events

In *Difference and Repetition*, *The Logic of Sense* and *What is Philosophy?* Deleuze cites the same passage from Péguy's *Clio*, an essay in the form of a dialogue between History and a pagan soul, written between 1909 and 1912 but not published until 1932. Péguy refers explicitly to Bergson in presenting History as proceeding on two levels: that of a public, worldly time in which different peoples and distinct periods acquire their character, and that of a *durée* which has its own rhythm, its own periods of contraction and relaxation, its own points of crisis, of suspension and of relief (Péguy 2002: 265). Péguy's muse, History, admits to the existence of moments in public life as in personal memory when all of a sudden a problem that had long proved intractable disappears and it is as if we became a different person or entered into a different world. The former person or the old world suddenly becomes foreign to us. And yet, in terms of the worldly time of historical events, nothing has happened:

> Suddenly, we felt that we were no longer the same convicts. Nothing had happened. Yet a problem in which a whole world collided, a problem without issue, in which no end could be seen, suddenly ceased to exist and we asked ourselves what we had been talking about. Instead of an ordinary solution, a found solution, this problem, this difficulty, this impossibility had just passed what seemed like a physical point of resolution. A crisis point. At the same time, the whole world had passed what seemed like a physical crisis point. There are critical points of the event just as there are critical points of temperature: points of fusion, freezing and boiling points, points of coagulation and crystallisation. There are even in the case of events states of superfusion which are precipitated, crystallised or determined only by the introduction of a fragment of some future event. (Péguy 2002: 269)[10]

In *Difference and Repetition*, Deleuze cites this passage immediately after the assimilation of structures-problems with events and the distinction referred to above between two series of events, one real and one ideal, where the ideal series is described as both transcendent and immanent in relation to the real. He presents Péguy's description of the event as illustrating these two series by deploying 'two lines, one horizontal and another vertical, which repeated in depth the distinctive points corresponding to the first, and even anticipated and eternally engendered these distinctive points and their incarnation in the first' (Deleuze 1994: 189). *The Logic of Sense* recounts broadly the same concept of structures as determined by the communication or resonance of two series, where a series is a set of singular points or singularities. Within any such structure, the redistribution, displacement and transformation of these singular points will determine a particular form of historicity. Deleuze here cites the same passage in support of the claim that Péguy 'clearly saw that history and event were inseparable from those singular points' (Deleuze

1990: 53). In both texts, this passage is used to support the idea that there are two levels or dimensions of time. The surrounding comments focus on the idea that historical events are the expression of singularities in a virtual structure that lies outside the order of worldly time rather than on the question of how Philosophy should respond to such events.

What is Philosophy? refers to the same passage in support of a different thesis. Much of the passage cited in *Difference and Repetition* is deleted and another line from further down Péguy's page is added: 'nothing happened and we are in a new people, in a new world, in a new humanity' (Péguy 2002: 269; Deleuze and Guattari 1994: 111, translation modified). Here, the emphasis is not so much on the conditions that render possible such experiences but on the experience itself and possible ways of responding. Péguy is said to have explained that there are two ways of considering an event. One is the way of the historian that consists in 'going over the course of the event, in recording its effectuation in history, its conditioning and deterioriation in history'. The other is the way of the philosopher. *Clio* is described as 'a great work of philosophy' and the passage is cited to illustrate a way of considering an event that consists in 'reassembling the event, installing oneself in it as in a becoming, becoming young again and aging in it, both at the same time, going through all its components or singularities' (Deleuze and Guattari 1994: 111).[11] The focus of Deleuze and Guattari's comments on this passage in *What is Philosophy?* is not so much the distinction between virtual and actual, becoming and history, but the philosophical response to the complexity that we find in all events. Péguy presents us with one of those occasions when, although on the historical surface nothing has happened, there has nonetheless been a sudden and unanticipated break with the past. Something happened on another level such that we find ourselves in a new world with new problems. The hermeneutical challenge is to 'make sense' of the event, to answer the question: what happened?

However, on Deleuze's account, History and Philosophy do this in different ways. History makes sense of the event by characterising it and providing an explanation. It tells us how the event came about, at some level of generality or duration, what prepared the way for it and made it possible, how it unfolded and eventually dissipated over time. In these terms, genealogy is still a form of historical explanation. Even with all due acknowledgement of the contingency and discontinuity it admits into history, and taking into account the structural rather than causal character of genealogical explanations of an event, it remains close to what Deleuze describes in the passages above as an historical approach.[12] While History tells us what actually happens and why, the task of

Philosophy is to give expression to the pure event in what happens. As we noted above, Deleuze defines the pure event as that part of every event that escapes its own actualisation. Pure eventness in this sense is the highest object of historical thought. It is what must be thought from an historical point of view, but at the same time that which can never, or never exhaustively, be thought since it is only given to us through what actually happens. A different approach is needed: one that creates concepts that take us inside the event, one that allows us to 'install' ourselves in the event as in a becoming.

One of the clearest examples of this approach to the nature of events is provided by the analysis of the different kinds of line of which individuals and groups are composed.[13] *A Thousand Plateaus* takes up Deleuze's argument in *The Logic of Sense* that the novella is a literary genre devoted to the question posed by every event, namely 'what happened?' As a result, the novella stands in a special relationship to the realm of pure eventness or becoming: 'It evolves in the element of "what happened" because it places us in a relation with something unknowable and imperceptible (and not the other way around: it is not because it speaks of a past about which it can no longer provide us knowledge)' (Deleuze and Guattari 1987: 193). The novella brings us into a relation to becoming by virtue of its treatment of the three kinds of line of which individuals and groups are composed. First, there is a molar or rigid line of segmentarity that corresponds to the social and institutional identities within which our public, private and professional lives are lived: family, school, work, etc. It is on this line that are defined the significant events that make up a biography or the history of a country. Second, there is a line of molecular or supple segmentation that is not divided into distinct segments but into quanta of deterritorialisation. On this line, Deleuze and Parnet suggest, we encounter a different kind of event; 'becomings, micro-becomings, which don't even have the same rhythm as our "history" . . . another politics, another time, another individuation' (Deleuze and Parnet 1987: 124). This line involves a conception of time closer to that which Deleuze earlier defined as the time of the event, Aion. It involves a present 'whose very form is the form of something that has already happened, however close you might be to it, since the ungraspable matter of that something is entirely molecularized' (Deleuze and Guattari 1987: 196). In F. Scott Fitzgerald's *The Crack-Up*, Deleuze's favoured example of the novella genre, these events are the imperceptible cracks in a person's make-up that occur independently of the signifying breaks that otherwise define the progress of a life. They are changes in the molecular structure of a personality, 'redistributions of desire such that when something occurs, the self that awaited it is already dead, or the one that would await it has not yet arrived' (Deleuze and Guattari 1987: 199). The 'something' that is referred to here can only be an 'historical' event of the kind that takes place on the first kind of line.[14]

Even so, the different kind of event that takes place on this second line still only amounts to a relative deterritorialisation of the segmentarity found on the first line. Deleuze and Guattari point to the existence of a third line that represents an even greater distance from the historical entities and identities of the first line, namely the line of flight or absolute deterritorialisation. This is a purely abstract line on which 'not only has the matter of the past volatilized; the form of what happened, of an imperceptible something that happened in a volatile matter, no longer even exists. One has become imperceptible' (Deleuze and Guattari 1987: 199). If the very form of the historical question has been lost, then it is on this line that individuals or groups escape history and enter into the element of becoming or pure eventness. They become imperceptible in the sense that they are identifiable only as haecceities or pure events, indistinguishable from one other but each in their own way.[15] They are reduced to an abstract line capable of actualisation in a multiplicity of traits. In this sense, as Deleuze and Guattari clarify later in *A Thousand Plateaus*, the imperceptibility of the line of flight or becoming is a way 'to enter the haecceity and impersonality of the creator' (Deleuze and Guattari 1987: 280).

Describing these lines as involving different kinds of event is only a first approximation. They might just as readily be described as referring to three levels within any event. Deleuze and Guattari indicate the intended scope of this analysis of the internal structure of events when they propose that the three kinds of line 'could equally be the lines of a life, a work of literature or art, or a society, depending on which system of coordinates is chosen' (Deleuze and Guattari 1987: 203–4). Lines of flight are primary in relation to the other two kinds, but as Deleuze and Parnet point out, this primacy is neither chronological nor eternal but rather 'the fact and right of the untimely' (Deleuze and Parnet 1987: 136). In *A Thousand Plateaus* Deleuze and Guattari assert that there is no act of creation that is not trans-, sub- or super-historical, with reference to Nietzsche's 'unhistorical atmosphere' without which creative acts would not be possible (Deleuze and Guattari 1987: 296). The prefix is less important than the fact that this *Untimely* is aligned with the event-like forms of individuation (haecceity), time (Aion) and change (absolute deterritorialisation) that are associated with the mobile transformative dimension of every assemblage: it is another name for 'the innocence of becoming (in other words, forgetting as opposed to memory, geography as opposed to history, the map as opposed to the tracing, the rhizome as opposed to arborescence' (Deleuze and Guattari 1987: 296). Even history is said to advance by way of the actualisation of absolute deterritorialisation in a given society at a given time: it follows lines of flight rather than 'signifying breaks' (Deleuze and Guattari 1987: 204).

We can now see more clearly the purposes served by the historical material in *A Thousand Plateaus*. On occasions, Deleuze and Guattari describe complex historical phenomena such as Nazism, the crusades or the decline of the Roman Empire in terms of their explication of the inner structure of events. In this manner, for example, a passage from Henri Pirenne's *Mohammed and Charlemagne* is used to illustrate the relationship between the rigidly segmented lines of the Roman Empire, the fluid lines of flight or deterritorialisation of 'the nomads who come in off the steppes', and the supple but ambivalent segmentarity of the migrant barbarians who oscillate between these two poles, sometimes becoming settled, occupying land and being incorporated into the Empire, sometimes allying themselves with the deterritorialising nomads and embarking on a line of conquest and pillage (Deleuze and Guattari 1987: 222). Similarly, the work of Mikhail Griaznov is used to show that their concept of nomadism does not refer to an anthropological or sociological kind of peoples but to 'a movement, a becoming that affects sedentaries, just as sedentarisation is a stoppage that settles nomads' (Deleuze and Guattari 1987: 430).

The continuity with Deleuze's earlier embrace of a structuralist conception of history is apparent in the remark that nomadism is a becoming and that all history does 'is to translate a co-existence of becomings into a succession' (Deleuze and Guattari 1987: 430). Deleuze and Guattari now say that lines of flight express different states of the abstract machines that define particular assemblages rather than the displacements and redistributions of singular points in ideal structures. Nevertheless, their conception of history still relies on the schema according to which virtual movements find expression in actual historical processes. Their overall concern is not to provide historical explanations, genealogical or otherwise, or even to characterise particular historical events, but rather to delineate the internal dynamisms of all kinds of events and the manner in which these unfold in reality. History provides them with one series of examples, alongside others, of surface phenomena where these are produced by the interaction of inner, virtual events or processes. Musical, psychological, anthropological and other phenomena also provide examples of different kinds of relationship between virtual and actual events and processes, for example when they draw upon Pierre Clastres's description of the mechanisms found in non-State societies that both anticipate and ward off the emergence of State power (Deleuze and Guattari 1987: 431).

Deleuze and Guattari sometimes rely on a narrow sense of the term 'history' that restricts it to molar and majoritarian identities and the processes that unfold in linear time. While history understood in this manner may be a surface phenomenon, the events that unfold in history cannot be dissociated from the 'unhistorical atmosphere' that surrounds them. Deleuze and Guattari create concepts that express the virtual dynamics of historical and other kinds of event. However the point is not to oppose history and becoming but to distinguish between them and to show that there are 'all kinds of correlations and movements back and forth between them' (Deleuze 2006: 377).[16] Even though Philosophy is experimental thought and experimentation is not historical, 'without history experimentation would remain indeterminate, lacking any initial conditions' (Deleuze 1995: 17). The line of flight or absolute deterritorialisation is the primary object of their analysis of the virtual dynamics of assemblages – whether as nomadology, schizoanalysis, pragmatics, micropolitics or noology – precisely because it is the source or condition of the emergence of the new. The exploration and elaboration of the realm of pure eventnesss or becoming is important because this dimension is immanent to the social field, its history and its public forms of individuation. Far from being opposed to history, or a matter of flight from the world, becoming, eventness and lines of flight are the condition of movement or change within the world.

References

Althusser, L. and Balibar, E. (1970), *Reading Capital*, London: New Left Books.

Battersby, C. (2003), 'Terror, Terrorism and the Sublime: Rethinking the Sublime after 1789 and 2001', *Postcolonial Studies*, 6 (1): 67–89.

Deleuze, G. (1990), *The Logic of Sense*, trans. Mark Lester with Charles Stivale, ed. Constantin Boundas, New York: Columbia University Press.

Deleuze, G. (1994), *Difference and Repetition*, trans. Paul Patton, London: Athlone and New York: Columbia University Press.

Deleuze, G. (1995), *Negotiations 1972–1990*, trans. Martin Joughin, Columbia: University of Columbia Press.

Deleuze, G. (1996), *L'Abécédaire de Gilles Deleuze avec Claire Parnet*, available on video cassette and CD-Rom (2003) from Vidéo Editions Montaparnasse.

Deleuze, G. (2003), *Deux Régimes de Fous. Textes et Entretiens 1975–1995*, ed. David Lapoujade, Paris: Minuit.

Deleuze, G. (2004), *Desert Islands and Other Texts 1953–1974*, trans. Michael Taormina, ed. David Lapoujade, New York: Semiotext(e).

Deleuze, G. (2006), *Two Regimes of Madness: Texts and Interviews 1975–1995*, trans. Ames Hodges and Mike Taormina, New York: Semiotext(e).

Deleuze, G. and F. Guattari (1987), *A Thousand Plateaus: Capitalism and Schizophrenia*, trans. Brian Massumi, Minneapolis: University of Minnesota Press.

Deleuze, G. and F. Guattari (1994), *What is Philosophy?*, trans. Hugh Tomlinson and Graham Burchell, New York: Columbia University Press.

Deleuze, G. and F. Guattari (2004), *Anti-Oedipus*, trans. Robert Hurley, Mark Seem and Helen R. Lane, London: Continuum.

Deleuze, G. and Parnet, C. (1987), *Dialogues*, trans. Hugh Tomlinson and Barbara Habberjam, London: Athlone Press.

Derrida, J. (2003), 'Autoimmunity: Real and Symbolic Suicides', in G. Borradori (ed.), *Philosophy in a Time of Terror*, Chicago and London: University of Chicago Press.

Foucault, M. (1972), *The Archaeology of Knowledge*, trans. A. M. Sheridan, London: Tavistock.

Foucault, M. (1997), 'What is Enlightenment?', in Paul Rabinow (ed.), *Essential Works of Foucault 1954–1984, Volume 1, Ethics*, trans. Robert Hurley and others, New York: The New Press.

Kant, I. (1978), *The Critique of Judgment* (1790), trans. J. C. Meredith, Oxford: Oxford University Press.

Kearney, R. (2003), 'Terror, Philosophy and the Sublime: Some Philosophical Reflections on 11 September', *Philosophy and Social Criticism*, 29 (1): 23–51.

Nietzsche, F. (1983), 'On the Uses and Disadvantages of History for Life', in *Untimely Meditations*, trans. R. J. Hollingdale, Cambridge: Cambridge University Press.

Nietzsche, F. (1994), *On the Genealogy of Morality*, trans. Carol Diethe, Cambridge: Cambridge University Press.

Nietzsche, F. (2001), *The Gay Science*, ed. B. Williams, Cambridge: Cambridge University Press.

Nietzsche, F. (2005), *Thus Spoke Zarathustra*, trans. Graham Parkes, Oxford: Oxford University Press.

Péguy, C. (2002), *Clio*, Paris: Gallimard.

Patton, P. (2008), 'History, the Event and the Untimely', in Hanjo Berressem and Leyla Haferkamp (eds), *Deleuzian Events – Writing|History*, Hamburg: Lit, 2008.

Patton, P. (2006), 'The Event of Colonisation', in Ian Buchanan and Adrian Parr (eds), *Deleuze and the Contemporary World*, Edinburgh: Edinburgh University Press.

Sibertin-Blanc, G. (2003), 'Les impensables de l'histoire: Pour une problématisation vitaliste, noétique et politique de l'anti-historicisme chez Gilles Deleuze', *Le Philosophoire*, 19: 119–54.

Smith, J. E. (1969), 'Time, Times and the "Right Time": *Chronos* and *Kairos*', *The Monist*, 53 (1): 1–13.

Notes

I am grateful to Moira Gatens, Craig Lundy and Claire Colebrook for helpful comments on earlier versions of this paper.

1. Deleuze and Guattari's text distinguishes between 'l'Histoire', meaning the intellectual discipline, and 'l'histoire', meaning the course of events. This distinction is obscured in the English translation when a sentence begins with 'History'.

2. In his 1967 essay on Structuralism, Deleuze writes: 'As regards time, the position of structuralism is thus quite clear: time is always a time of actualization,

according to which the elements of virtual coexistence are carried out [*s'ef-fectuent*] at diverse rhythms. Time goes from the virtual to the actual, that is, from structure to its actualizations, and not from one actual form to another' (Deleuze 2004: 180).

3. According to Althusser, 'For each mode of production there is a peculiar time and history, punctuated in a specific way by the development of the productive forces' (Althusser and Balibar 1970: 99). Since elements of different modes of production can coexist in a given social formation, this implies that different levels of the social formation will develop in their own relatively independent 'times'.

4. *Kairos* refers to 'a qualitative character of time, to the special position an event or action occupies in a series, to a season when something appropriate happens that cannot happen at "any" time but only at "that time", to a time which marks an opportunity which may not recur' (Smith 1969: 1).

5. In his 'Author's Note for the Italian edition of *Logic of Sense*', Deleuze comments:

   'the novelty for me lay in the act of learning something about surfaces. The concepts remained the same: "multiplicities", "singularities", "intensities", "events", "infinities", "problems", "paradoxes", and "propositions" – but reorganized according to this dimension. The concepts changed and so did the method, a type of serial method, pertaining to surfaces; and the language changed' (Deleuze 2006: 65).

6. Deleuze cites a passage to this effect from Nietzsche's 'On the Uses and Disadvantages of History for Life' (Nietzsche 1983: 60). See also 'Overturning Platonism' (Deleuze 1990: 265).

7. See also the description in *A Thousand Plateaus* of the May events as a molecular flow or 'line of flight' (Deleuze and Guattari 1987: 216); in *Dialogues* as the 'explosion of . . . a molecular line' (Deleuze and Parnet 1987: 132); and in *Negotiations* as 'pure reality breaking through' (Deleuze 1995: 144).

8. In *The Gay Science*, Paragraph 343, '*The meaning of our cheerfulness*', he describes the death of god as 'far too great, too distant, too remote from the multitude's capacity for comprehension even for the tidings of it to be thought of as having *arrived* as yet. Much less may one suppose that many know as yet *what* this event really means – and how much must collapse now that this faith has been undermined because it was built upon this faith, propped up by it, grown into it: for example, the whole of our European morality' (Nietzsche 2001).

9. Deleuze offers a more extended commentary on this passage from *The Archaeology of Knowledge* in 'What is a *Dispositif*?' where he writes: 'The novelty of a *dispositif* in relation to those that precede it is what we call its actuality, our actuality. The new is the *actuel*. The *actuel* is not what we are but rather what we are becoming, what we are in the process of becoming, that is to say the Other, our becoming-other. In every *dispositif* we must distinguish what we are (what we are already no longer) and what we are becoming: the part of history and the part of the actual' (Deleuze 2006: 345, translation modified). The original text reads: '*La nouveauté d'un dispositif par rapport aux précédents, nous l'appelons son actualité, notre actualité. Le nouveau, c'est l'actuel. L'actuel n'est pas ce que nous sommes, mais plutôt ce que nous devenons, ce que nous sommes en train de devenir, c'est-à-dire l'Autre, notre devenir-autre. Dans tout dispositif, il faut distinguer ce que nous sommes (ce que nous ne sommes déjà plus), et ce que nous sommes en train de devenir: la part de l'histoire, et la part de l'actuel*' (Deleuze 2003: 322).

10. See Deleuze 1994: 189; Deleuze 1990: 53; Deleuze and Guattari 1994: 111; Deleuze 1995: 170.

11. Compare the same account in Deleuze's interview with Negri: 'In a major philosophical work, *Clio*, Péguy explained that there are two ways of considering events, one being to follow the course of the event, gathering how it comes about historically, how it's prepared and then decomposes in history, while the other way is to go back into the event, to take one's place in it as in a becoming, to grow both young and old in it at once, going through all its components or singularities. Becoming isn't part of history; history amounts only to the set of preconditions, however recent, that one leaves behind in order to "become", that is, to create something new. This is precisely what Nietzsche calls the Untimely' (Deleuze 1995: 170–1).

12. Deleuze sometimes appears to suggest that Foucault's genealogical method is not historical (Deleuze 1995: 94). However, what he means is what he says more clearly in 'What is a *Dispositif?*', namely that Foucault, like Nietzsche, used history but for the a-historical purpose of diagnosing and reinforcing certain kinds of becoming-other in contemporary societies (Deleuze 2006: 346).

13. This analysis appears initially in Plateau 8: '1874: Three Novellas, or "What Happened?"' but reappears in Plateau 9: '1933: Micropolitics and Segmentarity' and in Chapter 4 ('Many Politics') of *Dialogues*. My discussion of these lines draws on all three of these presentations.

14. Guillaume Sibertin-Blanc, in an excellent discussion of this plateau in the course of an account of Deleuze's anti-historicism, describes the question raised by events of this molecular kind – 'what happened?' – as the 'form of expression of historicity as a pure form of thought' (*forme d'expression de l'historicité comme forme pure de la pensée*) (Sibertin-Blanc 2003: 137).

15. This phrase roughly translates Deleuze and Guattari's deliberately paradoxical formula in relation to 'becoming-imperceptible': 'One has become like everybody else but in a way that nobody else can become like everybody else' (Deleuze and Guattari 1987: 200, translation modified). Sibertin-Blanc describes the rupture effected on this line as a pure event, abstracted from any notion of the past. As such, it provides 'the unconditioned Idea which abolishes history, but the superior experience of which gives history to thought as a problem' (*Idée inconditionée qui abolit l'histoire mais dont l'expérience supérieure donne à la pensée l'histoire comme problème*) (Sibertin-Blanc 2003: 141). Note that in Deleuze's earlier discussion of Fitzgerald's *The Crack-Up* in *The Logic of Sense*, Series 22, 'Porcelain and Volcano', the third line is not mentioned. There is only a two level distinction in which Fitzgerald's crack is identified with the incorporeal pure event (Deleuze 1990: 155).

16. The translation of this passage is modified. The English text goes on to say that becoming is 'the opposite' of history, thereby eliminating all the nuance of Deleuze's use of the verb '*s'opposer*'.

Chapter 2

Of the Rise and Progress of Philosophical Concepts: Deleuze's Humean Historiography

Jeffrey A. Bell

In Deleuze and Guattari's *A Thousand Plateaus*, historical facts, dates and examples run throughout the text. From the use of dates as subtitles to each chapter, to the extensive use of historical examples, *A Thousand Plateaus* is brimming with history. And yet, as Deleuze and Guattari make clear, history is much more than an effort to represent the past as it *actually* happened. It is not just a matter of studying how one event causes another, how one actuality gives rise to another, but rather it ought also to entail a return to the conditions for the actualisation of the actual itself – conditions Deleuze will most frequently call the virtual. As Deleuze and Guattari put it in *What is Philosophy?*, to do such a history:

> It would be necessary to go back up the path that science descends, and at the very end of which logic sets up its camp (the same goes for History, where we would have to arrive at the unhistorical vapour that goes beyond the *actual* factors to the advantage of a creation of something new). (Deleuze and Guattari 1994: 140, emphasis added)

A Deleuzo-Guattarian history, therefore, entails two readings. There is first the effort to read history as accurately as possible, and thus Deleuze and Guattari will frequently rely upon the works of highly respected historians such as Fernand Braudel. The second reading is what we will call problematising history. This is the reading that affirms the virtual 'unhistorical vapour' that is inseparable from the actualities which are the subject of the first reading.

It is the second reading that will be the focus of the following essay. I will argue that there is an historical ontology implicitly at work in the writings of Deleuze (and Deleuze and Guattari) that is crucial to understanding and doing the type of history Deleuze and Guattari call for. To set this forth we will, in the first section, focus on Deleuze's early work on Hume, for in this work not only do we find Deleuze developing the conceptual tools he will use for much of the rest of his career, but we will also see how close Deleuze's philosophy is to that of Hume. More precisely, in extending Nicholas Phillipson's argument that Hume is 'the most genuinely historical of philosophers and the most subtly and profoundly philosophical of historians', I venture to claim that much the same can be said for the work of Deleuze (Phillipson 1989: 3).

From here we will then turn, in the next section, to Deleuze and Guattari's call for a problematising history. In a further elaboration of Hume, we will discuss eighteenth-century Scotland and the intellectual flowering that has come to be called the Scottish Enlightenment. In addition to reading the intellectual history of the Scottish Enlightenment as a series of solutions to problems – i.e., the standard reading that stresses the actualisations of the virtual – we will also discuss the problems of the Scottish Enlightenment that are inseparable from our current situation, problems that may, if one is attentive to them, allow for the creative transformation of the unquestioned actualities of daily life.

I

In his first published book, *Empiricism and Subjectivity*, Deleuze lays out what he takes to be the central problems at work in the philosophy of David Hume. The first problem, as Deleuze reads Hume, is how the multiplicity of ideas in the imagination 'become[s] a system' (Deleuze 1991: 22). This problem arises for Hume because of the externality of relations between impressions and the ideas that are the copies of these impressions. 'The mind', Hume says in his *Treatise*, 'is a kind of theatre', but immediately adds this caution: 'The comparison of the theatre must not mislead us. They are the successive perceptions only, that constitute the mind; nor have we the most distant notion of the place, where these senses are represented' (Hume 1978: 253). As a collection of impressions and ideas that lack any intrinsic, internal basis for relating one to the other, the mind is thus, as Deleuze puts it, 'a collection without an album, a play without a stage, a flux of perceptions' (Deleuze 1991: 23). How then, to restate the problem, does this multiplicity come to form an integrated system? The second problem follows from the first for Deleuze: 'The problem is as follows: how can a subject transcending the given be constituted in the given?' In particular, as Deleuze adds, how is it that this 'subject who invents and believes is constituted inside the given in such a way that it makes the given itself a synthesis and a system' (Deleuze 1991: 86–7). The problem of transforming a multiplicity into a system is thus related to the problem of accounting for the constitution of a subject within the given, a subject that nonetheless transcends the given, or is irreducible to the given.

The effort to respond to these problems will be the work of what Deleuze will call transcendental empiricism. We will discuss this effort below, but before doing so it will be helpful first to turn to a critical evaluation of Hume's philosophy, namely, the interpretation of Hume offered by David Pears, in his book *Hume's System* (1990). To be brief, Pears sees in Hume a 'general failure to mark the transition from his theory of ideas developed as a psychological analogue of a theory of meaning to its development as a theory of truth and evidence' (Pears 1990: 33). In other words, for Pears, Hume's famous argument that all our simple ideas are 'deriv'd from simple impressions . . . which they exactly represent' is the psychological analogue to a Fregean-Russellian theory of meaning which states that an utterance is meaningful if there is a content, x, which exactly corresponds to the utterance and gives the utterance a truth value – e.g. x is the argument that makes the function 'x is the author of Waverley' both true and meaningful when x is replaced by Scott. There is certainly ample textual support for Pears' argument. Pears himself cites the following passage from Hume's abstract to the *Treatise*:

> And when he [Hume anonymously referring to himself] suspects that any philosophical term has no idea annexed to it (as is too common) he always asks from what impression that presented idea is derived? And if no impression can be produced, he concludes that the term is altogether insignificant. (Hume 1978: 648–9)

Hume will make this exact point again in his first *Enquiry*, and thus it appears that one finds in Hume an anticipation of the critique of metaphysics proposed by the logical positivists – that is, a philosophical problem is a pseudo-problem if it cannot be referred to, or resolved by means of, a verifiable sense impression.

It is at this point that the problem in Hume's system emerges. If all our simple ideas are merely passive, mechanical copies of impressions, then a critic of Hume's system, as Hume himself admits, would need simply to find an idea that is not derived from an impression. Thomas Reid, for example, will take Hume up on this challenge, but one need not go to Reid for a possible counter-example.[1] Hume provides one himself. This is the well-known example of the missing shade of blue. Could one who has never had an impression of this missing shade nonetheless come up with the idea of it if 'all the different shades of that colour, except that single one, be plac'd before him, descending gradually from the deepest to the lightest'. Hume has no doubt that one would be able to do so, and yet rather than see this as 'proof, that the simple ideas are not always derived from the correspondent impressions', he simply moves on, dismissing this case as 'so particular and singular, that 'tis scarce worth our observing' (Hume, 1978: 6). For Pears, however, this difficulty should not be swept under the rug. To the contrary, by insisting on the externality of relations – i.e., the claim that everything can be reduced to being merely a collection of separable, distinct, simple and indivisible impressions – Hume is led to a form of atomism that will generate further problems for his system. For Pears, both Russell and Wittgenstein attempted to do this as well, 'but genuine simplicity proved unattainable', Pears claims, 'and he [Wittgenstein] soon abandoned his atomism in favour of holism. Hume should have done the same' (Pears, 1990: 27).

At the basis of Pears' critique, I argue, is an understanding of atoms that does not stand up to a close reading of Hume's *Treatise*. In particular, Pears assumes the atoms are indivisible identities, identities that come along to provide ideas with meaningful content. The problem with this view is precisely the assumption that the atoms are *identities*, identities that exist but without the type of 'lateral relations' Pears believes would help explain the idea of the missing shade of blue (Pears 1990: 20–1).[2] Identity, however, is for Hume, as we will see, *underdetermined*; rather than being the indefinable basis for Hume's theory, as Pears sees it, identity forever needs to be constituted, systematised and maintained. It is no wonder then that Deleuze, in his efforts to develop a philosophy of difference, found an initial inspiration in the work of Hume.

Hume's discussion of identity occurs at a crucial point in the *Treatise*, towards the end of Book I. After offering a summary of his system, and how it accounts for the 'idea of continu'd existence', Hume claims that the principle of identity is crucial for his system. And yet, he admits, identity cannot arise from the perception of 'one single object', for this 'conveys the idea of unity, not that of identity' – that is, not the continued identity of *this* object in time; nor can a multiplicity of objects convey this idea, for here one finds separable and distinct existences, not the continued self-identity of one and the same existence. Hume then offers the following solution:

> To remove this difficulty, let us have recourse to the idea of time or duration. I have already observ'd, that time, in a strict sense, implies succession, and that when we apply its idea to any unchangeable object [i.e., to a unity], 'tis only by a fiction of the imagination, by which the unchangeable object is suppos'd to participate of the changes of the co-existent objects, and in particular that of our perceptions. This fiction of the imagination almost universally takes place; and 'tis by means of it, that a single object,

plac'd before us, and survey'd for any time without discovering in it any interruption or variation, is able to give us a notion of identity. (Hume 1978: 200–1)

As Hume will clarify a few lines later, this fiction creates a difference within the unchanging object, a difference that enables us to see the object as the same as itself at a different time. Identity, in other words, is the result of an artifice, a fiction, and thus the identity of any object, whether it is an indivisible atom, a self, and so on, is inseparable from a generative, systematising process. And this brings us back to the problem in Hume that most interested Deleuze: how is this identity generated, and what is this systematising process, especially if we do not presuppose an overarching or founding *identity* as the basis upon which this process is to proceed?

Returning then to the transcendental empiricism Deleuze sees in the work of Hume, the transcendental component involves addressing the question, 'how can something be given to a subject, and how can the subject give something to itself?' (Deleuze 1991: 87). Most especially, how can the subject give something to itself that transcends the given? The empiricist aspect addresses the question, 'how is the subject constituted in the given?' (Deleuze 1991: 87). For Deleuze, Hume is quite clear as to how one goes beyond the given – it is through belief and invention: 'Belief and invention are the two modes of transcendence' (Deleuze 1991: 132). Moreover, it is precisely through the creativity of invention and belief that the multiplicity of ideas is transformed into a system: 'The subject invents; it is the maker of artifice. Such is the dual power of subjectivity: to believe and to invent, to assume the secret powers and to presuppose abstract or distinct powers . . . This subject who invents and believes is constituted inside the given in such a way that it makes the given itself a synthesis and a system' (Deleuze 1991: 86–7). These powers that constitute the subject within the given, and a subject able to invent and believe, are the principles of human nature. Deleuze is clear on this point:

> The most important point is to be found here. The entire sense of the principles of human nature is to transform the multiplicity of ideas which constitute the mind into a system, that is, a system of knowledge and of its objects . . . [but for this to be possible] we must give the object of the idea an existence which does not depend on the senses. (Deleuze 1991: 80)

The way in which the principles do this is through a double process. First, 'within the collection [multiplicity], the principle elects, chooses, designates, and invites certain impressions of sensation among others'. For example, 'the principles of passion are those that choose the impressions of pleasure and pain', and 'the principles of association . . . choose the perception that must be brought together into a composite'. As for the second process, the principle 'constitutes impressions of reflection in connection with these elected impressions' (Deleuze 1991: 113).[3] What does this mean? For Deleuze, what Hume means by this is that 'the principle produces a habit, a strength, and a power to evoke any other idea of the same group; it produces an impression of reflection' (Deleuze 1991: 114). Whenever a shade of blue appears, for instance, we are habitually able to place this shade into the series of resembling impressions that are felt to belong together by virtue of the selections made by the principles of association. This double process, however, mirrors a more profound double process for Hume, that being the processes associated with the passions on the one hand and the principles of association on the other. For Deleuze, as is well known, Hume gives clear primacy to the passions: 'Association gives the subject a possible structure, but only the passions can give it being and existence . . . the principles of the passions are absolutely primary' (Deleuze 1991: 120). To restate this using Deleuze's much later terminology of double articulation, the principles of human nature draw the multiplicity of ideas into a 'possible structure' through the association of ideas (first articulation), and the principles of human nature actualise this possible structure by way of the passions (second articulation). By prioritising the passions, therefore, Hume gives preference to the actual demands and passions, and the creativity of invention and belief are subordinate to these actual demands (hence Hume's famous statement that reason is and ought to be the slave of the passions[4]).

We can now restate, in Deleuze's terms, the process whereby the underdetermination of identity becomes determined. In the first articulation, an unchanging object becomes related, through a fiction or artifice that is nonetheless natural, to a series of others that change in time. In the second articulation, this series is then synthesised or actualised through an impression of reflection whereby what is constituted is the felt identity of an object in time. And now we can see why Hume dismisses the case of the missing shade of blue. It is worth noting, as well, that Hume offers the same counter-example in his first *Enquiry* and dismisses it with exactly the same words he used in his *Treatise*. Put simply, Hume dismisses the case of the missing shade precisely because it is singular; in other words, the idea of the missing shade of blue is subsumed by the felt identity of the synthesis of the resembling shades of blue, and thus the singularity of the missing shade does not derail the established, felt habits associated with 'blue' – i.e., it does not call for a new synthesis. In the case of the Laplanders, to take an example from Hume's first *Enquiry*, they can form no idea of wine because they have not even had the first in a series of wine-impressions, and thus they cannot even begin fictioning or synthesising the identity associated with wine. The process whereby identity comes to be generated is not instantaneous, and though there are examples in Hume, and in Deleuze as well, where a sudden transition seems to occur, more frequently and more importantly the identity of an object gathers strength over time. The very being and identity of these entities has a history – it is not all or nothing, being or nothingness – and it is this process that is referred to in using the term 'historical ontology'.

A few examples at this point may help to clarify what we mean. The subject who believes, for instance, is a subject subjected to processes that generate what it means to be a subject. As Deleuze puts it, for Hume, 'the mind is not subject; it is subjected' (Deleuze 1991: 31). Perhaps the most important of these processes for Hume is that whereby the subject becomes a subject motivated by a concern for humanity, for the public interest. Such a motivation does not arise naturally and immediately, Hume admits, for 'there is no such passion in human minds as the love of mankind' (Hume 1978: 481). Our natural inclinations, according to Hume, are always partial to our concrete, actual circumstances, and we are not naturally predisposed to get fired up about the more distant, remote and abstract interests of the public. Consequently, Hume claims that 'we must allow, that the sense of justice and injustice is not deriv'd from nature, but arises artificially, tho' necessarily from education, and human conventions' (Hume 1978: 483). Moreover, the emergence of justice and the protection of and respect for property that goes with this is, according to Hume, a belief or motivation that acquires strength over time. Hume is clear on this point: 'Nor is the rule concerning the stability of possession the less deriv'd from human conventions, that it arises gradually, and acquires force by a slow progression, and by our repeated experience of the inconveniences of transgressing it' (Hume 1978: 490).

The same applies, for Hume, to political and social institutions, education especially, and to the actions of politicians and others who subject subjects to the standards that create a cultured, moral subject. These very institutions and standards are themselves subject to a generative process. As Hume puts it with respect to the legitimacy of political power that magistrates and leaders have, 'time alone gives solidity to their right; and operating gradually on the minds of men, reconciles them to any authority, and makes it seem just and reasonable' (Hume 1978: 556). And again, in reference to the governmental institutions themselves, Hume argues that 'Time and custom give authority to all forms of government, and all successions of princes; and that power which at first was founded only on injustice and violence, becomes in time legal and obligatory' (Hume 1978: 566).

More recently, Bruno Latour has proposed a theory of 'relative existence' that is much in line with the historical ontology we find in Hume, and in Deleuze's extension of Hume. Central to Latour's theory is the notion that 'the terms "construction" and autonomous reality are synonymous' (Latour 1999: 275). In returning to Hume, and to the underdetermination of theories and beliefs by impressions that is integral to Hume's philosophy, Latour argues that the contrasting theories of Pasteur and Pouchet cannot be reduced to matters of fact:

> Pasteur and Pouchet disagree about the interpretation of facts because, so the historians say, those facts are underdetermined and cannot, contrary to the claims of empiricists, force rational minds into assent. So the first task of social historians and social constructivists, following Hume's line of attack, was to show that we, the humans, faced with dramatically underdetermined matters of fact, have to enroll other resources to reach consensus – our theories, our prejudices, our professional or political loyalties, our bodily skills, our standardizing conventions, etc. (Latour 2000: 263–4)

This Humean line of attack is central to what is called the strong programme in science studies. A guiding thesis of this programme, as spearheaded by David Bloor, is that sociologists ought to 'seek the same kind of causes for both true and false, rational and irrational beliefs' (Bloor 1991: 175). Whereas social causes are often sought to explain why certain false beliefs were once maintained, such causes are not looked for in accounting for why we hold to beliefs that are true. The assumption Bloor challenges is that 'true' beliefs are not socially caused but are caused by the autonomous reality of the facts themselves. It is at this point that the theory of underdetermination and Hume's line of attack comes in. If facts underdetermine the theories one adheres to, then one must look elsewhere than the facts themselves, and for Bloor and the strong programme we should look for social causes to account for the theories we support. The approach of the strong programme is more generally known as social constructivism, and it has been used to argue for the view that everything from quarks to mental illness is socially constructed (Hacking 1999).

At first it might appear that Latour's position should be seen as a version of social constructivism. If construction and autonomous reality are to be understood as synonymous, then is this not arguing for the social construction of reality? For Latour the answer to this question is

a resounding no, and for a very straightforward reason. Social constructivism presupposes, Latour argues, the duality of the human and the non-
human. It is the non-human world that is underdetermined and in need
of the human world to come along and speak for it, to provide the determinations the non-human world cannot provide itself. Scientific realism
adheres to this same view of reality. The entities of science, on this view,
are taken to be autonomous and independent of the social context within
which they may be discussed and disputed. In the case of scientific
realism, it is the autonomous reality of a scientific entity that ultimately
determines whether a scientific theory we construct is true or not; conversely, social constructivists argue that the truth of a scientific theory is
caused, because of the underdetermination of facts, by social factors.
Depite their opposing positions, they each base their understanding upon
a fundamental dualism – of subject and object, human and non-human.
'The acquiescence of the two archenemies, social constructivists and real-
ists, to the very same metaphysics for opposed reasons has', Latour notes,
'always been for me a source of some merriment' (Latour 2000: 264).

   What Latour offers in order to avoid the either/or options of scientific
realism and social constructivism is what he calls 'historical realism', and
key to historical realism is the notion of 'relative existence', by which he
means that scientific entities can be said to be 'existing somewhat, having
a little reality, occupying a definitive place and time, having predecessors
and successors'; or, as he puts it in *Pandora's Hope*, 'we insist and insist
again that there is a social history of things and a "thingy" history of
humans' (Latour 1999: 18). What this means for Latour, as for Hume and
Deleuze, is that reality is something that can be accumulated through
time, through an increasing number of associations. It is not all or nothing
regarding the existence of entities. As Latour puts it: 'An entity gains in
reality if it is associated with many others that are viewed as collaborat-
ing with it. It loses in reality if, on the contrary, it has to shed associates
or collaborators (humans and nonhumans)' (Latour 2000: 257). The
identity of such entities, in short, has a history, an historical ontology,
inseparable from it. In the case of Pouchet's theory of spontaneous generation, for example, the relative existence of spontaneous generation
was high in 1864, for it was associated with a heterogeneous number of
human and non-human elements. Latour lists 'commonsense experience,
anti-Darwinism, republicanism, Protestant theology, natural history
skills in observing egg development, geological theory of multiple creations, Rouen natural museum equipment [the lab where Pouchet
worked]', as among the associations that were inseparable from the relative existence of spontaneous generation at the time (Latour 2000: 257).

By 1866, however, Pasteur's theory of fermentation displaced Pouchet's by acquiring its own heterogeneous network of associations. Today Pasteur's theory has become an unquestioned 'black boxed' (to use Latour's term) fact, not only by being incorporated into the textbooks, but also, and more importantly for Latour, as a result of establishing a heterogeneous field of human and non-human associations. 'I live', admits Latour, 'inside the Pasteurian network, every time I eat pasteurized yogurt, drink pasteurized milk, or swallow antibiotics' (Latour 2000: 263).

For Hume, Deleuze and Latour then, on our reading, whatever identity we choose to say *is* – whether this is the simple identity of atoms on Pears' reading of Hume, Pasteur's microorganisms, or the established forms and institutions of government – this identity has a history. Every identity, in short, is in itself underdetermined and requires an historical, inventive process to establish and maintain its actuality. If understood in only this way, however, we would be following the path from the virtual to the actual, as was mentioned at the beginning of this essay. For Deleuze, by contrast, the hope is to begin with the identities that are actual and given, and then move to the generative, inventive processes that remain inseparable from these actualities. Hume, moreover, seeks to do the same thing. 'In England', Hume notes, there are 'many honest gentlemen, who being always employ'd in their domestic affairs, or amusing themselves in common recreations, have carried their thoughts very little beyond those objects, which are every day expos'd to their senses' (Hume 1978: 272). Hume, of course, sought to carry his thought beyond everyday actualities, and associated with the effort to do this is what I would call doing historical ontology.

II

Turning now to the theme of problematising history, and incorporating the discussion of historical ontology, I want first to compare this type of history to two similar versions set forth by contemporaries, or near contemporaries, of Deleuze himself. The first and most obvious is that of Foucault. In fact, during a lecture delivered towards the end of his life at Berkeley in 1983, Foucault argued that his work had been an effort to do a 'history of thought' rather than a 'history of ideas'. Foucault describes the difference between the two as follows:

> Most of the time a historian of ideas tries to determine when a specific concept appears, and this moment is often identified by the appearance of a new word. But what I am attempting to do as a historian of thought is

something different. I am trying to analyze the way institutions, practices, habits, and behavior become a problem for people who behave in specific sorts of ways, who have certain types of habits, who engage in certain kinds of practices, and who put to work specific kinds of institutions. The history of ideas involves the analysis of a notion from its birth, through its development, and in the setting of other ideas which constitute its context. The history of thought is the analysis of the way an unproblematic field of experience, or set of practices, which were accepted without question, which were familiar and 'silent', out of discussion, becomes a problem, raises discussion and debate, incites new reactions, and induces a crisis in the previously silent behavior, habits, practices, and institutions. (Foucault 2001: 74)

Deleuze's project is quite in line with Foucault's. They are each concerned with addressing the unquestioned actualities of life through 'histories', or 'archaeologies' as Foucault also frequently called them, that reveal the contingencies associated with what have become the durable actualities of today. There are a number of examples of this analysis at work in Foucault, from his early work on madness which studied the problematisation of the insane and the attendant discourse which medicalised them, to the theme of the lectures from which the above quote was taken: how *parrhousia* (Greek for frank, open and free speech) became problematised as the Demos of Ancient Greece began to claim a right to *parrhousia* themselves. In both cases, and in most if not all of his work in between, the problems Foucault analyses are problems inseparable from our current ways of thinking, though our view of these problems may lie hidden beneath certain unquestioned assumptions.

Foucault will even on one occasion use the term historical ontology to describe his project.[5] However, as Ian Hacking is correct to point out, the constituted being with which Foucault is most concerned is the subject. In particular, he is concerned with how the 'truth' and 'legitimacy' of certain discourses constitute ourselves as objects of knowledge. Second, Foucault is concerned with the power through which we constitute ourselves as agents able to act upon, or be acted upon, by others. And finally, he was concerned with the ethical implications of how we are constituted as moral subjects, subjects with obligations and duties towards ourselves and others. Where Hacking – who once held the chair at the Collège de France that Foucault had himself held – differs from Foucault is on the stress he places on the ontological implications of the latter's project. For Hacking:

Historical ontology is about the ways in which the possibilities for choice, and for being, arise in history. It is not to be practiced in terms of grand abstractions, but in terms of the explicit formations in which we can constitute ourselves, formations whose trajectories can be plotted as clearly as those of trauma or child development . . . Historical ontology is not so much about the formation of character as about the space of possibilities for character formation that surround a person, and create the potentials for 'individual experience'. (Hacking 2002: 23)

Now perhaps this is splitting hairs, but for Hacking historical ontology will be less a study of the institutions that legitimise and embody the practices and discourses associated with the way in which the self is constituted, and hence will be less political, but will instead provide a chart and mapping of the possible ways in which we can 'be' as subjects. To take Hacking's example of trauma, trauma is an object of knowledge that has not always existed, and yet it is now something with very real effects upon how we see ourselves and how we respond to events. An historical ontology of 'post-traumatic stress syndrome' becomes, therefore, on Hacking's view, less a history of the institutions and discourses that legitimise and control the practices associated with trauma – though certainly their role is significant – but rather a history of how we can come, in our everyday life, to see ourselves as *being* a person of a certain type, whether this is someone who suffers from post-traumatic stress disorder, or, as was the topic of one of Hacking's early books, someone with multiple personality disorder.

Now the historical ontology I see at work in Deleuze is quite in line with that of Foucault and Hacking, but it extends the analysis beyond that of examining how the subject is constituted to seeing how both human and non-human subjects and entities are constituted. This is already evident in Deleuze's book on Hume, for although the problems associated with transcendental empiricism dealt with how a subject is constituted, the constitution of the subject was inseparable from non-subjective factors. In fact, it is fair to say, I think, that Deleuze's historical ontology is concerned with how the very subject–object dichotomy itself is just one of many entities that come to be constituted, and the double articulation model discussed above comes then to be an appropriate tool for understanding the generative processes associated with the emergence of entities ranging from sedimentary rock to subjects and nation states.[6]

With these general comments in mind, we can turn now to examine how a Deleuzian historical ontology could be used to understand intellectual and cultural change. To do this, we return again to Hume, for this was equally a concern of Hume's. We saw earlier how the multiplicity of ideas is transformed, through a double process, into the impressions of reflection that come to be actualised as beliefs – for example, the belief in causation – that are irreducible to what is actually given. This same process is at work within socialisation, or what we might call acculturation, though this time the multiplicity that comes to be transformed into a system or unity is the multiplicity of partialities, passions and interests, or what Deleuze will call a social multiplicity in *Difference and Repetition* (Deleuze 1994: 193). Deleuze is quite clear on this point: 'Partialities or particular interests cannot be naturally totalised, because they are mutually exclusive. One can only invent a whole, since the only invention possible is that of the whole' (Deleuze 1991: 40). Hume is thus led, for Deleuze, to understand society as not being founded upon a law that allows us to escape our nature (*à la* Hobbes), but rather as a series of invented institutions, inventions that are themselves indistinguishable from human nature in that they follow from the principles of human nature:

> The main idea is this: the essence of society is not the law but rather the institution . . . institution, unlike the law, is not a limitation [as Hobbes would understand it] but rather a model of actions, a veritable enterprise, an invented system of positive means or a positive invention of indirect means. (Deleuze 1991: 45–6)

What such institutions attempt to do, then, is not to function as representatives of a general interest or a general will, but rather to operate so as to make 'the general interest an object of belief' (Deleuze 1991: 51). Such an operation, if successful, will 'enter the natural constitution of the mind as a feeling for humanity or as culture' (Deleuze 1991: 130). And it is through this constitution or invention of social institutions that the multiplicity of partialities and interests comes to be transcended by the feeling for humanity, whereby one becomes a polished, polite and cultured subject of good breeding.

With this latter move, we come to a core concern of Hume's – namely, the relationship between society and what Hume calls, in an essay of the same name, 'the rise and progress of the arts and sciences'. In this essay Hume recognises that since the geniuses of the arts and sciences are frequently few in number, to discuss the conditions that give rise to them may seem a futile task. However, he then argues that though they

> be always few in all nations and all ages, it is impossible but a share of the same spirit and genius must be antecedently diffused throughout the people among whom they arise, in order to produce, form, and cultivate, from their earliest infancy, the taste and judgment of those eminent writers. (Hume 1993: 58)

It is this diffusion of 'the same spirit and genius . . . throughout the people' – or what Deleuze might call the drawing of a multiplicity of interests into a plane of consistency (first articulation) – that is the antecedent condition allowing for the actualisation (second articulation) of the great geniuses, and hence for the rise and progress of the arts and sciences.

Hume's concern with understanding the conditions for the emergence of creativity, in this case of creative geniuses in the arts and sciences, and just as importantly his concern for understanding the conditions that lead to the decline of creativity within society, are especially relevant to Deleuze's work. Hume's reasoning in regard to the necessary decline of creativity in a particular culture (or 'nation') is quite straightforward:

> A man's genius is always, in the beginning of life, as much unknown to himself as to others; and it is only after frequent trials, attended with success, that he dares think himself equal to those undertakings, in which those who have succeeded have fixed the admiration of mankind. If his own nation be already possessed of many models of eloquence, he naturally compares his own juvenile exercises with these; and, being sensible of the great disproportion, is discouraged from any further attempts, and never aims at a rivalship with those authors whom he so much admires. (Hume 1993: 75–6)

At this point we again merge with Deleuze's project, especially with his transcendental empiricism. In an experimental philosophy, or a philosophy that begins with the actual in an effort to release the virtual inseparable from it, one must not prejudge or predetermine what new actualities might result from this process (Deleuze 1994: 143–4). An historical practice that will engender creative thinking thus cannot allow itself to be reduced to, or be predetermined by, the identity of any model or standard, just as the genius, according to Hume, can only come to rival the other great authors they admire when there is no already established national model, and when this developing genius, without knowing where their work will develop, is able to progress through 'frequent trials' and experimentations.

Turning our attention to more recent work in intellectual history, we can find in the work of Fritz Ringer a significant parallel to Deleuze's Humean approach to intellectual history. In his essay 'The Intellectual Field, Intellectual History, and the Sociology of Knowledge', Ringer expands upon a thesis of Pierre Bourdieu and argues that original and coherent thought is to be understood as a 'kind of clarification, an emergence toward clarity', and what is clarified are the 'tacit assumptions of a cultural world', or what he calls the 'cultural preconscious' (Ringer 1990: 273). What the creative, original intellectual is able to do, in other words, is to put forth a work that holds together a 'disparate multiplicity of practices' within the intellectual world of the time. This holding together 'clarifies' the work of this field by making explicit what was already implicitly at work in the writings, discussions, and so on, of other contemporary intellectuals. The creative intellectual is not, on this view, the self-caused genius who, like a pied piper, sets the terms that all other intellectuals in the field follow. Others follow only because they were already implicitly doing what the creative intellectual does, but does more clearly. For an intellectual to become a 'star' or leader they must articulate (first articulation) in a consistent manner the diverse, heterogeneous intellectual field of which they are a part (i.e., the cultural preconscious), and as others come increasingly to recognise this clarified field the clarifier then comes to be identified as being (second articulation) the canonical figure in the field. This cultural preconscious, however, is an already ordered and consistent field – the creative intellectual simply expresses the order of this field to others; they do not, of themselves, order the field. Thus, from a Deleuzian and Humean perspective, the intellectual, on Ringer's account, is not truly thinking beyond the intellectual field, beyond what is given. They are not experimenting with the actual relationships that compose the intellectual field – be they textual, interpersonal and institutional – so as to intensify them and force a reordering of the field, and with it the clarifying work Ringer discusses. For Ringer, the creative intellectual simply clarifies for others the givens with which they were already working, but without conscious awareness (hence the cultural preconscious). For Deleuze and Hume, however, this is not creative thinking, thinking beyond what is actually given; it is an unmasking or revealing of what is already actually given.

There is an additional problem with this view and others like it that attempt to make society, or social institutions and factors, the already established and constituted element that prefigures intellectual life. Whether it is an intellectual field, a class interest, an ideology, etc., we need to be wary, as we have seen Latour argue, of assuming that society functions as an already constituted causal subject that constitutes individuals, or intellectuals, as its objects. Such a view simply repeats the metaphysical subject–object dualism Latour rejects. Latour similarly rejects the notion that historical events simply follow from their causal antecedents. Such an understanding of history, as Latour makes quite clear, forecloses upon any possibility for creativity, for moving beyond the actual. If history has no other meaning than to activate potentiality – that is, to turn into effect what was already there in the cause – then no matter how much juggling of associations takes place, nothing, no new thing at least, will ever happen, since the effect was already hidden in its cause, as a potential. Causality follows the events and does not precede them (Latour 1999: 152).

As with problematising history, the history Latour seeks to undertake is similarly interested in moving beyond the actual to the conditions that allow for something new to take place. To the extent then that the effect is already in the cause as its hidden potential, the actualisation of this potential merely comes to realise what was already there and is not the upsurge of anything new. This is precisely Deleuze's point and explains why he repeatedly argues that the virtual in no way resembles the actual, for only in this way can something truly new come to be (Deleuze 1994: 211–12). For Latour and Woolgar, then, as they put it in *Laboratory Life*, '"reality" cannot be used to explain why a statement becomes a fact, since it is only after it has become a fact that the effect of reality is obtained' (Latour and Woolgar 1979: 180). In other words, only when a heterogeneous number of associations and links between human and non-human elements are networked together (first articulation) do we acquire actualisations that come to be taken as the factual reality that accounts for cause-effect relationships. Once actualised as a fact, or black boxed, the historical processes come to be eclipsed by the actualised fact. Likewise for Deleuze, the reality of the virtual, although presupposed by and inseparable from the actual, comes to be eclipsed and hidden by the actualisation of the actual.[7] As Hume might put it, the frequent trials and experiments of the would-be genius start to lose their contingency, fragility and unpredictability once the genius becomes actualised as a canonical figure and model. Once seen in this light, it is the actual nature of the genius that leads one to see the emergence of the genius as an inevitable consequence of actualising and revealing an already present reality. But for Hume nothing is certain. Success is not assured, and the presence of predetermining national models and exemplars only increases the likelihood of failure.

It is at this point that the problematising history we find in Deleuze becomes most relevant to intellectual history. In analysing Humean concepts a Deleuzian intellectual history will see them not as tools with a predetermined use and application, but rather as the inventive by-products of a generative process, a process that focuses not on what has been thought, but rather on the problems associated with thinking itself, the problems associated with trying to think beyond what has actually been thought. The rise and progress of philosophical concepts is not, for Deleuze, the story of problems that come to be solved by way of conceptual representations that function as solutions by mapping these representations onto previously undiscovered entities (viz., ideas). To the contrary, a Deleuzian problematising history begins with concepts as solutions in order to move towards the virtual fields and problems that are inseparable from these functional concepts and representations; and it is this virtual field that makes new work possible – that is, the mapping and representational work of functional concepts. Thus, although intellectuals may begin with certain texts and traditions, the very *identity* of what these texts mean needs forever to be reconstituted, and in this process accepted meanings may be violated, or new readings may arise that problematise the intellectual field. Approached in this way a study of intellectual history (or the history of philosophy) would not satisfy an antiquarian or scholarly interest in what the great thinkers of the past thought, but it would, hopefully, engender creative thinking, a thinking that might open up possibilities in today's world beyond those already offered and already tried. It was this type of creative thinking that took place during the Scottish Enlightenment, of which Hume was a part, and which engendered many of the unquestioned ways we actually think about ourselves and our place in the world today. It will be a similar creative thinking that will bring forth the unquestioned actualities of tomorrow.

References

Bell, J. (2006), *Philosophy at the Edge of Chaos*, Toronto: University of Toronto Press.

Bloor, D. (1991), *Knowledge and Social Imagery*, Chicago: University of Chicago Press.

Bonta, M. and J. Protevi (2004), *Deleuze and Geophilosophy*, Edinburgh: Edinburgh University Press.

Deleuze, G. (1991), *Empiricism and Subjectivity: An Essay on Hume's Theory of Human Nature*, trans. Constantin V. Boundas, New York: Columbia University Press.

Deleuze, G. (1994), *Difference and Repetition*, trans. Paul Patton, London: Athlone and New York: Columbia University Press.

Deleuze, G. and F. Guattari (1994), *What is Philosophy?*, trans. Hugh Tomlinson and Graham Burchell, New York: Columbia University Press.

Foucault, M. (1984), *The Foucault Reader*, ed. Paul Rabinow, New York: Pantheon Books.

Foucault, M. (2001), *Fearless Speech*, Los Angeles: Semiotext(e).

Hacking, I. (1999), *The Social Construction of What?* Cambridge, MA: Harvard University Press.

Hacking, I. (2002), *Historical Ontology*, Cambridge, MA: Harvard University Press.

Hume, D. (1978) *Treatise of Human Nature*, ed. L. A. Selby-Bigge, Oxford: Oxford University Press.

Hume, D. (1993), *Selected Essays*, ed. Stephen Copley and Andrew Edgar, Oxford: Oxford University Press.

Latour, B. (1999), *Pandora's Hope: Essays on the Reality of Science Studies*, Cambridge, MA: Harvard University Press.

Latour, B. (2000), 'On the Partial Existence of Existing and Non-existing Objects', in *Biographies of Scientific Objects*, ed. L. Daston, Chicago: University of Chicago Press, 263–4.

Latour, B. and Woolgar, S. (1979), *Laboratory Life: The Social Construction of Scientific Facts*, Beverly Hills: Sage Publications.

Pears, D. (1990), *Hume's System*, Oxford: Oxford University Press.

Phillipson, N. (1989), *Hume*, New York: St. Martin's Press.

Reid, T. (1997), *An Inquiry into the Human Mind on the Principles of Common Sense*, University Park, PA: The Pennsylvania State University.

Ringer, F. (1990), 'The Intellectual Field, Intellectual History, and the Sociology of Knowledge', *Theory and Society* 19: 269–94.

Notes

1. For Reid's counter-example, see Reid 1997: 259.
2. 'So his [Hume's] phenomenological division of ideas follows lines laid down by definitions until it reaches indefinables. That is how Russell too and Wittegenstein in his early period saw the task of logical analysis . . . His [Hume's] concentration on this kind of definition, reinforced by the metaphor [of dividing an apple into parts], drives him to atomism. For it makes him neglect the lateral connections of any thing whose idea is under analysis' (Pears 1990: 20–1).
3. In support of the constitutive role of impressions of reflection, Deleuze (1991: 97) cites the *Treatise* (Hume 1978: 36–7). The text runs as follows: 'Five notes play'd on a flute give us the impression and idea of time; tho' time be not a sixth impression, which presents itself to the hearing or any other of the senses. Nor is it a sixth impression, which the mind by reflection finds in itself. These five sounds making their appearance in this particular manner, excite no emotion in the mind, nor produce an affection of any kind, which being observ'd by it can give rise to a new idea. For that is necessary to produce a new idea of reflection, nor can the mind, by revolving over a thousand times all its ideas of sensation, ever extract from them any new original idea, unless nature has so fram'd its faculties, that it feels some new original impression arise from such a contemplation'. Such a new original impression is an impression of reflection, and these impressions are the results of the principles in their constitutive role.
4. Hume 1978: 415: 'Reason is, and ought only to be, the slave of the passions'.
5. Foucault does so in his well-known essay on Kant, 'What is Enlightenment?' (Foucault 1984: 45).
6. See Bell 2006: 213–18, where these points are discussed.
7. See Bonta and Protevi 2004: 36: 'one of the key theses of Deleuze's philosophy is that the extensive properties of actual substances hide the intensive nature of the morphogenetic processes that give rise to them'.

Chapter 3

Theory of Delay in Balibar, Freud and Deleuze: *Décalage, Nachträglichkeit, Retard*

Jay Lampert

This chapter explores some relations between delay, retroactivity and history.

State history (which Deleuze and Guattari often refer to simply as 'history') describes an ordered succession of regimes, while revolutionary history (which Deleuze and Guattari generally call 'becoming', but sometimes also call 'history') assembles contemporaneous series from across the historical field. But of course, contemporaneous becomings cannot all occur at the same time. History therefore consists of diachrony within synchrony; or, to put it in reverse, succession is delayed simultaneity.

In another text (Lampert 2006a), I discussed Deleuze and Guattari's analyses in *Anti-Oedipus* and *A Thousand Plateaus* of simultaneity and delay in history. At a certain point in this chapter, that discussion would be relevant; but rather than rework that material here, I will switch gears. My goal is to examine two of Deleuze's resources for a theory of delay: Balibar and Freud. In Chapter 2 of *Différence et répétition*, Deleuze says that 'there is no question as to how a childhood event acts only with a delay (*retard*). It *is* this delay' (Deleuze 1969: 163). Applying this thesis in the 'Apparatus of Capture' Plateau of *Mille Plateaux*, Deleuze and Guattari discuss the historical encounters that made capitalism possible, encounters that allow capitalism to capture all past ages in its historicisations and at the same time allow something post-capitalist to become what will always have been escaping from it. The passage in *Différence et répétition* refers to Freud; the second passage, from *Mille Plateaux*, footnotes Balibar (Deleuze and Guattari 1980: 565).

Balibar offers a great deal of concrete material for a Deleuzian philosophy of historical delay. I will indicate the points at which Balibar fails to make a sufficiently thoroughgoing use of his own concept of delay, but rather than then move to Deleuze and Guattari's use of delay in their philosophy of history in particular, I will move to Deleuze's critique of delay in Freud, in order to sketch a theory of universal delay. To schematise the three concepts of delay to be discussed here: Balibar's concept of delay (*décalage*) makes delay a consequence of complex synchrony; Freud's concept of delay (*Nachträglichkeit*) makes synchrony an artifact of delayed reaction; Deleuze's concept of delay (*retard*) treats synchrony as delay itself.

Balibar

Balibar in general treats diachrony as a structural variation following from a synchronous situation. Over many years, he has been speculating on how serial contemporaneities pass through delays. Deleuze and Guattari footnote Balibar on a crucial point, namely on the encounter between the independent histories of wealth and labour in the creation of capitalism (Deleuze and Guattari 1980: 565). Balibar adds valuable concreteness to Deleuze and Guattari's account of the delayed emergence of, and then the delays within, capitalism. But elsewhere in *Mille Plateaux*, Deleuze and Guattari construe delay more abstractly. The delays in economic transformations, and the accelerations in the global free market, express a more universal delay inherent in becoming. Deleuze and Guattari define all movement on the plane of immanence in terms of 'the infinite slowness of the wait . . . and the infinite speed of the result' (Deleuze and Guattari 1980: 343). They cite speed and delay (*tardivité*) as diagrammatic traits of abstract machines (Deleuze and Guattari 1980: 176–7). They say that 'the renunciation of external pleasure, or its delay (*retardement*), its infinite distance, testifies to an achieved state where desire no longer lacks anything but fills itself and constructs its own field of immanence' (Deleuze and Guattari 1980: 193). In short, '*retard*' and its cognates describe historical delays as functions of abstract machinic delays. On the one hand, this means that concrete details of history are already abstract. On the other hand, it is only in concrete cases that history becomes abstract enough to delay its co-existence.

(a) Reading Capital: Diachrony and décalage

Balibar confronts the classical problem of historical continuity and discontinuity by introducing two principles: diachrony to analyse 'periods', and synchrony to analyse temporary invariance (Balibar 1965: 204). Classical historiography seeks 'the right break' between two historical periods, but fails to see that different sorts of breaks are 'structured' by different economic modes of production (Balibar 1965: 206). A structure is a complex of combinations and distinctions (Balibar 1965: 216), a 'relation of relations' that replaces what traditional historians used to assume was 'transitive causality' (Balibar 1965: 224). The old focus on breaks and periods, using exclusively diachronic analysis, without appeal to synchronic systems to explain why elements interact as they do, assumed a 'mechanistic thought of temporality' (Balibar 1965: 236–7). Balibar promises to show that the apparently diachronic, periodic transitions are dependent on synchronic modes of production. What looks like successive events are often just variations on a constant structure.

In this sense, Marxism is anti-evolutionary. 'The possibility of finding the periods of modes of production according to a principle of *variation* of combinations, alone deserves to hold our attention' (Balibar 1965: 225). Differences between modes of production are defined by 'non-correspondence' across their functions, structurally rather than genetically. The transition, for example, from animal-driven to steam-driven ploughs comes about not through a 'lineage' of the tool, since the new plough has a different function, determined by a new labour process. It is thus better to speak of transitions as 'displacements than as a continuity' (Balibar 1965: 243) or 'development' (Balibar 1965: 247). Strictly speaking, Marx is not exactly a 'structuralist', since structuralism posits a 'formal combinatory', whereas Marx grounds structures on concrete modes of production (Balibar 1965: 226).

Modes of production are difficult to define, since they consist less of specific technologies than of 'rhythms' and 'patterns' (Balibar 1965: 235). A mode of production is a 'synchronic' system, yet it is realised only with the 'chronological *dislocation* ([or time-lag], *décalage*)' (Balibar 1965: 236) whereby advances made in one industry are spread across different industries, labour pools, legal systems, and so on. A system like capitalism aims to employ its favoured modes of production 'simultaneously' (Balibar 1965: 237), but temporal dislocations are part of its extended simultaneity. Delay within a synchronic system is an essential feature of the simultaneity's complexity.

Because not every succession is historical in the same sense, depending on how it relates to a pre-existing structure, there is no 'history in general'. Even a restricted phrase like 'the history of labour' wrongly assumes a continuous 'referent' or 'subject' (Balibar 1965: 249). Indeed, historical analyses are inherently problematic, requiring decisions about what phenomenon should be individuated as the successor of what. The 'different forms of historical individuality' (Balibar 1965: 252) constitute 'not a multiplicity of centres but the radical absence of a centre' (Balibar 1965: 253). To put this in the terms of a theory of delay, the de-centred object of an historical series implies a dislocation precisely in succession. Even though history is a series of synchronies, the reference of each element in one synchronous state is deferred until we see which element in the following synchronous state corresponds to it.

The only means of determining what succeeds what hangs on the 'repetition' of processes across time periods (Balibar 1965: 259). Elements in the so-called phases in the 'accumulation of capital', for example, are different across almost every parameter, for example, across different types of labour, wealth, property owners and banking systems. Yet in spite of being problematic, variation by repetition can help to identify a phenomenon across differences. For in general, reproducing a process in a new context forces old and new phenomena to become commensurable (as old and new currencies can be added together and spent on a single commodity.) Indeed, the paradigm of a phenomenon that is individuated only after it has been re-produced in a different form from its original production is capital itself. Capital is produced only during its second cycle (Balibar 1965: 263): not merely as exploitation but as self-perpetuating exploitation. Re-production turns a series into a synchronised system. In short, Marx turns the 'transformation of succession into synchrony, into "simultaneity" (in his own term: *Gleichzeitigkeit*)' (Balibar 1965: 264). But individuating what exists in that simultaneity depends on what is re-produced afterwards; otherwise, it is only a 'fictive contemporaneity' (Balibar 1965: 264).

The problem of history is how a synchronous state has a subsequent history: 'how each of these times, for example the time of the "tendency" of the mode of production, *becomes* a historical time' (Balibar 1965: 302). We have said that two phenomena only fall into a synthesis once they are individuated and combined synchronically. Only an eventual simultaneity can explain a succession capable of leading to it. On the one hand, this means that we no longer need to ask how labour and wealth ever got combined in capitalism, since it is only once capitalism's second cycle is in process that the relevant precursor phenomena can even be defined. So once capitalism does exist as a synchronous system, the relevant forms of labour and wealth will already be operating together. Once the concrete synchronic structure is in existence, its elements, and their respective histories, are already, and within that synchronous period, 'eternally' co-existing (Balibar 1965: 272). It is only an illusion that one can debate which, of labour and wealth, is 'the preceding and the succeeding' (Balibar 1965: 271).

The twist in Balibar's analysis is that it is only once a result, like capitalism, exists all at once, that its pre-history, like the accumulation of capital, is a genuine succession. The accumulation prior to capitalism is an effect within the simultaneity of capitalism. Yet Balibar does not construe causal succession purely as retroactive interpretation, which he regards as idealist; there really are actual transitions. Nevertheless, he does want the transitions to depend on simultaneous structures. He wants to affirm real historical transitions, even 'ruptures' (Balibar 1965: 268), while denying succession prior to concrete periods of social history. He wants to make simultaneity precede, but not abolish, succession. Or in my terms, he wants to contrast simultaneity not with succession but with delay. Furthermore, Balibar wants to explain the possibility of transitions without a general theory of transition. He needs to differentiate forms of transition, each defined by the particularities of the structures before and after it. To that end, he describes two transitions: (1) the 'pre-history' of capitalism in 'primitive accumulation'; and (2) the 'tendency' towards the dissolution of capitalism. In the course of the former, Balibar critiques retroactivity; in the course of the latter, he affirms temporal pluralism.

Transition 1: Pre-history versus retroaction

The primitive accumulation of capital begins only once there is already surplus value, that is, once the threshold of capitalism has already been crossed. It is a myth to say that capitalism gradually developed out of a pre-capitalist right to property, and that only later did people begin to sell their labour power. Balibar calls this sort of myth 'retrospective projection' (Balibar 1965: 276), culturally subjective 'memory' at the service of capitalism's self-justification, rather than genuine 'history' (Balibar 1965: 278). The origins of capitalism have to be capitalism's own early stage, capitalism's own 'pre-history' (Balibar 1965: 278), distinct from and prior to mature capitalism's retrospective self-image. The twist in Balibar's account is that only if an early stage is taken to occur *within* a period can that stage be held distinct as pre-history from the mature stage within that period; if the early stage is taken to have occurred before the period, it is too easily co-opted into an anachronistic apologetics of the mature period. Retroactive interpretation is admittedly appealing in that it sees correctly that earlier stages of capitalism occurred while the elements in capitalism were still relatively independent, that is, when finance capital, labour exploitation, and so on, made up a still undecided 'diversity of historical pathways' (Balibar 1965: 282). But what is wrong with retroactivity is that it ignores the 'find' (*trouvaille*) whereby independent processes were forced into the same result (Balibar 1965: 282).

At first, it seems that in rejecting retrospective interpretation Balibar is affirming genuine succession: an event that really took place before capitalism. But Balibar's subtle point is that capital accumulation took place *before* capitalism, but *also during* capitalism, and that this sort of paradoxical sequence, neither an a-historical rupture nor a normal occurrence within a pre-given structure, is precisely what we call 'transition'. In my terms, a transitional sequence is neither a moment in a succession that includes capitalism later, nor a phenomenon simultaneous with other capitalist events, but precisely a delay-event. Balibar is not saying, as Deleuze will, that the same event occurs both during childhood and during adulthood, but he is saying that the adult's past occurs at a moment when one's adulthood is still in its childhood state.

In sum, it is an illusion to use retroactivity to claim that pre-capitalist build-up was an innocent process prior to it; it is also an illusion to claim that all societies have included capitalism more or less (perennialism is not retroactive, since it does not recognise transitions at all); in contrast, it is right to identify pre-history as the moment at which non-capitalist processes become differences with a common result. These two pervasive Balibarian themes – the plurality of genealogical pathways and the structural synchrony of their effects – will generate his theory of time. If Balibar's theory is difficult, it is so for the same reasons that Deleuze's is, namely that it has to combine the diversity of forces with a plane of consistency, temporal synchrony with temporal distance.

Transition 2: Differentials, double references, and *décalages*
The dissolution of capitalism begins with a 'tendency' in its 'dynamic' (Balibar 1965: 283; 285). Indeed, any structure is in a 'movement towards its historical future' simply due to 'its existence in time' (Balibar 1965: 285). In materialist terms, to be 'in' time does not mean that events fall under pre-existing temporal co-ordinates that map the 'chronology of a succession' (Balibar 1965: 285), but rather that the dynamic of the process plays the event out in stages. The law of a process determines its dissolution 'in the long run'. The theory of the 'long run' is in turn a theory of 'retarding causes' (Balibar 1965: 286), namely causes that specify, yet delay, indeed specify as delay, the rhythm of the process's 'counter-effects' (Balibar 1965: 287). Historical contradiction implies that a delayed result is simultaneous with the process that precedes it: a 'synchrony (Marx calls it a "simultaneity")' whose structure is a simultaneity-delay 'double': *doppelseitige Wirkung* (Balibar 1965: 289) or *zweischlägtig* (Balibar 1965: 290). As different as are the two transitions described by Balibar (one an encounter of forces, the other a tendency

towards dissolution), the theory of transition requires a synchrony whose first movement and final tendency are diachronous. Balibar here cites Althusser's call for a theory of 'historical temporality' (Balibar 1965: 293). Too many philosophies of history take for granted an abstract philosophy of time. They assume time is 'continuous, linear, and unique', 'order, unfolding, and duration', pivoting on the 'contemporaneous present' (Balibar 1965: 294). They assume that all events that occur at the same moment in time 'belong to the same history' (Balibar 1965: 294). The most they can say regarding temporal diversification in history is to contrast short-term events with long-term invariants (wrongly called 'structures', Balibar adds) (Balibar 1965: 294). The classical theory of historical 'periods' assumes this model, excluding 'true diversity' from within a period (Balibar 1965: 294). Of course, even naive historians notice different tempos within a mode of production (for example, the time it takes to expend a day's labour versus the time it takes to produce a commodity). But their descriptions at best 'insert different times one within another' (Balibar 1965: 295), for the sake of overall forecasting. Theoretically, their reduction of rhythms to homogeneous time-segments is neither diachronic (since it excludes novel temporal structures) nor synchronic (since it measures empirical successions rather than systems).

In truth, though, the same synchronic structure can include different models of time: the generation of profit includes the 'time of social labour' with its rhythms and time-scales; the turnover of capital includes rhythms of production and circulation; resolving crises of overproduction accelerates transportation time (Balibar 1965: 298–9). These multiple time-lines within a single period make a system 'dynamic'. They are what permit 'backward' and 'forward' development, or, to be precise, the phenomenon that two processes may occur successively in one nation and simultaneously in another (Balibar 1965: 300).

In 'differential analysis', whenever we see non-corresponding functions co-existing (synchronically), we will describe this by saying that a (diachronic) passage is taking place (Balibar 1965: 307). A so-called 'period of transition' is primarily just a 'double reference to the structure of two modes of production' (Balibar 1965: 307). This is the 'theory of décalages': time-lags. A period of transition is *the co-existence of two modes of production (or more) in a single "simultaneity" and the dominance of one over the other* (Balibar 1965: 307). Methodologically, 'problems of diachrony must be thought within the problematic of a theoretical "synchrony"' (Balibar 1965: 307).

This theory of multiple co-existing yet differential time-lines is helpful in accounting for historical (and indeed all) phenomena. I am not going to compare, contrast and force encounters between each of Balibar's fine-grained points and those of Deleuze and Guattari in *Mille Plateaux*, as useful as such a project might be. Instead, I want to pose a general question for Balibar. Given the theory of differential time-lines and time-lags, why does he still need a division between synchronic structures within an historical period and diachronic transitions between them? Balibar thinks that synchronicity is a necessary condition for the co-existence of different time-lines, presumably because only a systematic mode of production can co-ordinate rhythms of labour, production and circulation. But the transition events he refers to, namely accumulation-encounters and tendency-generators, seem by themselves capable of juxtaposing differential temporal determinators, whether structural synchrony is posited or not. For that matter, the temporally differential processes seem capable of accounting for the very difference, if there really needs to be one, between structural and transitional processes.

If the division between synchronic and diachronic phenomena were legitimate, it would support a distinction between phenomena appropriate for their own period and those exhibiting deep delay. But if that division can be tampered with, it might allow a freer use of categories of delay within the simultaneity of a differentiated structure, as well as freer use of categories of simultaneity during and across diachronic transitions. The paradox for Balibar's solution is that once periods are explained by means of diachrony and synchrony, and diachrony and synchrony are explained by means of simultaneity and delay, and simultaneity is explained by a systematics of delay, then delay turns out to be the only one of these categories that is finally necessary. And yet, once delay is given its due, the picture of history is going to look different. In his later texts, which we will now examine, Balibar extends the role of delay into more uncertain futures, into synchronous periods before transitions take off, and into sub-stages within synchronous periods. The result will be to introduce subjective as well as epistemological elements into the theory of delay, alongside its socio-temporal elements. And the long-term result will be to push towards what I am calling a universal theory of delay.

(b) The Philosophy of Marx: dialectic and deferral

In *Masses, Classes, Ideas*, the locus of delay will be the historical time remaining in capitalism before the historicity of the revolution. But in *Race, Nation, Class* and *The Philosophy of Marx* (Balibar 1995: 80–110), the historicity of the revolution is itself described in terms of delay.

Delay is now extended along a longer line of events past the end of capitalism. But more deeply, there are now two sorts of delays: the delay of the telos, no matter how uncertain, contingent and deferred; and the delay that reassembles variations in between the end of one system and the presence of the next.

Balibar begins with Marx's criticism of those capitalist economists who read pre-capitalist societies historically but read capitalism ahistorically (Balibar 1995: 81). Balibar equally criticises 'postmodernists' who ridicule the idea of progress yet assume their own views are progressive (Balibar 1995: 88). Balibar wants to defend the progressivist model of irreversible improvement in history, without relying on general teleology.

For Balibar's anti-generalism, 'dialectics' means above all that history does not follow 'models' (Balibar 1995: 96). It is true that dialectical causality, the idea that 'in the last instance' an economic base determines a superstructure, is, in an abstract sense, teleological. We might even say that the superstructure of philosophy is a delayed reaction to material conditions.[1] But what that structure produces is precisely a state in which classes struggle; what historical progress leads to is precisely multiple simultaneous possibilities, a situation that does not have a single telos. In short, Balibar rejects the 'general form' of progress, but affirms 'differential' 'accelerations' of forces (Balibar 1995: 101). The paradigm is found in the double status of proletarians: as capitalism's workers, and as revolutionary agents. It is the doubling of a single phenomenon, the multiple dynamics co-existing simultaneously within a single moment, which makes history irreversible whether a certain plan succeeds or not. The differential within capitalism implies the impossibility of capitalism arriving at its own limit, and hence a telos beyond capitalism. In the vocabulary of Race, Nation, Class, we might have said that diachrony is the double of synchrony.

The 'endlessly deferred impossibility' of capitalism not only generates a proletarian revolution, but also generates time as such (Balibar 1995: 101). 'Historicity' itself is the delayed result of the simultaneous contradiction between production and its impossible fulfilment. Historicity is the opposite of narrative finality (Balibar 1965: 102); it is the difference between a force of production and itself; it is immanent delay. Yet while Balibar suggests this idea that history is universal delay, the rest of his text delimits delay to more local points.

Balibar focuses on two problems that have faced Marxism during the long delay between its inception and the allegedly imminent revolution (Balibar 1995: 103). First, why did Marx say that a dictatorship of the proletariat was a necessary stage in the transition to communism?

Second, why did Marx say that industrialisation had to occur before communism? Is there not evidence that these transitional stages did not facilitate, but rather extended, the delay of revolution?

At the empirical level, Marx's answer is that the proletariat needed time to become self-conscious, even if this means a transition within a transition, a will to diachrony while capitalism is still a synchrony. No doubt Balibar is right to give this defence of delay. But at a more abstract level it seems that Balibar depends on the truth of revolutionary politics being not so much about naming its stages as about the quality of transition. In revolutionary history, it is 'as if time were to open up or stretch out to make the way, "between" the present and the future, for a practical application of the "classless society" in the material conditions of the old one' (Balibar 1995: 106). In this passage, Balibar seems to mean something more like a Derridean motif, wherein a question opens up the time of a revolutionary delay, than a Deleuzian motif, wherein a temporal assemblage is itself revolutionary. What is important for Balibar is that Marx's insistence on extra transitional phases, even if they increase suffering and dictatorship, is made understandable by the idea that between immanence and progress there is inherent 'provisionality': 'historical time's 'non-contemporaneity with itself'' (Balibar 1995: 106). Balibar's final statement that some societies might need transitions that others would not seems empirically plausible but theoretically mild. No doubt there is 'a concrete multiplicity of paths of historical development' (Balibar 1995: 108). But the structures of delay that Balibar unfolds in order to reach this conclusion seem like they should lead beyond an apologies for slow progress, and towards a theory of revolutionary delay as such.

(c) Race, Nation, Class: genesis and hesitation

As Balibar moves from structuralist to genetic analyses of history, inserting delay at more points, and perhaps softening his earlier anti-evolutionism, one might expect a different role for simultaneity. What is interesting is that a reduced role for simultaneity does not lead to a reduced role for delay. Delay does not have to mean the staggered presence of the double reference of a synchronous event; it can mean the undecidable status of the results of genetic succession.

Balibar's focus here is on the historicity of the nation. The narrative of the 'nation' is illusory in assuming a continuous project of nation-building through many generations. It assumes that we can retroactively select moments in the past and see them as stages in a destiny (Balibar 1991: 86). In reality, there are multiple origins of a nation, different dates of interactions across language, monarchy, currency, church, law, government and police, all of which are brought into play once the nation is later formed. The issue is not the coherence of the founding phenomena, but the 'threshold of irreversibility' at which categories of nation become a 'system' (Balibar 1991: 88).

Though Balibar says that we cannot 'deduce' the nation from one phenomenon alone, he does emphasise the proletarianisation of labour in nation-construction. He says (as do Deleuze and Guattari) that the division of the world into capitalist nations inevitably generates a division between 'core' and 'periphery', hence colonisation. Balibar's main point is that differentiated historical pathways, in their simultaneous potentialities, are indeterministic: non-national states co-existed with, and competed with, early nations, and early bourgeois classes 'hesitated over' whether the nation state was the best way to control armies, rural populations, and so on. (Balibar 1991: 90).

Multiplicity thus explains the 'time-lags' in the emergence of the nation in the early days of capitalism (Balibar 1991: 90). For it takes time to resolve hesitations. If during the time-delay there exists a 'simultaneous genesis of nationalism and cosmopolitanism' (Balibar 1991: 90), it is because delay is identical to simultaneous possibilities competing over which will become the hegemonic eventuality.

Balibar does not classify delay-forms, but we can read his text with that in mind. When Balibar says that 'renouncing linear developmental schemas' allows us to see that there are pressures favouring pre-national forms even after nations become prominent (Balibar 1991: 90–1), we can say that delay-as-anachronism follows from delay-as-dispute. When Balibar asks, 'for whom today is it too late' to become a nation? (Balibar 1991: 91), wondering whether decolonised societies can become nations if they have no backward peripheries to define themselves against, no single language, and no protected markets, we might say that after too much delay, no new comparable delays are possible.

What Balibar does make explicit is that since nations are in part illusory, they are incompletable. Even old nations suffer 'delayed nationalization': 'so delayed is it, it ultimately appears as an endless task' (Balibar 1991: 92), for example as the endless task of excluding immigrants. Delay-as-unstable and delay-as-unfinished follow from delay-as-contestation. In the final analysis, the delay-structure of nationalism means that it is too late to believe that the successful nation state will still arrive. The national event did not come in its proper time (since no precursor was proper to it), but having been delayed, it is too late for it to arrive at some later time.

Of course, we have to admit the *relative* stability of capitalist nations, and the production of the narrative of a 'people', even if its threshold is never met (Balibar 1991: 92-3). But the very unity of the narrative depends on dipping into a multiplicity of resources from military glories to census statistics to collective interpellations. The nation does not just 'territorialize', Balibar says (no doubt referring to Deleuze and Guattari, though without citation), but *de*-stratifies pre-existing relations in order to reconstruct them into an imaginary signifier.

By the end of Balibar's essay, the topic of delay takes a back seat. His remarks on the way that language and race can only ever partially constitute ethnicity are convincing on their own terms (Balibar 1991: 96–103). But it would also have been interesting to draw out the way in which national language idealises an 'uninterrupted chain' of communication: undelayed national consciousness; whereas racial identity depends on the purity of future generations: delayed confirmation. Balibar's essay ends with the remark that we cannot predict whether European nations will stabilise, reform, or dissolve. No doubt this is correct. Nevertheless, multiplicity historiography, hesitation subjectivity, and the logic of delay, are not used to full value in this sort of delayed ending.

(d) Masses, Classes, Ideas: delay during the delay

Marx criticised bourgeois historians for failing to imagine a history after capitalism. Now, Balibar criticises Marx for failing to see history *during* late capitalism, namely during the time in which capitalism's dissolution into communism is delayed. Balibar begins with the problem of why Marx only rarely names the 'proletariat' in *Capital*. The short answer is that while the bourgeoisie has a 'historical character' throughout capitalism, the proletariat only achieves this towards the end of capitalism. Before that, the proletariat plays a real but amorphous role as the 'non-subject of history' (Balibar 1994: 142–3). Even when the proletariat does emerge, its 'class' structure (a condition for revolutionary history) must still become a 'mass' movement (the agent of history) (Balibar 1994: 144–5). The problem is that many attempts to explain the agency of the proletariat during late capitalism (via ideology [Marx] or via the Party [Lenin]) underplay the historical transformations of the proletariat during the course of late capitalism (for example, the transformations of unionism) (Balibar 1994: 160). In short, Marx posits the historicism and transience of capitalism, but does not trace enough history within it. As Balibar puts it, this makes Marx's philosophy a 'historicism without history' (Balibar 1994: 148; 156–61).

Balibar says that a theory of the masses as '"motor forces" of history' must go 'much further than the simple idea of a "retro-action" (*Rückwirkung*)' (Balibar 1994: 156), further than 'Althusser's principle of "action at a distance", an "absent causality"' (Balibar 1994: 157). What we need is not a general promise that the proletariat will have been guiding history before it existed as a unified force, but a concrete account of what happens between events, of motors that are non-totalisable, and of programs that are never fulfilled. In short, we need an historical materialism that is nevertheless incompletable both in time and in theory (Balibar 1994: 174).

Without using the phrase, Balibar is demanding a historicity *with* history, a description of historical events during the period of delayed historicity. This articulation is still some distance from Deleuze's principle that an event before its maturation *is* its delay. Deleuze is more interested in undecidability than in uncompletability, more interested in affirming chance than in epistemic unpredictability, more interested in preserving inclusive disjunctions than in waiting to see which exclusive disjunct will resolve a dispute. Nevertheless, Balibar shares with Deleuze the view that history is the in between of historicity, and that neither retroactive interpretations, nor distant former presents with slow fuses – in short, neither the afters nor the befores – explain the delayed motors of history.

Over the course of several texts, Balibar has developed three broad roles for delay. The first pertains to multiple time-forms at work in the same historical period. Second, once a 'period' is defined as a synchronous structure of a mode of production, delay pertains to diachronic transitions across periods. Third, delay pertains to unfulfillability: either the incompletability of a synchronous structure or the unachievability of its supposed successor. We could say that the first delay is based on multiplicity, the second on chronology, and the third on finitude. Together we might call this a theory of delay as historical *différance*. But Balibar tends to keep these phenomena relatively distinct. While each level of historical phenomena is characterised by a certain kind of delay, his theory of delay remains at some remove from the definition of events themselves. Balibar is not led to say, as Deleuze does, that an earlier event '*is* the delay'. In order to use Deleuze to consider what happens to a theory of delay when it is universalised, I will switch from cases of national and mass histories to Deleuze's use of a case history from Freud. Perhaps it is inevitable that historiography (the theory of transitions) *with* a history (that is, in all its in betweens) should require a logic that is not restricted to political history but can be exemplified in everything from childhood sagas to literary traditions to social regimes.

Deleuze

(a) Difference and Repetition: It is this delay

Deleuze's most concentrated statement on delay appears near the end of the chapter on time in *Différence et répétition*: 'There is no question as to how the childhood event acts only with a delay. It *is* this delay' (Deleuze 1969: 163). Whereas Balibar finds elements within synchrony that spark a delayed reaction, producing diachrony immediately before, during and after a transition, Deleuze finds synchrony itself to be a kind of diachrony, so that temporally distant events occur as one singular event. Deleuze sees delayed reaction not as a consequence of multiple co-existing historical pathways but as the temporal condition of those pathways themselves. In fact, Balibar was beginning to move in this direction when he said that multiple historical potentialities imply multiple forms of time. But he tended to soften this point in his conclusions. The case that Deleuze uses concerns the delayed reaction of a series of childhood events upon a series of adult events.

> The essential point is the simultaneity . . . of all the divergent series, the fact that all coexist. From the point of view of the presents . . ., the series are certainly successive, one 'before' and the other 'after'. It is from this point of view that the second is said to *resemble* the first. However, this no longer applies from the point of view of the . . . object = x which runs through them . . ., which establishes communication between [two events] or the forced movement which points beyond them . . . The question arises how to explain the phenomenon of 'delay' (*retard*) that is involved in the time it takes for the supposedly original infantile scene to produce its effect at a distance in an adult scene that resembles it and which we call 'derived' . . . The two series coexist in an intersubjective unconscious . . . The childhood event is not one of the two real series but, rather, the dark precursor that establishes communication between the basic series, that of the adults we knew as a child and that of the adult we are among other adults and other children . . . There is no question as to how the childhood event acts only with a delay. It *is* this delay, but this delay itself is the pure form of time in which before and after coexist . . . What is originary . . . is not one series in relation to the other but the difference between series. (Deleuze 1969: 162–3)

Deleuze's theory is that what makes an adult react to the past is not the slow causality of the past, and not the retroactive interpretation of the present, but the overlay of past and present narratives, and that the difference between them – not the resemblance but the difference – defines both, and distributes them in time. Delayed reaction presupposes the pure past as the co-existence of distant events, as well as the future as the desire within each event to communicate across time. Deleuze is offering a subtle alternative to Freud's conception of 'delayed reaction', *Nachträglichkeit*,[2] in his early text, *Project for a Scientific Psychology* (1895). Freud's case study concerns a young woman who has a phobia against going into a shop by herself. Under analysis, she remembers that when she was twelve, two shopkeepers laughed at her clothing. After more analysis, she remembers that when she was eight, a shopkeeper grinned and tried to touch her through her clothing. Why can she not go shopping alone now? Considered as quantitatively separate events, having been present at distant moments in succession, the childhood and adult events would have to interact on the basis of qualitative similarities, for example in that they both involve a girl and older men, clothing and grins. On the basis of those similarities, the girl would expect another similarity, namely danger. But Freud does not think the similarities are strong enough to explain the exaggerated fear. Indeed, if the patient consciously generalised that 'shopkeepers are molesters', that would be a motive for avoiding shops. But the point is that she does not know why she cannot go into shops. Why is the reaction delayed, masked and magnified? Freud's explanation is that it is only at the age of puberty that children realise what sexuality is, and at that age they retroactively interpret their previous experiences in sexual terms. During the first experience, the girl was pre-puberty. At that moment, the event was unpleasant, but no big deal; she could remember or forget it indifferently. At puberty, she realises that years earlier, the man was assaulting her. Furthermore, now that she has sexual feelings, she wonders if she had been complicit. The remembered event has now become unbearable, so now the memory is repressed. It has become important and at the same time inexpressible; therefore it comes out symptomatically as phobia. The early experience cannot have its nature, or its effects, when it happens. It is 'premature'. It achieves its meaning too late, because it occurs too early (Freud 1950 [1895]).

This is delayed reaction by retroactive interpretation: an event that cannot be processed in the normal flow of anticipations and fulfilments, whose effects are excessively slow to manifest, and which later appears as a sudden onslaught of the past, as if after a delay the past speeds right up to the present without delay. Freud calls it a *proton pseudos*, a false origin.

Now, Freud soon changed his mind about key features of this account, possibly for bad reasons, but we do not have to worry about this. Delayed reaction clearly plays a role in many psychic phenomena, and the theory of retroactive interpretation seems on the face of it plausible.

However, Deleuze's theory of time claims to render retroactive interpretation obsolete, construing delayed reaction instead as co-existence through difference. Deleuze and Freud agree that overlaying the difference between child and adult viewpoints, between what we might call innocence and desire, is what makes the early event traumatic (innocence infected by desire), and the later one phobic (desire blocked by regression to innocence). For Deleuze, what dramatises the memory is not that one now interprets the event through adult eyes instead of a child's, but that one now relives it at both stages of life at once. Merely retroactively learning what a childhood event meant, or merely retroactively attributing adult motives to the child, would not make a person obsessively try to avoid it now, unless one felt oneself a child again *while* going about one's present business. And conversely, one would not feel complicit in the childhood event, and so try to compensate for it now, unless one felt that qua child one was always already forming an adult sensibility. It is as if capitalism, its feudal past, and its communist future, were all overlapping variants undergoing shifting integrations and de-integrations – synchronic in the sense that the same (inter-)subjectivity struggles with them all at once, yet diachronic in the sense that its subjectivity is serially self-divided. To be sure, such a phenomenon could still be called 'retrospective interpretation', even though Balibar restricts that term to capitalism's attempt to justify itself on the basis of a mythical past, and Deleuze restricts it to refer to an Oedipalised subject's obsession with chastising herself on the basis of a mythical lost innocence. But the phenomenon as Deleuze describes it might better be called reciprocal causality with reversible inter-subjectivity. For that matter, delay might better be called simultaneity at a distance.

Deleuze argues that Freud's theory of delay erroneously depends on a 'solipsistic unconscious' rather than an 'intersubjective unconscious' (Deleuze 1969: 162), namely the communication between the child one is and the adult one is. We might define schizoanalysis precisely as a theory of internal inter-subjectivity through delayed temporal effects across intersecting series of thoughts, memories and affects. It is not hyperbolic phenomenological description to say that when faced with an experience today I run through one series of reactions that calls into play my eight-year-old self, and another my fifty-year-old self. Whenever a person walks into a store, a child is walking into the store and an adult is walking into the store at the same time. The primitive accumulation of childhood refers less to pre-historical events in chronology than to a diagram of virtual possibilities that I, or anyone, might put into operation at any time. The many subjectivity diagrams at my disposal constitute the co-existence of different moments of my personal history.

The childhood series: looking up to adults, uncertainty about what things mean, powerlessness, a struggle for self-identity, becomes entangled with an adult series: self-recognition, generalisation, socialisation, sexual politics. The similarities provide only a minimal assemblage: girl, entrance, storekeeper, clothing, grin. But once the two series are overlaid, then the childhood question, 'what do adults want from me?' is superimposed onto the adult question, 'how do I manage desire?' The two different perspectives together create figurative resemblances: 'shamefully, the storekeeper when I was a kid was a man like the men I desire'. Or, 'all the men I want are aggressive'. Or, 'everything they have for sale is repellent'. The resemblance is a running effect of two different interpretations targeting the same object = x. In short, on Deleuze's model of delayed reaction, it is not that there exist two events separated in time, the multiple potentials in the earlier getting resolved in the later, or the later gathering up and reacting to the earlier; rather, there is one event occurring at two distant moments in time at once. At its best, the overlay need not subsist as trauma or reaction, but as a poetics of time regained or a politics of inter-subjective historical modes of productivity.

Any given event might have a crossover point with an event stored in the past, whose gears it engages for a while. The force behind cross-temporal assemblage might or might not be voluntary. It could be economic, biological, technological, political, linguistic, or philosophical; a gift, a germ, a spur, a wave of immigration, a pun, or a concept of delay could set in motion a whole history of delayed reactions. The point is that delay is a structure of time before it is a matter of psychic, economic, or some other specific kind of development. Delay is any immediate co-existence of events that come before and after one another in time, operating as a single experience. Now, it might seem preferable to have a less general definition of delay, that is, to explain a particular delay with reference to a specific mechanism that prevents an event from occurring on schedule and forces it into co-existence with a temporally distant event. And indeed, Deleuze's focus on delay *in* time is intended to keep the assemblage of the event and its delayed reaction concrete. In the texts with Guattari, Deleuze of course gives concrete models of delay, particularly of the way capitalism uses regions of delayed development as lawless zones capable of sparking accelerated development. Yet what emerges in different ways from the accounts of delay in Balibar and in Freud is that sometimes, when we are offered a concrete mechanism of delay, whether the mechanism of delay is the restrospective discoveries of puberty or the apologetics of capitalism, the mechanism of delay seems too specific, and creates the illusion that the delaying phenomenon, the transition to its successor, and the successor itself, are distinguishable temporal phenomena. And then it seems preferable to say after all that the source of delay is a universal structure of temporality.

(b) Cinema 2: too late

I cannot here prove thoroughly that a pure-time theory of delay offers a concrete political historiography, so I will end this chapter with a small scale case for study.

On the last pages of the 'Crystals of Time' chapter in *Cinema 2*, Deleuze (1985) says that in Visconti – and later he adds, in Syberberg – '*something* arrives too late' (*trop tard*). It's the SS; it's Hitler. 'History growls at the door.' We do not exactly experience it, yet we more than experience it; history is never just 'scenery'. If that something could have been 'caught in time' (*pris a temps*), we might have averted it, but 'it is History, and Nature, itself, the structure of the crystal, that makes it impossible for something to arrive in time' (Deleuze 1985: 126). It is not just that Visconti is nostalgic; history is an 'autonomous factor', and being too late is the very 'rhythm' of history, 'a dimension of time', the universalisation of Poe's 'Nevermore'.

And yet, 'history arrives too late *dynamically*' (Deleuze 1985: 127). It (fascism, capitalism, childhood) arrives too late, so we cannot stop it, so it remains forever, but it is too late, so it never was where we looked for it, so if we stop looking for it so obsessively, we do not have to keep finding it, so it no longer has to be there. Because of its dynamic, the too-late has three exceptions. First, the work of art thrives on the too-late. It is too late for the human, phenomenological eye to see, but as Vertov would say, the camera eye can see it, and by extension, I would say, the History-Eye can see it. Second, the too-late destroys every human chance at success with one exception: the too-late succeeds at time itself, 'time regained' (Deleuze 1985: 128). Third, Deleuze says surprisingly in the 'Conclusion' to *Cinema 2* that when cinema sees the too-late, it 'defeats Hitler' (Deleuze 1985: 352–3). What is Deleuze saying? It is too late to defeat Hitler. But what is Hitler? Strangely, Deleuze assesses Hitler in a way similar to that most famous too-little-too-late text in philosophy: the interview where Heidegger says that the problem with Nazism was its inauthentic communications technology, its reduction of discourse to information. Surely that says too little. But Deleuze says it too: Hitler succeeded by convincing his people that what he said was what he said it was, that what he said was, that what was was what he said, in short, by creating the cinematic illusion that expression is simultaneous with content, by synchronising sound and picture. Defeating this requires a different kind of cinema, to create a delay between speech and the visible, to make each too late. Perhaps this counterattack of the too-late should have been caught at the time. Some Godard should have made *Medium Cool* at Nuremburg. In fact, already in 1935 Ernst Bloch (Bloch 1991: 104–16) was arguing that Hitler was succeeding in harnessing the power of 'non-contemporaneous' social forces and that Hitler's opponents had to find a way to defeat him with their own non-contemporaneities. It may be an accident that the too-late was discovered too late, but it is not too late to discover it now, it is not too late to make history, but to do it is to unweave the one-at-a-time event-units that claim they will not be no longer for a thousand years, to make history now is to make an act that *is* the delay, an act in which the now is not merely now but simultaneously stretches along staggered time, to act on trauma and proletarianisation in the dimension of the too-late, though of course, hopefully, in time.

Why is there always one extra transition before a revolution can occur? Why is history one long hesitation? If the answer is that history is essentially non-contemporaneity, then delays are not so much obstacles to, as forms of, decisive events. Overlapping at a distance, or simultaneity at a delay, will be a strategy for defeating dictators, a therapy for childhood traumas, an alternative to capitalism's rewriting of history. This only works if synchrony doubles itself with internal time-differentials, and if diachrony doubles back the externality of succession. To be fair to Balibar, if he does not go this far in the direction of pure-time historiography, that is a deliberate choice on his part. In a recent text (Balibar 2007: 8), he worries that unless the 'rupture of time' is 'determined in the last instance' by material history, it may lead to something more 'demonic' than revolutionary. Deleuze may be less worried about demons than Balibar. Nevertheless, the ongoing challenge to Deleuzian philosophy of history is to show how concrete assemblages of abstract temporalities can do the work that revolutionary historiography used to do with the succession of modes of material production.

References

Althusser, L. (1969), *Lénine et la philosophie*, Paris: Francois Maspero.
Balibar, É. (1965), 'Sur les concepts fondamentaux du matérialisme historique', in Louis Althusser et al., *Lire le Capital*, Paris: Presses Universitaires de France, 1965.

Balibar, É. (1991), *Race, Nation, Class: Ambiguous Identities*, trans. Chris Turner, London: Verso.

Balibar, É. (1994), *Masses, Classes, Ideas*, trans. James Swenson, New York: Routledge.

Balibar, É. (1995), *The Philosophy of Marx*, trans. Chris Turner, London: Verso.

Balibar, É. (2007), '*Préface*' to Y. Sato, *Pouvoir et Résistance: Foucault, Deleuze, Derrida, Althusser*, Paris: L'Harmattan.

Bloch, E. (1991), *Heritage of Our Times*, trans. Neville and Stephen Plaice, Berkeley: University of California Press.

Deleuze, G. (1969), *Différence et répétition*, Paris: Presses Universitaires de France.

Deleuze, G. (1985), *Cinéma 2: L'Image-temps*, Paris: Les Éditions de Minuit.

Deleuze, G. and F. Guattari (1980), *Mille Plateaux*, Paris: Éditions de Minuit.

Freud, S. (1950 [1895]), *Project for a Scientific Psychology*, Standard Edition of the Complete Psychological Works of Sigmund Freud, ed. J. Strachey, vol. 1, London: The Hogarth Press.

Lampert, J. (2006a), *Deleuze and Guattari's Philosophy of History*, London: Continuum.

Lampert, J. (2006b), 'Derrida's Solution to Two Problems of Time in Husserl', *The New Yearbook for Phenomenology and Phenomenological Philosophy*, VI: 259–79

Notes

1. According to Louis Althusser (1969): 'Philosophy exists only by lagging behind (*en retard sur*) the drive towards science' (23). 'On the basis of the concept of this necessary delay, many other difficulties can also be clarified' (25). There has by now been enough delay since Marxist science arose for us to do Marxist philosophy (in a way that Marx, Engels and Lenin could not yet do), so the delay can be 'in part overcome' (26). Yet in other respects, 'it is we who are lagging behind Lenin' (27).

2. There is a lot to say about this term, including Derrida's discussion of why Husserl was reluctant to use it (see Lampert 2006b).

Chapter 4

Geohistory and Hydro-Bio-Politics

John Protevi

It seems that in *A Thousand Plateaus* Deleuze and Guattari prefer geography to history. Do they not come right out and say 'nomads have no history; they only have a geography' (Deleuze and Guattari 1987: 393)? Geography has three registers for them, corresponding to their three ontological registers. There is (1) actual geography, the production of maps (or better, 'tracings') of extended space, most often in the service of the State and its traditionally primary mode of spatialisation, striated space (Deleuze and Guattari 1987: 12); (2) intensive geography, the 'cartography' that follows lines of becoming, the mapping of 'longitude' and 'latitude' of bodies (Deleuze and Guattari 1987: 260–1); and (3) virtual geography, the map of the abstract machines of coding, overcoding and decoding, as they are actualised in the machinic assemblages of tribes, empires and war machines (Deleuze and Guattari 1987: 222).

Before we go any further, we should note that the production of smooth spaces by the armed forces and surveillance technologies of contemporary States and quasi-State corporations, as well as the demand for identity cards and fixed addresses by asylum seekers, economic migrants, and other displaced persons, prevents any naive 'postmodernist' privileging of the smooth as somehow progressive or always beneficial and the striated as always retrograde and repressive.[1] After all, the main text of *A Thousand Plateaus* ends with the line: 'Never believe that a smooth space will suffice to save us' (Deleuze and Guattari 1987: 500).

History, by contrast, is the time-keeping and self-fulfilling prophecy of States. It is the constructed sequence of significant events that seemingly obliterates geography, the earth, and the non-historic presignifying and countersignifying regimes: 'the defeat of the nomads was such, so complete, that history is one with the triumph of States' (Deleuze and Guattari 1987: 394). Deleuze and Guattari's view of 'official' history is as hostile as their view of geography is sympathetic. They take for granted that history is a fabrication by sedentary societies to justify their importance and centrality. Even at its best, 'all history does is translate a coexistence of becomings into a succession' (Deleuze and Guattari 1987: 430); that is, history establishes conditions for translation of co-existing diagrams, for the actualisation of virtual multiplicities. In this way, 'the task of the historian is to designate the "period" of coexistence or simultaneity of these two movements' (deterritorialisation and reterritorialisation) (Deleuze and Guattari 1987: 221).

As always with Deleuze and Guattari, however, the *de jure* opposition of geography versus history is matched by the recognition of their *de facto* mixing. Thus in the section on geophilosophy in *What is Philosophy?*, Deleuze and Guattari call for 'geohistory', following Braudel: a materialist history sensitive to the earth, an historical geography or geographical history (Deleuze and Guattari 1994: 95). In thinking about the 'geo' of geohistory, we have to recognise first of all that *terre* in *A Thousand Plateaus* has various meanings which interweave ontology and politics in what I have elsewhere called 'political physics' (Protevi 2001). We will explain the technical terms here later, but let us note that *terre* has at least four registers, the first three of which are equivalent to the English 'earth', and the fourth to the English 'land'.[2] In *A Thousand Plateaus*, 'Earth' is (a) equivalent to THE Body without Organs, the virtual plane of consistency upon which strata are imposed (Deleuze and Guattari 1987: 40); (b) part of the earth–territory [*terre–territoire*] system of Romanticism, the gathering point, outside all territories, of 'forces of the earth' for intensive territorial assemblages (Deleuze and Guattari 1987: 338–9); and (c) the 'new earth' (*une nouvelle terre*), the correlate of absolute deterritorialisation, tapping 'cosmic forces' or new potentials for creation (Deleuze and Guattari 1987: 423; 509–10). 'Land', by contrast, is *terre* that is constituted by the overcoding of territories under the signifying regime and the State apparatus (Deleuze and Guattari 1987: 440–1).

When we look for examples of Deleuze and Guattari's interest in geohistory as the interweaving of ontology and politics, we find, among the more interesting references in *A Thousand Plateaus*, Karl Wittfogel's Cold War epic, *Oriental Despotism* (1957). Wittfogel claimed that a particular form of social organisation, 'Oriental despotism' – characterised in its most intense form by the State being the largest landowner, by the bureaucratic organisation of landlords, capitalism and the gentry, and by a form of 'weak private property' allowing for 'total power' rooted in the State – came from State origination and control of massive irrigation projects. Deleuze and Guattari refer to Wittfogel at several points in

Anti-Oedipus and *A Thousand Plateaus* concerning the State as apparatus of capture. We cannot take Wittfogel at face value, for even the most
superficial schizoanalysis shows that his libidinal investment was anti-
communism; he left behind his geohistorical focus when he tried to show
that Stalinist totalitarianism could be traced to cultural influences via
some unspecified sort of contact with Oriental despotism. Although
himself a victim of Nazism, spending nine months of 1933 in concentration camps before being freed as the result of intense negotiation and
family contacts (Ulmen 1978: 162–9), he never traced the 'total power'
of the Nazi regime (which certainly had no connection with irrigation),
nor did he investigate power and stratification in American West water
works (admittedly not 'total' power, but power and stratification
nonetheless) (Worster 1985: 28–9). Nonetheless, Wittfogel does point us
to an important aspect of geohistory: the management of water leading
to what we can call hydro-bio-politics. To see the contours of this
complex arena, let us trace the ontology and politics of water.

Ontology

For Deleuze and for Deleuze and Guattari, being is production. The production process (intensive difference driving material flows resulting in
actual or extensive forms) is structured by virtual Ideas or multiplicities
or 'abstract machines'. Multiplicities are composed of mutually defined
elements with linked rates of change ('differential relations') peppered
with singularities. In mathematical modeling of physical systems, singularities are points at which the graph of a function changes direction.
Singularities in models represent thresholds in intensive processes, where
a system undergoes a qualitative change of behaviour. Being as production is symbolised in *A Thousand Plateaus* by the slogan, 'the world is
an egg' (Deleuze and Guattari 1987: 251). What this means is that
'spatio-temporal dynamisms' or intensive processes are that which actualises or 'differenciates' Ideas. These processes, however, are hidden by
the constituted qualities and extensities of actual products. The example
of embryology shows this differenciation of differentiation, as the
dynamic of the egg's morphogenesis implies a virtual Idea unfolding in
such a way that there are things only an embryo can do or withstand.
The world is thus a progressive determination going from virtual to
actual. Thought, however, is vice-diction or counter-effectuation: it goes
the other way from production. It is a matter of establishing the
Idea/multiplicity of something – 'constructing a concept' – by moving
from extensity through intensity to virtuality.

Following water is a great way to think in the Deleuzian manner.

1. We can measure water *extensively* in its three forms: solid, liquid, gas: the thickness in feet of the Greenland ice shelf; the number of cubic kilometres of ocean water; the percentage humidity at one time and place, and so on.

2. We can follow water flows as *intensive* processes. Differences in temperature, density, and so on, provoke material flows, for example, the manifold ocean currents: to name only a very important one, the Gulf Stream brings equatorial heat north, warming northwestern Europe, and sinking off Greenland as temperature drops, density and salination increase, and the stream plummets to the ocean floor to join the sub-surface ocean currents. (One of the real threats of global warming is that melting Greenland ice will dilute the Gulf Stream, inhibit its sinking, and rearrange the ocean current system so that northwestern Europe gets colder even as the average temperature of the planet climbs.)

3. And we can construct the *virtual* Idea of water. Among its dimensions would be that which governs the hydrological cycle: linked rates of change of difference-driven intensive processes of evaporation, precipitation, runoff, with singularities marking phase transitions as events: from solid to liquid to gas. At all its points of transition, we see the 'becoming' of water, and can name its affects: 'to flow, to become denser, to expand while freezing, to float as ice, to boil, rain, snow, sleet', and so on.

These physical affects are mostly of interest to us as they enter into bio-assemblages. Thus we have to see how water is 'perplicated' with Ideas of other natural cycles, involving all the 'spheres' that contemporary geographers talk about: hydrosphere of course, but also lithosphere, atmosphere and biosphere (Wood 2004). But, as Deleuze and Guattari delight in saying after explaining some very complex point, 'this is much too simple'. The spheres are *de jure* distinct, but *de facto* mixed. Not only are they composed of immensely complex nested sets of coupled cycles at many scales, but their intersection zones – their 'zones of indiscernibility' – are intermixed. For instance, the atmosphere is not a collection of gases, but is better thought of as 'air', and air has plenty of organisms (spores, microbes), minerals (dust) and water in it. Similarly, the hydrosphere is not just chemically pure H_2O but is 'water', which has plenty of organisms, air and minerals in it. The lithosphere in turn is not just minerals, but its top layer is 'soil', which has in it plenty of air, water and organisms. Finally, the biosphere's organisms are made of water and minerals and cycle air through them. In Louisiana, I can testify, the air you're breathing is an unholy mixture of soil, water and organisms, the vaporised bayou wafting into your lungs: sometimes you just don't know if you're breathing, drinking or chewing.

There are other linked cycles: calcium is a very important one (bones!), but let's just talk about the carbon cycle: photosynthesis and respiration. Photosynthesis takes CO_2 and H_2O and uses solar energy to produce carbohydrates and O_2. Respiration takes O_2 and releases the energy used in the chemical bonds of carbohydrates, releasing H_2O and CO_2 back into their cycles. Bio-energy is just hydrocarbon-mediated solar energy. So you can see the link of the water and carbon cycles. Organic life is just an eddy in the flow of these and many other elements. Organic life uses solar energy to tap into these elemental cycles, to capture and hold some of these flows in other, smaller and tighter cycles: the 'organic syntheses' we see in the discussion of the first synthesis of time (Deleuze 1994: 73).

But that's not a good formulation, 'tap into the cycles', as if life were exterior to the elemental cycles. We remember that we need to avoid any 'ridiculous cosmic evolutionism' (Deleuze and Guattari 1987: 49). Water is not just a support for organic life. In one sense, the creative burst of life on land IS water. Let's recall the dual definition of life in *A Thousand Plateaus*: (1) a set of beings ('organisms'), 'a particularly complex system of stratification' (Deleuze and Guattari 1987: 336); (2) the creativity of complex systems, 'a surplus value of *destratification* . . . an aggregate of consistency that disrupts orders, forms, and substances' (Deleuze and Guattari 1987: 336; italics in original). In the second sense, then, life is not limited to the organism form: 'the organism is that which life sets against itself in order to limit itself' (Deleuze and Guattari 1987: 503). No, life as speciation via alliance rather than filiation, as creative 'involution' (Deleuze and Guattari 1987: 238), is part of the cycles: the hydrosphere, lithosphere and atmosphere are coupled with the ever-changing biosphere. Let us also note here in discussing non-organic life that the Gaia hypothesis need not take the extreme position often attributed to James Lovelock, in which Gaia is an organism; Lynn Margulis's 'ecosystem' perspective, coupled with her 'serial endosymbiosis theory' stance on evolution, is much more defensible – and much more Deleuzian for that matter, since it relies upon a notion of Gaia as an Idea or set of linked rates of change of differentially defined elements (the different 'spheres') punctuated by singularities (the 'events' of profound geo-evolutionary change: e.g., the oxygen explosion and the rise of the aerobic bacteria) (Margulis 1998: 119).

More detail on bio-water will help us appreciate the way that considering water can help us understand Deleuze and Guattari's call for geohistory. In *A Thousand Plateaus*, they give the following as an example of a line of flight: 'When the seas dried, the primitive Fish left its associated milieu to explore land . . . now carrying water only on the inside, in the amniotic membranes protecting the embryo' (Deleuze and Guattari 1987: 55). This is an exemplification of the principle that 'an organism that is deterritorialized in relation to the exterior necessarily reterritorializes on its interior milieus' (Deleuze and Guattari 1987: 54). This development is non-organic life: instead of staying in its territorialised way of life, its habits linked to the milieus with which it interacts, the fish folding water inside itself is forming new habits and with them a new, internal, milieu. Again, we must insist that non-organic life is not always non-biological life. It can be simply a change of living patterns: to use the terms of *Difference and Repetition*, organic life is locked into 'bare' repetition while non-organic life is differenciation. But of course, returning to *A Thousand Plateaus* and following one of the theorems of deterritorialisation, it's always on the most deterritorialising factor that reterritorialisation occurs, even when in the case of the absolute deterritorialisation of nomadism (Deleuze and Guattari 1987: 384) that reterritorialisation is on deterritorialisation itself (Deleuze and Guattari 1987: 381). We will see the way the portable water skin allows for this recursive relation of nomadism, how it enables the nomad to be at home while breaking habits and forming a new milieu.

We see an interesting illustration of the interplay of re- and deterritorialisation in the concept of 'Hypersea', in which the environment of life on land is the deterritorialised sea (McMenamin and McMenamin 1994; Wood 2004: 120–2; Margulis 1998: 109). In a memorable image, the authors of the thought-provoking book *Hypersea* tell us that organisms are 'lakes' of Hypersea, separated by membranes and connected by ingestion, sex, parasitism and other forms of communication: 'The appearance of complex life on land was a major event in which a kind of mutant sea invaded the land surface. . . . The land biota represents not simply *life* from the sea, but a variation of the sea itself' (McMenamin and McMenamin 1994: 25). What's different about the Hypersea organisms is that they have to stick closely together in tightly bound systems enclosed by a membrane to replicate in an enclosed space the organic functions that are distributed in the sea.

> Organisms, which are all primarily water, can interact at arm's length, so to speak, only in water. On land, direct physical connections become essential. Overall, terrestrial organisms had to build for themselves structures and

components that could perform the environmental services that marine organisms can take for granted. (McMenamin and McMenamin 1994: 4)

Land life is physically bonded capture – organic land life is an 'apparatus of capture' or, more melodramatically put, we're all vampires: thus a notion of geo-hydro-political physiology underlies that of the organism. Because of this self-contained structure, 'bodies of macroscopic terrestrial plants and animals are the setting for extremely active, if miniaturized, ecological interactions. . . . These interactions constitute Hypersea' (McMenamin and McMenamin 1994: 13). The most elementary of those ecosystems, of course, is the eukaryotic cell, as we see in the serial endosymbiosis theory of Lynn Margulis. The mitochondria were originally oxygen-using bacteria that under pressure of the 'oxygen holocaust' came to live together with other cell elements, providing energy to the emergent unity, the nucleated cell (Margulis 1998: 42). A question then for a certain type of political physiology: are the mitochondria slaves or partners?

Politics

We could go on in this way exploring physiology as politics for quite some time, but let's shift to think politics as physiology: the body politic as a body, a system of material flows. The State as apparatus of capture on top of organic apparatuses, the State as meta-vampire, seeking always control of flows, especially flows of water. Because water is such a great solvent, it dissolves rock and picks up minerals. Thus, unfortunately for land plants and animals, most of the water on earth – that in the oceans – is too salty. Although we are 'hypersea', we're much more dilute than sea water, so we need 'fresh' water; we'll supply the minerals in carefully controlled doses. How humans have directed fresh water from where there's a lot of it – rivers and aquifers – to where we can use it for drinking or feeding to plants and animals (agriculture) – the process of irrigation – is an important story discussing hydro-bio-politics.

To return to Wittfogel's highlighting of the State/water relation, we should recognise that despite his failings, he does point us to an important truth: aridity is the key to the connection of stratified societies and irrigation. Studies on the American West show how the large-scale state and federal investment in irrigation could only produce stratified societies in arid conditions, where control of water grants a key power position (Worster 1993). (Recall the plot of *Chinatown*!) Although Deleuze and Guattari affirm that 'there is no going back on Wittfogel's theses on the importance of large-scale waterworks for an empire' (Deleuze and Guattari 1987: 363), they do acknowledge that some parts of Wittfogel's work have been 'refuted' (Deleuze and Guattari 1987: 19). Although they do not enter into the details of this refutation, when we do, we find they affirm some of Deleuze and Guattari's central theses on the State.

Let's take the example of Egypt. Ancient Egyptian irrigation was basin irrigation rather than canal irrigation. In basin irrigation earth banks run parallel and perpendicular to the river, creating basins. Sluices would direct floodwater into a basin where it would sit for a month until the soil was saturated. Then the water would be drained to the next basin and the soil in the first basin would be ready for planting. This system sustained Egypt's remarkable continuity (the only ancient irrigated society to have a continuous existence). Once-a-year planting didn't deplete the soil, which was replenished by the next year's flood. Nor did basin irrigation result in salination, as the water table during the dry season was well below the root level, so that flood waters would push accumulated salts down into the water table, below the root level (Butzer 1976). Karl Butzer has shown how basin irrigation using the Nile floods arose as a decentralised, locally controlled system, and was later overcoded by the apparatus of capture of the State. Butzer writes:

> All of the information that can be brought to bear on Dynastic land use in Egypt shows a simple pattern of winter agriculture, largely confined to the flood basins, with their crude but effective system of annual flood irrigation. Despite the *symbolic association* [my italics; read 'overcoding'] of the pharaoh with this inundation, Dynastic irrigation technology was rudimentary and operated on a local rather than national scale . . . Perhaps the only centralized aspect was the traditional link between tax rates and the potential harvest [State as 'apparatus of capture'], as inferred from the height of each Nile flood . . . no form of centralized canal network was ever achieved in Dynastic times. (Butzer 1976: 50)

In this same vein, we can also talk about Stephen Lansing's work in Bali, which also shows local, decentralised control of canals in the mountains of Bali (Lansing 2006). With Butzer and Lansing, the contours of the bio-litho-hydro-political multiplicity begin to come into focus. There is more than one singularity and the role of chance is irreducible. The multiplicity behind the morphogenesis of political structure includes geological factors such as ground slopes and surface friction; biological factors such as the type and strength of local flora and fauna; hydrological factors such as river currents, channels and wave strengths; and social factors such as the speed capacity of available transportation assemblages, which are social/technical at the same time: man–sandal–spear–shield assemblages; horse–man–stirrup assemblages; and all the assemblages formed with chariots, wagons, sailing ships, rowing ships, and so on. Wittfogel's mistake was seeing a single pathway – control of irrigation – in the morphogenesis of Oriental despotism. This may actually have been the pathway for ancient Mesopotamian empires, which needed flat river valleys for irrigation-intensive agriculture and to install garrisons in outlying towns which could be quickly supported: the *corvée* supplies labour for roads as well as for irrigation and monuments. Once past a certain threshold, we find a positive feedback loop: the bigger the territory under control, the more solar energy is captured in agriculture and the larger the bureaucracy and the army that can be fed with the surplus. These can then enlarge and administer the territory and put more peasants to work producing and funneling surpluses and building roads for more expansion, and so on. Butzer, however, shows that in Egypt the key factor for Pharaonic absolutism was the ecological embeddedness of 'nomes' or basic territorial/political social units.

> These primeval nomes appear to have provided the necessary political infrastructure for the military ventures that over several generations of strife led to the unification of Egypt. In this sense Pharaonic civilisation remains inconceivable without its ecological determinants, but not in the linear causality model [sc. of Wittfogel] of stress → irrigation → managerial bureaucracy → despotic control. (Butzer 1976: 111)

In other words, Butzer does not deny Egypt was united under a despot nor that its political structure was ecologically embedded. He just denies that irrigation control was the sole determinant of that imperial scale despotism. Here we see an important question of scale: for Butzer, the 'nome' or local unit qualifies as a State – perhaps even a hydraulic state – but not as an empire.

In fact, it has recently been argued that centralised national state control of Egyptian irrigation – based on a change from basin irrigation to a centralised canal grid system – is a nineteenth-century phenomenon that was represented as a return to the supposedly centralised irrigation control of the Pharaohs. So the argument would be that with regard to Egypt at least, Wittfogel mistook modern propaganda for ancient reality (Kalin 2006). Butzer (and by extension Lansing) thus contradicts Wittfogel, who stresses the State as the origin of large-scale water works, and confirms Deleuze and Guattari's theses that the imperial State overcodes local arrangements.

We should recognise in conclusion, however, that the State has no monopoly on hydro-bio-politics, for there is a 'hydraulic model of

nomad science and the war machine . . . [which] consists in being distributed by turbulence across a smooth space' (Deleuze and Guattari
1987: 363). We need to add to Deleuze and Guattari's discussion of the
nomad in order to bring ontology and politics more closely together in
the study of hydro-bio-politics. For the portable water container, the
animal skin, is as fully a part of the nomad assemblage as the more
famous stirrup, and the machinic phylum had to encompass this technological supplement to Hypersea to allow the nomad occupation of the
smooth space of the arid steppes.

References

Butzer, K. (1976), *Early Hydraulic Civilization in Egypt: A Study in Cultural
Ecology*, Chicago: University of Chicago Press.
Deleuze, G. (1994), *Difference and Repetition*, trans. Paul Patton, New York:
Columbia.
Deleuze, G. and F. Guattari (1987), *A Thousand Plateaus: Capitalism and
Schizophrenia*, trans. Brian Massumi, Minneapolis: University of Minnesota Press.
Deleuze, G. and F. Guattari (1994), *What is Philosophy?* trans. Hugh Tomlinson and
Graham Burchell, New York: Columbia University Press.
Hardt, M. and A. Negri (2000), *Empire*, Cambridge, MA: Harvard University
Press.
Kalin, M. (2006), 'Hidden Pharaohs: Egypt, Engineers and the Modern Hydraulic',
2006 MA thesis, Wolfson College, University of Oxford.
Lansing, S.J. (2006), *Perfect Order: Recognizing Complexity in Bali*, Princeton:
Princeton University Press.
McMenamin, M. and D. McMenamin (1994), *Hypersea*, New York: Columbia
University Press.
Margulis, L. (1998), *Symbiotic Planet: A New Look at Evolution*, New York: Basic
Books.
Protevi, J. (2001), *Political Physics: Deleuze, Derrida, and the Body Politic*, London:
Athlone.
Ulmen, G.L. (1978), *The Science of Society: Toward an Understanding of the Life
and Work of Karl August Wittfogel*, The Hague: Mouton.
Weiszman, E. (2007), *Hollow Land: Israel's Architecture of Occupation*, London:
Verso.
Wittfogel, K. (1957), *Oriental Despotism: A Comparative Study of Total Power*,
New Haven: Yale University Press.
Wood, D. (2004), *Five Billion Years of Global Change*, New York: Guilford.
Worster, D. (1985), *Rivers of Empire: Water, Aridity, and the Growth of the
American West*, New York: Oxford University Press.
Reisner, M. (1993), *Cadillac Desert: The American West and its Disappearing Water*,
2nd ed., New York: Penguin.

Notes

1. See Eyal Weiszman (2007) for the practical application by the Israel Defense Force
   of Deleuze and Guattari's theories of smooth and holey space in operations in
   Palestinian urban space (holey space?). Michael Hardt and Antonio Negri call

attention in their *Empire* (2000) to the desire for stability and identity on the part of many displaced persons today.

2. In translating *Mille Plateaux* into English, Brian Massumi uses two English words to translate the French *terre*, which can mean both 'earth' in the astronomical sense of our planet and 'land' in the geographical sense of a cultivated area. There is no consistency in Deleuze and Guattari's use of the majuscule in the French text; both *Terre* and *terre* are used in the sense of 'earth' and 'land'. The Anglophone reader should keep in mind the close proximity of *terre* ['earth' and 'land'] with *territoire* ['territory'].

Chapter 5

The Thought of History in Benjamin and Deleuze

Tim Flanagan

Regarding a Reading

The sentences from the final chapter of *Le Pli* in which Deleuze briefly cites Walter Benjamin's *Ursprung des Deutschen Trauerspiels* (1925) are far from straightforward. And yet these comments nonetheless deserve close attention since the very complexity of their reflection adduces the conditions by which the philosophical significance of the baroque – a significance that informs each of these arcane studies – might be explored. In keeping with the declaredly monadological propaedeutics with which Benjamin prefaces his study, the opacity of Deleuze's patient (even meditative) consideration of the earlier work exhibits both thinkers' understanding that, for a baroque synthesis of things, no thesis suffices to be conceptualised categorically but rather is informed by the peculiarly historical analysis which emerges in regard to a written work's before and after.

At the outset of his section on 'The World as a Cone: Allegory, Emblem and Device', Deleuze declares that

> Walter Benjamin made a decisive step forward in our understanding of the Baroque when he showed that allegory was not a failed symbol, or an abstract personification, but a power [*puissance*] of figuration entirely different from that of the symbol: the latter combines the eternal and the momentary, nearly at the centre of the world, but allegory uncovers nature and history according to the order of time, it produces a history from nature and transforms history into nature in a world that no longer has its centre. (Deleuze 1993: 125; 1988: 170–1)[1]

According to Deleuze, Benjamin's study reveals how the baroque is comprehended through a uniquely temporal schematism and yet, although for both thinkers the contrast between allegory and symbol is best rendered theoretically in terms of duration, what is integral here is a sense of order *simpliciter* whose form is not subject to any substantive theory of time.[2] Indeed as suggested by the cryptic remainder of the passage, what is so remarkable for Deleuze about Benjamin's study of the 'history' of these plays is that the *Trauerspiel* thesis itself functions as a transcendental critique of logic by interrogating the very possibility of concept construction.

If we consider the logical relation of a concept to its object, we discover that the linkage can be surpassed in a symbolic and in an allegorical way. Sometimes we isolate, purify or concentrate the object; we cut all its ties which link it to the universe, and thus we raise it up, we put it in contact not with its simple concept, but with an Idea which develops this concept morally or aesthetically. Sometimes, on the contrary, the object itself is broadened according to a whole network of natural relations. The object itself overflows its frame in order to enter into a cycle or series, and now the concept is found increasingly compressed, interiorised, wrapped in an instance that can ultimately be called 'personal'. Such is the world as a cone or as a cupola, whose base, always in extension, no longer connects it to a centre, but tends towards an apex or a summit (Deleuze 1993: 125; 1988: 171).

For all the suggestion, then, that the baroque is to be understood in terms of history and nature – or rather through the peculiarly combinatorial sense in which history is both produced from and transformed into nature – Deleuze's reading unfurls by addressing the complex logical implications of the baroque world. Whereas Benjamin's study had ostensibly interrogated the theatrical absurdity of such a world, here, through the figure of the architectural cupola, Deleuze proposes to focus on the ways in which the dramatic perdition of the world's centre might be articulated by means of more traditional philosophical discourse. And yet while this announcement would look to concentrate on something that is seen to be centrifugally rent by the forces of nature and history, any apparent difficulty in this regard no more jeopardises Deleuze's reading of Benjamin than it does the sublime philosophical project common to both thinkers. For just as the construction of Benjamin's own disputation (the subject of his thesis) is designed to articulate the relative, or rather superlative, reprobation of seventeenth-century German drama (the object of his thesis), so too Deleuze is interested less in the simple literality of what the *Trauerspiel* monograph actually says, or whether this could or should have been said differently, than with the concern to exhibit the philosophically discursive conditions that inform the thesis at all. Indeed in this way Deleuze's 'personal' reading of Benjamin is completely problematic in that his reflections identify, and perhaps even go so far as to define, the limits of what is conceptually possible in terms of the earlier study.

The Multiplication of Judgement

By means of an intimidating, albeit patient, scholarship which considers not only the literary intricacies of the plays but also the technical sophistication of their stagecraft, Benjamin's study evidences how, in the *Trauerspiel*, providence ultimately includes damnation as much as salvation. This perspicacious demonstration of the historically awry nature of baroque dramaturgy is significant for Deleuze, since the sense in which dramatic narrative never really concludes with an ultimate resolution of things provides a stage for the very production of philosophy to be acted out in the intrigue between Kant and Leibniz.

Importantly for Deleuze, the baroque study adduces the unique experience of philosophy's own conditions by showing how ultimately in such a drama the skies remain open-ended and so, like the cupola, without a final or absolute point. For although there remains an Alpha and Omega, their time cannot be assigned with any certainty since here damnation and salvation are shown to be no longer timeless values themselves but rather aspects of dimensions whose continued presence emerges relatively through non-linear terms – terms that are 'not always conditions of experience in the Kantian fashion that still turns them into universals, but the conditions of a problem to which the thing responds in one case or the other, the cases referring to values of the variable in the series' (Deleuze 1993: 48; 1988: 64). Indeed as Deleuze explains in his 1978 preface to D. H. Lawrence's *Apocalypse*,[3] or earlier in the discussion of axiomatics in *Difference and Repetition* and of the proposition in *The Logic of Sense*, what is of significance here is less any final word on things and more the reality presented by discursive terms themselves.

For this reason, silhouetted against the setting of Kantian subjectivity, Deleuze repeatedly invokes the significance of the famous closing sections of Leibniz's *Theodicy*, where the goddess Pallus presents Theodorus with a 'theatre of history' which cannot be realised through any cathartic point of view (Deleuze 1998: 371–2). Anticipating thereby the work of Brecht, which both Benjamin and Deleuze acknowledge as declaredly non-Aristotelian, the performance of such a drama concerns 'less the development of actions than the presentation of conditions [*Zustände darzustellen*]' (Benjamin 1996–2001, Vol. IV: 304; 1972–91, Vol. II.2: 535, translation modified) since the experiential encounter with such theatre is not produced as an underlying representation of or for a subject, but rather emerges as an ingenuous relation of the tension present between audience and performance. Moreover, significantly for philosophy, this dislocation of historical time affects apperceptive unity as much as the very possibility of thought. As Theodurus experiences, how all the events of history (with their necessary selections of some series over others) could ever be represented so that they might be combined in any determinate conception of things is a seemingly impossible problem – a problem, for Deleuze, that not only engenders the originality of Benjamin's study but is, moreover, 'exactly the problem that has disturbed philosophy since its beginnings', or at least, 'ever since there was logic' (Deleuze 1980).

What attests to this affinity between Benjamin and the author of the *Theodicy* is the way in which the twentieth-century study of German baroque theatre responds to the very paradox whose reckoning constitutes the 'infinite' even 'impossible task' Leibniz himself undertook when he committed himself to showing in what way [*à montrer de quelle manière*] all propositions can be linked [*ramenées*] to the judgement of attribution, notably propositions that state relations, that state existences, that state localisations, and that, at the outside, exist, are in relation with, can be translated as the equivalent of the attribute of the subject (Deleuze 1980).

For just as Benjamin's disputation on the function of allegory fails so conspicuously to propose a completely determinate concept of the German *Trauerspiel*, Leibniz's undertaking to show a subjective equivalence between all the different propositions in terms of an attributive scheme must similarly fail. And yet the very failure (indeed the necessity of this failure) to reduce or to reify [*ramener*] the world into a subject/attribute schema says less about the possible adequacy of these propositions and more about judgement itself. Against the Kantian model of modality this failure shows how, in the baroque scheme of things, any apodicticity only ever emerges from the fact that the assertoric eventually reveals itself to be insufficient. What this failure presents is the way in which the possibility of judgement, if not philosophical discourse at all, is conditioned problematically by an internal limit adduced through the crisis of the baroque. For the only way in which something might be said in regard to the overwhelmingly paradoxical presence of the theatre of history without remaining a profanity is if the terms which produce the series of statements cohere with one another in a 'virtual' relation.

In this way, following a key moment in Leibniz's *Discourse on Metaphysics* (Leibniz 1991: 8), Benjamin and Deleuze develop the sense in which the very essence ('individual substance' or 'haecceity') of things can never be spoken of sufficiently, if defined primitively, since it is evident that all true predication has some basis in the nature of things and that, when a proposition is not an identity, that is, when the predicate is not explicitly contained in the subject, it must be contained in it virtually. That is what the philosophers call *in-esse*, when they say that the predicate term is in the subject. Thus the subject term must always contain the predicate term, so that one who understands perfectly the notion of the subject would also know that the predicate belongs to it.

Notwithstanding the commitment here to 'identity propositions',[4] Leibniz's virtual form of predication suggests to Benjamin and Deleuze an ontological thesis proper to the grammar of the baroque – a 'grammar', Deleuze explains, 'in which the predicate is above all a relation and an event, and not an attribute' (Deleuze 1980: 53; 71). For crucially the discursive elements of this constitution are not to be found in terms of the rectitude of their legislation, but rather problematically – in the very possibility of legislation itself. As evidenced in Carl Schmitt's considerable influence on Benjamin's study and later work, a 'parliamentary crisis' might well be said to loom since the baroque reveals there to be no jurisprudential equivalence or even primacy between the order of the higher and lower faculties. As Deleuze explains in his chapter on conic sections and the mathematics of variation, here 'fluctuation of the norm replaces the permanence of a law' (Deleuze 1993: 19; 1988: 26) since the potential order and structure of any assemblage – the capacity to organise and distribute power – only ever comes about through a uniquely bicameral tension that continuously threatens double dissolution.[5]

What matters for the baroque, then, is not so much the jurisdiction of laws but rather the transcendental conditions realised in the varying force or potency (*pouvoir*, *Gewalt*) of their power (*puissance*, *Mächtigkeit*). Accordingly, Deleuze proposes that 'Leibnizian transcendental philosophy, which bears on the event rather than the phenomenon, replaces Kantian conditioning' (Deleuze 1993: 120; 1988: 163) since the form of discursive logos in Kant is modelled all too 'naturally' on the parliamentary, and ultimately bourgeois, propriety of what is actually said or what must be said, rather than on the turbulent 'history' of those (virtually antecedent) conditions that might eventually prompt even the utterances or gestures of speech at all – conditions both Benjamin and Deleuze describe as truly baroque.

History as the Consequence of 'Double Antecedence'

As suggested not least of all by the term's etymology (through Early-Modern Spanish *berruga/berruca*, from the Latin *verruca*), the very notion of the term 'baroque' resonates with the ancient topic whereby, for all their aspiration to be conceived logically as objects of thesis, parts of speech nonetheless remain acroamata bound to the realm of phusis.[6] For both Benjamin and Deleuze, such an irreconcilable discord between sound and meaning reveals the uniquely philological character of baroque discourse as something whose ultimate historical realisation is duplicitous rather than upright, no longer (or perhaps not yet) literal but musical – in short: determined reciprocally, from within, rather than transitively, from without.[7]

The philosophical significance of the baroque is not, however, amenable to this simply onomatopoetic discord between sound and meaning. For while this serves to illustrate the linguistic character of such discourse, as Benjamin explains at length throughout his study and as Deleuze keenly appreciates, what is integral to the logos of the baroque is the manner with which written script is regarded as historical. Indeed, Deleuze's interest in Benjamin must be seen in the context of the uniquely transcendental combination of seeing with reading described in §61 of the *Monadology* – a combination which testifies to the intensely exegetical and even eschatological obsession with lexicography that absorbed dramatists of this period.

As Benjamin himself explains in a key section on 'The Origin of Modern Allegory' (Benjamin 1990: 167–70; 1978: 146–50) with regard to the enduring significance of pictorial script, following medieval humanism's interest in the *Hieroglyphica* of Horapollon, the understanding that underpins baroque and contemporary allegory functions according to the essentially determinable nature of phonetics with regard to the essentially unassignable problematic or 'history' of hierogrammatics. For whereas the sonorous form of an object's thesis either suffices to be content through the immediacy of a particular iteration or remains an indeterminate clamour, the written form by contrast (although far from unequivocal) continually proposes something that provokes discourse to begin.[8] For this reason, Benjamin insists that:

> it will unmistakenly be apparent, especially to anyone familiar with allegorical textual exegesis, that all of the things which are used to signify derive, from the very fact of their pointing to something else, a power [*Mächtigkeit*] which makes them appear no longer commensurable with profane things, which raises them onto a higher plane and which can,

indeed, sanctify them. Considered in allegorical terms, then, the profane world is both elevated and devalued. This religious dialectic of content has its formal correlative in the dialectic of convention and expression. For allegory is both: convention *and* expression; and both are inherently contradictory [*von Haus aus wiederstrietend*]. (Benjamin 1990: 174–5; 1978: 152–3)

Although inherently discursive, categorically speaking the very being of allegory is metaphysical rather than logical since it is neither literary nor linguistic but rather the expression of the conditions that provide for discourse at all. Following Deleuze's own descriptions *passim*, allegory can thus be seen as ineluctably baroque since it refers to an operative function rather than an essence, to a relation, a verb or *concetto* that is predicative rather than attributive. In keeping not only with its very etymology but so too its significance for the theological tradition, an allegorical synthesis of terms, then, does not propose to overcome antithetical differences but rather to repeat the ingenuousness of their thesis through the ostensive profanity of a different or at least 'other presentation in the world' (*allos agoreuein*).

As Benjamin explains above, drawing on his early essays on language, if the theological tension between sacred and profane composes the content of allegory then this corresponds to the sense in which the allegorical form of writing is at once the 'profanity' of what is said in terms of the logic of any literary convention but also, and moreover, the metaphysically 'sacred' expression of those conditions that provide for such conventions at all. In other words what is integral here is the sense in which allegorical expression does not allow for a naive distinction between what is said and its being said since, formally speaking, these are only ever merely combinations of varying orders.

For his part, Deleuze explains that the relation of these two halves cannot be represented in terms of simple identity, but rather coheres presently in a complex and infinitely determinable reciprocity. For while the dialectic of the theologically sacred/profane (and the correlative of expression/convention) together constitute what is set forth in allegory, neither enjoys primacy with respect to the other. The reason for this, as Benjamin demonstrates, is that the very expression of such content is informed as much by a logic of elementary terms as their extra-propositional or metaphysical combination with one another – a combination, in other words, which is not in the end amenable to whatever can or should be said (that is, to what can be represented symbolically, once and for all) but rather which takes place in the presence of what Deleuze describes in Benjamin as irresolvable 'networks of natural relations'.

For example, if a collection of markings within a given hieroglyph is assigned a hierogrammatical function, then its relation with other as yet undetermined hieroglyphs informs their subsequent understanding. Equally, if such an element of a hieroglyph is found to occur in contexts that were not anticipated or in interpretations not revealed in earlier exegeses then this may lead to a serious reconsideration of the value previously assigned to those individual markings. In this way, then, there are two halves of the object: one half is the logical participation of the object in a profane drama of pure relations, where this set of strokes is said to determine the value of that hieroglyph, while the other half of the object is its dialectical (or, following Deleuze, differential) participation in a metaphysical 'salvation drama' where, despite appearances, one set of strokes allows a hieroglyph to mean one thing in one context and yet also another thing in a different context. As Deleuze explains, paraphrasing Hegel's admiration for the calculus,

> we have a first part, a first moment of the object, the object as perceived or the world as expression. But there persists the question of knowing what the other part may be which now corresponds to the initial equation: pure relations are no longer at stake, but differential equations and integrations that determine the efficient causes of perception, that is, which have to do with a matter and the bodies that perception resembles. Such is the second moment of the object, no longer expression, but content. (Deleuze 1993: 101; 1988: 134–5)

Corresponding to the dialectic of allegory stated in Benjamin, for Deleuze the philosophical object is here distributed according to the reciprocity of two different orders – according, that is to an architecture of 'two floors, separated by a fold that echoes itself' (Deleuze 1993: 29; 1988: 41). For unlike the Romantic synthesis of things, where the harmony of these orders is resolved transitively through the auto-apotheosis of nature (or in works of art and their aesthetic reflection in genius), allegorical synthesis is historically rent both by the gravamen of tradition and the harbinger of prophecy. Confronted by a theodicy but no eschatology, allegory must not only 'throw together' (*syn-ballein*) both the sensible and supersensible (what Deleuze describes as the momentary and the eternal) but, significantly, must continue to do the same *ad infinitum*; that we can express the hope for beatitude and sanctification does not guarantee that we may be its subject, and yet we can only continue to hope since our very inclusion in the world repeats the world or, as Benjamin continues:

> just as baroque teaching conceives of history as created events [*überhaupt Geschichte als erschaffenes Geschehn begriffe*], allegory in particular,

although a convention like every kind of writing, is regarded as created, like holy scripture. The allegory of the seventeenth century is not convention of expression but expression of convention. (Benjamin 1990: 175; 1978: 153)

For both thinkers, then, these 'two halves' of the world are not resolvable because they are not equal to one another, and so when they enter into relation with one another this does not so much complete things as merely repeat them in a different way. And it is for this reason, against Kant's 'theological rationalism' (Benjamin 1990: 66; 1978: 48), that Benjamin warns against Romanticism's absolutising of the symbol as a simple aesthetic object which supposedly overcomes the 'paradoxical' relation of the sensible and the supersensible by rendering them in terms of appearance and essence (Benjamin 1990: 160; 1978: 139). More specifically:

> The undialectic neo-Kantian mode of thought is not able to grasp the synthesis which is reached in allegorical writing as a result of the conflict between theological and artistic intentions, a synthesis not so much in the sense of a peace as a *treuga dei* between the conflicting opinions. (Benjamin 1990: 177; 1978: 155)

The harmony of a baroque synthesis, then, is only ever provisional – a ceasefire of hostilities, as Benjamin here suggests, rather than a cosmopolitan peace, since the differences between things are never entirely overcome in any one declaration. Instead, in any truly philosophical thesis there emerges an accord of things or, as the title of Deleuze's final chapter suggests, an ideal relation that obtains in the form of a New Harmony. For like the cupola itself, here any and every point of view becomes problematised so as to reveal the minimal conditions for any perspective at all. In short, indeed following the account of Archimedian geometry from *Difference and Repetition*, here synthesis is shown to be no more than the present limits of analyses in a given function. For just as intuition 'sees' and the understanding 'reads', the real difficulty comes about in determining a value for the reciprocal simultaneity and instantaneity of these two aspects of experience.[9] Describing the truly theological torsion of this inversion of God ($^\circ/1$) which Kant has the confidence to ignore, Deleuze explains how

> the point [*la question*] is effectively that of knowing how the unit of a numerator is at once combined with the infinite of the denominator ($1/\infty$) but with the distinctive variable value ($1/n$, necessarily holding for $1/2$, $1/3$, or $1/4$. . .). . . . each monad expresses the world $1/^\circ$, but clearly expresses only one particular zone of the world $1/n$ (with n in each case having a very specific [*précise*] value). Each monad includes the world as an infinite series

of infinitely small parts, but establishes differential relations and integrations only upon a limited portion of the series, such that the monads themselves enter into infinite series of inverse numbers. In its own portion of the
world or in its clear zone, each monad *thus presents accords*, inasmuch as
an 'accord' can be called the relation of a state with its differentials, that is,
with the differential relations among infinitely small units that are integrated
into this state. Whence the double aspect of the accord, insofar as it is the
product of an intelligible calculus in an affective [*sensible*] state. (Deleuze
1993: 129–30; 1988: 177–8)

Significantly, the 'double aspect of the accord' presented in this manner
corresponds to the way in which the baroque conditions for philosophy
are for Benjamin articulated textually (or scripturally) through allegory.
And while, entirely true to its form, the very disputation of such a thesis is
ineluctable from the event of its complete articulation throughout each
thinkers' respective monograph, the most thoroughgoing demonstration
of this affinity is to be found in the reflections on philosophy's presentation (*Darstellung*) from the *Erkenntniskritische Vorrede*. For there, like
Deleuze, Benjamin shows that the task of the philosopher is to interrogate
by way of concepts the ingenuousness of things found in the multiplicity
of their Idea. In a passage from the *Vorrede* that resembles his own interest in Maimon, relegated to a draft of the study (Benjamin 1972–91, Vol.
I.3: 934), Benjamin explains that a truly philosophical thesis emerges as a
relation of the seemingly different orders regarding the logic of what is said
and the metaphysics of those conditions that provide for its presentation.

Tirelessly the process of thinking makes new beginnings, returning in a
roundabout way to its original object [*geht es auf die Sache selbst zurück*].
This continual pausing for breath is the mode most proper into the process
of contemplation. For by pursuing different levels of meaning in its examination of one single object it receives both the incentive to begin again and
the justification for its irregular rhythm. Just as mosaics preserve their
majesty despite their fragmentation into capricious particles, so philosophical contemplation is not lacking in momentum. Both are made up of the
distinct [*Einzelne*] and the disparate; and nothing could bear more powerful testimony to the transcendent force of the sacred image of truth itself.
The value of fragments of thought is all the greater the less distinct their relationship to the underlying idea [*Grundkonzeption*], and the brilliance of
their representation [*Darstellung*] depends as much on this value as the
brilliance of the mosaic does on the quality of the glass paste. The relationship between the minute precision of the work and the proportions of
the sculptural or intellectual whole demonstrates that truth-content
[*Wahrheitsgehalt*] is only grasped through the immersion in the most minute
details of the subject matter [*Sachgehalts*]. (Benjamin 1990: 28–9; 1978: 10)

In this way, whereas other discourses claim historical progress, philosophy always remains both historically underdetermined and overdetermined; what makes philosophical texts timeless is that they do not so much assert answers to questions, or even propose further questions, but rather present the conditions that provide for the conceptual presentation of the Idea that informs any and every treatise.[10] Quite literally, then, in this way the logos of such a pre-linguistic interrogation of the world – what Benjamin describes variously as *Urvernehmung* (Benjamin 1990: 36; 1978: 18, 19) and *ursprüngliche Vernehmen* (Benjamin 1990: 37; 1978: 19) – takes place through a form of discourse that at each moment predicates itself to the world anew as if on the First Day. This peculiarly baroque 'philology', however, is not the same thing as some proto-linguistic or etymological order of substantive truth but rather merely the presence of the conditions that engender discourse at all. For the philosophical treatise must, by means of concepts, set forth the original (*ursprüngliche*) form – the Idea – of any and every encounter with the world. This, at least, is what Benjamin explains in what is if not the most quoted then the most turgid passage from the *Vorrede*:

> Origin [*Ursprung*], although an entirely historical category, has, nevertheless, nothing to do with genesis. The term origin is not intended to describe the process by which the existent came into being, but rather to describe that which emerges from the process of becoming and disappearance. Origin is an eddy in the stream of becoming, and its current swallows the material involved in the process of genesis. [*Der Ursprung steht im Fluß des Werdens als Strudel und reißt in seine Rhythmik das Enstehungsmaterial hinein*]. That which is original is never revealed in the naked and manifest existence of the factual; its rhythm is apparent only to a dual insight [*Doppeleinsicht*]. On the one hand it needs to be recognized [*erkannt*] as a process of restoration and re-establishment, but, on the other hand, and precisely because of this, as something imperfect [*Unvollendentes*] and incomplete. There takes place in every original phenomenon a determination of the form in which an idea will constantly confront [*auseinandersetzt*] the historical world, until it is fulfilled, in the totality of its history. Origin is not, therefore, discovered by the examination of actual findings, but is related to their history and subsequent development [*Vor- und Nachgeschichte*]. The principles of philosophical contemplation are recorded in the dialectic which is inherent in origin. This dialectic shows singularity and repetition to be conditioned by one another in all essentials. (Benjamin 1990: 45–6; 1978: 28)

The function of this 'historical category' is further developed in Benjamin's subsequent work where, as here, what is stressed is the undertaking to interrogate the logos of things by means of what he describes above as the dialectic of 'singularity and repetition [*Einmaligkeit und Wiederholung*]'.[11] The philosophical treatise must, from the beginning and 'at all times', be attended by its own metaphysical justification and so by definition cannot be completed in terms of the self-same discourse that any one treatise proposes since any 'science in conflict with the language of its investigations is an absurdity' (Benjamin 1990: 42; 1978: 24).[12] Moreover sufficient knowledge of a thesis can only be said to have come about following its original 'rhythm' which considers not only what things happen to say or what they could have said (their *Vorgeschichte*) but so too with anything that that they might yet still have to say (their *Nachgeschichte*). For the very happening of philosophy, which is as much to say the conditions of its possibility, is given through what Benjamin describes here as a '*Doppeleinsicht*' and indeed corresponds to the 'double antecedence' (Deleuze 1993: 52; 1988: 69) of monads that Deleuze develops in response to the classical proportions of 'before and after' from book IV of Aristotle's *Physics*.

For both Benjamin and Deleuze, then, the more centrally or genetically the terminology of any conceptual scheme is asserted with respect to the discursive order of things the more it attracts suspicion and, so too, the higher the burden of proof must be for its claims. 'Conceptual distinctions', Benjamin explains, 'are above all suspicion of destructive sophistry only when their purpose is the salvation of phenomena in Ideas, the Platonic *ta phainomena sozein*' (Benjamin 1990: 33; 1978: 16).[13] For the philosophical truth of a thesis cannot be revealed simply in terms of its continuity with the logical abductions, deductions and inductions of whatever else is said, but must also accord with the very conditions that motivate discourse at all. The reason for this is that, as elements of discourse, concepts do not obtain categorically as logical representations of things, but rather are constructed and exhibited metaphysically, through writing, as allegories of Ideas, as monads.

The Tradition of Thesis in Kant

If, however, the baroque understanding of philosophy's thesis is adduced through such double antecedence, then the problem of formulating any discourse is that there seem to be no possible limits at all as to what can be said – no criteria, in other words, to adequately adduce Ideas through concepts or generate the latter from the former. The endlessness of such a discourse would indeed appear so pointless that, contra Aristotle, 'who . . . at one point proposed in the *Metaphysics* a very beautiful formula: it is indeed necessary to stop (*anankstenai*)', philosophical discourse would simply not say anything and instead, like Klee's *Angelus Novus*, would exhibit only the very conditions of speech by letting out 'a great scream . . . in front of the chasm of the interconnection of concepts' (Deleuze 1980). Accordingly, as Benjamin explains in his section 'The Word as Idea', 'the task of the philosopher [is] to restore, by representation [*durch Darstellung*], the primacy of the symbolic character of the word, in which the idea is given in self-consciousness, and that is the opposite of outwardly-directed communication' (Benjamin 1990: 36; 1978: 18–19). For what is metaphysically singular or sacred about a word (the presence of its Idea as multiplicity) cannot be determined objectively, through conceptually profane terms, as a being of simple logic.

Instead, the very concept of the philosopher's object – the thesis – must itself be informed by the originally theological sense of the symbol. What this requires is that the thesis be defined through its terms' 'historical' relation (*Vor- und Nachgeshichte*) to the world, which at once provides for and yet also problematises and pullulates the formation of concepts rather than facilitating their consolidation within simple discursive series. Against this, however, not only does the Kantian understanding of the symbol propose to conceptualise the discursive ingenuousness of philosophical terms in a transitive synthesis, so too this forces philosophy to surrender the metaphysical rigour of its dialectical interrogation (or analysis) of those 'networks of natural relations' whose objects give rise to theses on the world at all. Through such a misappropriation, the philosophical thesis is thereby conceived logically in terms of completely determinate objects that are assigned as part of a universal attributive scheme.

Against this, however, as the baroque shows, philosophical theses emerge as conceptual dramatisations of an Idea such that their very object is no longer amenable to simple logic but rather to the metaphysics of those transcendental conditions of historical antecedence that adduce a thesis's virtual significance in the world at all. Since no thesis can assert (*kategorein*) the final word with respect to the concept of an object, to define an object simply by what a given concept has to say abstracts from the original reality that prompted something to be said in the first place. And yet while this discrimination is necessary so that formal discourse might be possible, whereas the allegorical selection of discursive elements is nothing if not inclusive, the symbol operates by way of exclusion. For Benjamin and Deleuze, then, the integral difference with respect to the articulation of the concept/object relation is whether in the final analysis[14] things are said to be external or internal to the world – that is, symbolised categorically by an attribute or allegorised 'historically' as a predicate.

In this way, the function not only of Deleuze's commentary on Benjamin but also of each philosophical thesis is something truly allegorical. For example, if Benjamin's published interest in the *Ursprung* of German mourning-plays is taken as a predicate term, then, following their shared development of the virtual, the subject of the dissertation must be conceptualised as something which reciprocates with the reality of those conditions that give rise to the entire 'object' of *Trauerspiel*. For essentially, Benjamin is concerned neither with the definition of the prototypes of this drama nor the archetypal identification of these plays as a genre. Although both of these literary representations are aspects of the study, the truly 'historical' concern of Benjamin's project is neither an account of the inception of these plays (their *res gestae*) nor a catalogue of their reception in previous criticism (their *historia rerum gestarum*) but rather a presentation that proposes to articulate through concepts the very Idea of this drama. Indeed as developed at the outset in the study's recondite proem, the term *Ursprung* functions to adduce the complex philosophical (or *Kritische*) set of conditions by which the singularity of these plays can be known (or *Erkennt*).

In a similar manner, for all the topological imagery of *Le Pli*, Deleuze's own study of the baroque is not simply an extended metaphor with respect to an age whose only sense of transcendence came immanently in the form of variations of hope and fear implied within the self-same world. And so while the study ends with the claim that thought discovers 'new ways of folding . . . because what always matters is folding, unfolding, refolding', this is more than a droll literary technique. Instead, as with the extended philological consideration of the mathematical 'singularity',[15] here the use of the term *pli* is both rigorous and productive. For the thoroughgoing articulation of the 'fold' echoes the way in which differenciation and differentiation explicate the original 'duplicity' implied in the rhythm of One and the Many which no thesis could ever assert categorically.

For neither Benjamin nor Deleuze, then, are the respective uses of the terms *Ursprung* or *Pli* purely symbolic in the sense developed by Kant in §59 of the *Critique of Judgement*. For there Kant proposes an understanding of certain symbolic words which do not reciprocate the logic of what is actually said with the metaphysical conditions of their being said:

> Our language is replete with such indirect exhibitions [*Darstellungen*] according to an analogy, where the expression does not contain the actual schema for the concept but merely a symbol for our reflection. Thus the

words 'foundation' (support, basis), to 'depend' (to be held from above), to 'flow' (instead of to follow) from something, 'substance' (the support of accidents, as Locke puts it), and countless others are not schematic but symbolic hypotyposes; they express concepts not by means of a direct intuition but only according to an analogy with one, i.e., a transfer of our reflection on an object of intuition to an entirely different concept, to which perhaps no intuition can ever directly correspond [*der Übertragung der Reflexion über einen Gegenstand der Anschauung auf einen ganz andern Begriff, dem vielleicht nie eine Aunschauung direkt korrespondieren kann*].

For both Benjamin and Deleuze, that reflection is 'carried across' in this way (literally, 'trans-ferred' or 'trans-ported': *über-trug*) 'to an entirely different concept, to which perhaps no intuition can ever directly correspond' betrays an insufficient element in Kant's transcendental project. For whereas baroque discourse exhibits the philosophical problematic of how a thesis relates to the world by means of an historical duplicity – not so much through what is actually said but rather through the virtual conditions which provide for speech at all – here Kant subscribes uncritically to certain categorical assertions about the discursive relation of philosophy to the world.

Rather than interogating the metaphysical ingenuousness of things from within, and thereby attesting to the historical relation of a thesis's Idea to the world of concepts, certain 'symbolic hypotyposes' in Kant propose simply to outsource the task of philosophy (the interrogation of logos) to linguistic analogues. In this way, the conceptual construction of philosophical theses does not so much provide for an ingenuous judgement of things as for the supposedly objective adjudication of categorical prejudices. And while this is not to say that such a discourse is not possible, or even quite effective, the elements of philosophical discourse that Benjamin and Deleuze look to propose are what they refer to historically as those 'baroque' moments which behove a certain reconsideration of the sense of *Darstellung* in Kant's transcendental project.

References

Benjamin, W. (1972–91), *Gesammelte Schriften*, Vols 1–7, hrsg. von Rolf Tiedemann and Hermann Schweppenhäuser, Frankfurt am Main: Suhrkamp.
Benjamin, W. (1978) [1925], *Ursprung des deutschen Trauerspiels*, Frankfurt: Suhrkamp.
Benjamin, W. (1990), *The Origin of German Tragic Drama*, trans. John Osborne, London: Verso.
Benjamin, W. (1996–2001), *Selected Writings*, Vols 1–4, ed. Marcus Bullock, Howard Eiland, Michael Jennings and Gary Smith, Cambridge, MA: The Belknap Press of Harvard University Press.

Benjamin, W. (1999), *The Arcades Project*, trans. Howard Eiland and Kevin McLaughlin, Cambridge, MA: The Belknap Press of Harvard University Press.

Deleuze, G. (1980), *Leibniz* <http://www.webdeleuze.com/php/sommaire.html>

Deleuze, G. (1988), *Le Pli: Leibniz et la Baroque*, Paris: Les Éditions de Minuit.

Deleuze, G. (1993), *The Fold: Leibniz and the Baroque*, trans. Tom Conley, London: Athlone.

Deleuze, G. (1995), *Kant's Critical Philosophy*, trans. Hugh Tomlinson and Barbara Habberjam, London: Athlone.

Deleuze, G. (1998), *Essays Critical and Clinical*, trans. Dan Smith and Michael Greco, London: Verso.

Kant, I. (1987), *Critique of Judgement*, trans. Werner Pluhar, Indianapolis: Hackett.

Leibniz, G. W. (1991), *Discourse on Metaphysics and Other Essays*, ed. and trans. Daniel Garber and Roger Ariew, Indianapolis: Hackett.

Leibniz, G. W. (1998), *Theodicy: Essays on the Goodness of God, the Freedom of Man and the Origin of Evil*, trans. E. M. Huggard, Chicago: Open Court.

Notes

1. References for each thinker's study are given by their English pagination first and respective French or German pagination second.

2. Elsewhere, for example, regarding Kant's third *Critique*, Deleuze describes a sense that 'is no longer the aesthetic of the *Critique of Pure Reason*, which considered the sensible as a quality which could be related to an object in space and time; it is not a logic of the sensible, nor even a new *logos* which would be time. It is an aesthetic of the Beautiful and of the Sublime, in which the sensible is valid in itself and unfolds in a *pathos* beyond all logic, which will grasp time in its surging forth, in the very origin of its thread and giddiness. It is no longer the Affect of the *Critique of Pure Reason*, which related the Ego to the I in a relationship which was still regulated by the order of time; it is a Pathos which leaves them to evolve freely in order to form strange combinations as sources of time; "arbitrary forms of possible intuitions"' (Deleuze 1995: xii).

3. There, describing the problem presented by scripture, Deleuze contrasts allegory against the confidence and certainty of symbolism where 'we make a true decision: we turn into ourselves, upon ourselves, ever more rapidly, "until a centre is formed and we know what to do". Just the opposite occurs in allegorical thought, which is no longer an active thought but a thought that ceaselessly postpones or defers. *It replaced the force [puissance] of decision with the power [pouvoir] of judgement.* Furthermore, it wants a final point as the last judgement. And it places these provisional points, between each sentence, as so many stages in a path preparing for the second coming. No doubt it is the sense of sight, books, and reading that have given us this taste for points, segmentary lines, beginnings, ends and stages. The eye is the sense organ that separates us: allegory is visual, whereas the symbol evokes and unites all the other senses. When the book was still scrolled, it perhaps retained its power as a symbol. But how, precisely, can we explain the strange fact that the book of the seven seals is supposed to be a scroll, and yet that the seals are broken successively, in stages – apart from the fact that the Apocalypse needs to put points everywhere, to install segments everywhere? . . . The Apocalypse reveals its own aim: to disconnect us from the world and from ourselves' (Deleuze 1998: 49).

4. Earlier in the *Logic of Sense* and *Difference and Repetition*, Deleuze shows how the principle of identity in truths of essence and truths of existence entails for Leibniz the eventual exclusion of incompossible series. And while in his lecture

notes he laments that 'from this perspective Leibniz remains within classical logic' (Deleuze 1980) in a footnote to the study in question, against Couturat and Guerolt, Deleuze asserts that 'for Leibniz the incompossible is an original relation irreducible to any form of contradiction. It is a difference and not a negation. That is why in the following pages we are proposing an interpretation based only on convergence or divergence of series' (Deleuze 1993: 150; 1988: 79–80). For Benjamin's position, see especially his early fragments on language and logic.

5. 'The theological-juridical mode of thought, which is so characteristic of the century, is an expression of the retarding effect of the over-strained transcendental impulse [*spricht die verzögernde Überspannung der Transzendenz*], which underlies all the provocatively worldly accents of the baroque' (Benjamin 1990: 65–6; 1978: 48).

6. On this tradition see the discussion of the baroque theory of language (Benjamin 1990: 202–3; 1978: 180). See too Benjamin's comments on Herder's (1772) *Essay on the Origin of Language* (Benjamin 1996–2001, Vol. III: 69; 1972–91, Vol. III: 453–4).

7. Consider Deleuze's discussion of the inner 'prehensive' quality of sound in his short chapter on Whitehead in *Le Pli*. 'The phonetic tension in the language of the seventeenth century', for Benjamin, 'leads directly to music, the opposite of meaning-laden speech [*sinnbeschwerten Rede*]' (Benjamin 1990: 211; 1978: 186–7).

8. 'Spoken language is thus the domain of the free, spontaneous utterance [*ursprünglichen Äußerung*] of the creature, whereas the written language of allegory enslaves objects [*Dinge*] in the eccentric embrace of meaning' (Benjamin 1990: 202; 1978: 179–80). 'Whereas the speaker uses voice and gesture to support individual sentences, even where they cannot really stand up on their own, constructing out of them – often vaguely and precariously – a sequence of ideas, as if producing a bold sketch in a single attempt, the writer must stop and restart with every new sentence' (Benjamin 1990: 29; 1978: 11).

9. 'We have to understand literally – that is, mathematically – that a conscious perception is produced when at least two heterogeneous parts enter into a differential relation that determines a singularity' (Deleuze 1993: 88; 1988: 117). With respect to the post-Kantian development of the concept in Fichte and Maimon, Deleuze discusses how, rather than 'having perception presuppose an object capable of affecting us, and conditions in which we would be apt to be affected, the reciprocal determination of the differentials (dy/dx) brings about the complete determination of the object as a perception, and the determinability of space-time as a condition' (Deleuze 1993: 89; 1988: 118).

10. 'In the great philosophies the world is seen in terms of the order of ideas. But the conceptual frameworks within which this took place have, for the most part, long since become fragile. Nevertheless these systems, such as Plato's theory of ideas, Leibniz's Monadology, or Hegel's dialectic still remain valid as attempts at a description of the world. It is peculiar to all these attempts that they still preserve their meaning, indeed they often reveal it more fully, even when they are applied to the world of ideas instead of empirical reality. For it was as descriptions of the world of ideas that these systems of thought originated. The more intensely the respective thinkers strove to outline the image of reality, the more they were bound to develop a conceptual order which, for the later interpreter, would be seen as serving that original depiction of the world of ideas which was really intended' (Benjamin 1990: 32; 1978: 14).

11. 'Indeed this is where the task of the investigator begins, for he cannot regard a fact as certain until its innermost structure appears to be so essential as to reveal

it as an origin. The authentic – the hallmark of origin in phenomena – is the object of discovery, a discovery which is connected in a unique way with the process of recognition. And the act of discovery can reveal it in the most singular and eccentric [*Singulärsten und Verschrobensten*] of phenomena, in both the weakest and clumsiest experiments and in the overripe fruits [*Erscheinungen*] of a period of decadence' (Benjamin 1990: 46; 1978: 28–9).

12. In his notes to a similar *Vorrede* for the *Arcades Project*, Benjamin seeks to 'Say something about the method of composition itself: how everything one is thinking at a specific moment in time must at all costs be incorporated into the project then at hand. Assume that the intensity of the project is thereby attested, or that one's thoughts, from the very beginning, bear this project within them as their telos. So it is with the present portion of the work, which aims to characterize and to preserve the intervals of reflection, the distances lying between the most essential parts of this work, which are turned most intensively to the outside' (Benjamin 1999: N1, 3).

13. Deleuze ends his lectures on Leibniz: 'There is a philosophical sensibility, it is the art of evaluating the consistency of a group [*ensemble*] of concepts' (Deleuze 1980).

14. 'Leibniz is infinite analysis, Kant is the grand synthesis of finitude', begins Deleuze in the final sentence from his Leibniz lectures (Deleuze 1980).

15. 'The singular has always existed in a certain logical vocabulary. "Singular" designates what is not difference, and at the same time, in relation to "universal". There is another pair of notions, it's "particular" that is said with reference to "general". So the singular and the universal are in relation with each other; the particular and the general are in relation. What is a judgment of singularity? It's not the same thing as a judgment called particular, nor the same thing as a judgment called general. I am only saying, formally, "singular" was thought, in classical logic, with reference to "universal". And that does not necessarily exhaust a notion: when mathematicians use the expression "singularity", with what do they place it into relation? One must be guided by words. There is a philosophical etymology, or even a philosophical philology. "Singular" in mathematics is distinct from or opposed to "regular". The singular is what is outside the rule' (Deleuze 1980). Note thus 'the honeymoon of the singularity and the concept' (Deleuze 1990: 67; 1988: 91).

Chapter 6

The Cannibal Within: White Men and the Embodiment of Evolutionary Time

Eve Bischoff

On Pentecost Sunday, 1924, a strange spectacle presented itself to visitors to the German city of Hanover: men, women and children alike gathered in crowds on the numerous bridges, catwalks and gutters along the small river Leine, and frantically started fishing for bones, skulls and other human remains. A few days later, the police blocked the stream and searched the riverbed. The officers discovered more than 500 different parts of several human bodies. In the previous months, rumours had spread like wildfire: of human flesh sold on the market in Hanover, of traps set to snatch young men or boys, and of a werewolf looking for his prey. The hysteria infected the neighbouring villages and scared maidservants refused to enter the city for minor errands such as shopping (Lessing 1973: 17–18).

Eventually, on 23 June 1924, one Friedrich (Fritz) Haarmann was taken into custody. Born in Hanover in 1879, Fritz was known to the police to be a petty criminal and a homosexual. According to his confessions, Haarmann took advantage of the desperate situation many young men found themselves in when they arrived in Hanover. The city was a hub for the nationwide migration of young labourers during the first years of the Weimar Republic, and many of the men resorted to male-to-male prostitution as a means of survival. Haarmann invited such men to his flat, entertained them with food and drink, had sex with them and then killed some of them. To make matters more disturbing, Haarmaan had dealt in meat, mostly on the black market, selling it to neighbours and offering it in exchange for sundry services or his rent. Since the official investigations could not confirm the origin of his supplies, rumour had it that he had sold the flesh of his victims. Stories circulated: about minced meat, self-made sausages, and aspic. Suddenly, contemporaries saw themselves confronted with the resurrection of the 'beast of prey, the cannibal, the wolf in human shape' (Frey 1959: 60) Theodor Lessing, philosopher, intellectual and author of critical political essays, entitled his study on the case from which the above description is taken: *Haarmann: Story of a Werewolf*. Referring to a sexual killer as a 'were-wolf' was a common practice in daily and weekly newspapers of the 1920s.[1]

As described in Deleuze and Guattari's *A Thousand Plateaus*, the were-wolf is the paradigmatic demonic animal, characterised by its capability to establish 'unnatural participations' (Deleuze and Guattari 1987: 267). In contrast to 'Oedipal animals' and 'State animals' that build molar structures and fixed identities either on a personal or a social level, demonic animals form molecular connections. These connections are transformative by nature: they change those between whom they have been established (Deleuze and Guattari 1987: 265–7). These transforma-tive relations follow from Deleuze and Guattari's concept of 'becoming' as an ongoing process of deterritorialisation, which 'disrupts signifying projects' and undermines fixed identities. Thought of as a process of transduction, becoming realises a multiplicity, a rhizomatic network of connections and relations, of intensities and lines of deterritorialisation (Deleuze and Guattari 1987: 257, 262). Accordingly, Deleuze and Guattari assert that werewolves transform others into themselves, into part of the pack, into a part of the multiplicity, propagating not by filia-tion but by contagion, reproducing not sexually but by infection (Deleuze and Guattari 1987: 266–7). As we will see later on, they hereby also cel-ebrate the violent character of these infections, which disrupt existing molar structures. This might be taken to imply that cannibalistic sex-crime is somehow laudable. Nothing could be further from my inten-tions. Instead, the aim is to locate Deleuze's and Guattari's notion of the werewolf within its historical context, to retrace its connections to white male hegemonic masculinity, and to demonstrate that this celebration of male violence has in fact its own history. As a consequence, I propose to re-evaluate 'becoming' as a political strategy intended to destablise patri-archal and capitalistic structures of domination. My argument will be twofold: I will use Deleuze's and Guattari's notion of the rhizomatic char-acter of all identities to explore the relation between masculine self and cannibal other, while simultaneously using their concepts to reconstruct the history of becoming.

'Becoming' is certainly the concept most often referred to in Deleuzian thinking. In the context I will discuss here, two aspects of the transfor-mative processes that constitute a so-called 'block of becoming' are of central importance. First, all such blocks are stimulated by a heteroge-neous term, an 'Anomalous' term, or 'Outsider', which has several functions: it is the 'precondition for the alliance necessary to becoming' and it borders and 'determines the temporary or local stability' of every multiplicity. Moreover, it 'carries the transformations of becoming or crossings of multiplicities always farther down the line of flight' (Deleuze and Guattari 1987: 275). Therefore, in contrast to traditional perspectives, such as Hegelian philosophy or Lacanian psychoanalysis, Deleuze and Guattari perceive the other not as the negative-image of the self but as the point of flight towards which lines and connections strive. The self is in turn 'a threshold, a door, a becoming between two multiplicities'. Leaning towards one of them, the self is 'the continuation of another multiplicity that works it and strains it from the inside' (Deleuze and Guattari 1987: 275). As such, the other and the self become real simultaneously. The second central aspect is the gender-political dimension of Deleuze's and Guattari's thoughts on becoming. In *A Thousand Plateaus* they present 'becoming-woman' and 'becoming-animal' as the two privileged ways to exit majoritarian structures of domination; they also refuse the possibility of 'becoming-man'. According to them, 'man' implies the 'state of domination', or the majoritarian structures which are to be subverted in the first place. According to them, all becomings begin with 'becoming-woman', since 'woman' has operated as the definitive other of Western patriarchal society (Deleuze and Guattari 1987: 320–1). As demonstrated by Rosi Braidotti, this emphasis on 'becoming-woman' ignores the different subject positions of men and women with regard to power. From her perspective, becoming is 'far from being the dissolution of all identities in a flux' and is instead a process that is in fact 'sex-specific, sexually differentiated, and consequently take[s] different forms according to different gendered positions' (Braidotti 1994: 121). She concludes that male and female subjectivities should pursue different lines of flight according to their distinct starting points.

To develop my argument, I will take up Braidotti's insistence on the specificity of becoming and look closely at the case of Fritz Haarmann, in order to map the historical configuration of male identity in Germany in the 1920s. By following the flows of sperm and blood, the dissemination of homosexuality and cannibalism, I will reconstruct the transformative processes that connected the male self with the anomalous other of the homosexual cannibal killer. Re-evaluating historical material such as Richard von Krafft-Ebing's *Psychopathia Sexualis*, Cesare Lombroso's *Criminal Man*, and the records of Haarmann's case, I will first demonstrate that the male heterosexual self and the homosexual cannibal other were far from clear-cut and distinct identities. Thus, I will demonstrate the rhizomatic character of hegemonic white male masculinity and engage in the kind of feminist intellectual project Elspeth Probyn and Elizabeth Grosz called for, the project of 'making queer all sexualities' (Grosz and Probyn 1995: xi).[2] Second, I will argue that there is in fact such a thing as 'becoming-man' even if such a becoming is ugly, mean and violent. By historicising the notion of the werewolf, I will demonstrate that this becoming is permeated by relations of power and discourse and in doing so will thereby question Deleuze and Guattari's vision of becoming as a way of exiting phallogocentric structures of domination and exploitation.

Blood

In April 1918, shortly after he was released from a prison sentence of over five years, Haarmann rented a small shop where he started a thriving business in meats of diverse origin. The chaotic economic situation at the end of the First World War provided him with both requisites: meat and customers. Most of his supplies were stolen goods, brought to him by young men, whose frequent visits were closely watched by his neighbours. Some of these men were his sexual partners, as became obvious when the police raided the establishment, following a neighbour's complaint. Twice the officers found him in bed with an adolescent man, both of them naked.[3] The meat, such as poultry or rabbit, was not sold at the counter but on the black market. He continued his trade after having closed the shop and moved to another place of residence in November of the same year. When questioned on the origin of his meat supplies, either by his customers, the police, or by the judge chairing the trial, Haarmann declared that it was horseflesh and that he had bought it from a man named 'butcher's Karl' in the nearby town of Ricklingen. However, as this butcher could not be found, the jury concluded that the origin of his commodity was unknown.[4] Rumour had it, however, that Haarmann had in fact sold the flesh of his victims. By distributing his commodity on the black market, he allegedly introduced human flesh into the commodity sphere: he fed the mouth-machine its own flesh, thereby producing cannibals. The suspicious neighbours called him names: 'Good morning, man-butcher [Menschenschlachter].'[5] Two women, who suspected Haarmann of manufacturing his own aspic from the flesh of his victims, snatched pieces of meat out of a bowl in his flat, carried them to a police station and insisted on an examination. The result was negative: the police physician, Dr Schackwitz, declared it to be veal or pork.[6]

The occurrence of cannibal killers was interpreted as a sign of the general moral deprivation and decay of a nation that had been a colonial power until the end of the First World War. The social-democratic news-paper *Vorwärts*, for instance, noted that it was only against the back-ground of an economic predicament which was more severe in Germany than anywhere else that the idea of trading human flesh to satisfy the individual craving for meat could appear in the brains of certain degen-erated humans (Kannibalen 1924).

In contemporary public discourse, cannibalism was usually associ-ated with the indigenous populations of far-away, colonised spaces. As demonstrated by numerous studies, this prejudice against indigenous people was part and parcel of the colonial project itself (Arens 1987: 165–85; Kilgour 1998: 242–3; Obeyesekere 2005: 9–14). In one of the most influential anthropological studies on the topic at the beginning of the twentieth century, entitled *Die Anthropophagie*, its author, Richard Andree, described various forms of cannibalism practised by so-called 'savages' (Andree 1887).[7] Generally, he assumed, anthropophagy arose in situations of extreme famine. Afterwards, this makeshift response became habit and a tradition was established. The kind of cannibalism Andree characterised as the most disgusting and morally depraved was the one allegedly practised by the Azande, an ethnic group living in central Africa on a territory which today is part of the Democratic Republic of the Congo, the Sudan and the Central African Republic. Theirs was one of the last precolonial African empires at the beginning of the twentieth century. The Azande were also called the 'Niam Niam', an onomatopoeic term meaning 'great eaters' taken from the language of the Dinka, a neighbouring African ethnic group (Schweinfurth 1918: 287). The Azande, according to Andree and his fellow anthropologists, ate slaves, prisoners and their own relatives, including their own chil-dren, whom they supposedly considered a special delicacy. Moreover, they sold the flesh of human bodies on their markets like any other regular commodity. Both practices, consuming their own offspring and selling human flesh as a staple good, were marked as the most terrible forms of anthrophagy conceivable (Andree 1887: 103).

Apart from habit, greed and particular tastes, contemporary scientists assumed superstition to be the other main reason for cannibalism. And just as superstitious beliefs were thought to be widespread, so were can-nibalistic practices. This perspective was shared not only by anthropolo-gists but also by juridical or criminological experts, for whom cannibals practically lived next door. They were members of the so-called lower classes, workers, or residents of rural areas: in short, those living on the fringes of bourgeois 'civilisation'. As the cannibalistic practices were usually performed either to cover up criminal acts or were criminal in the first place, the experts spoke of 'criminal superstitious beliefs' (Groß 1903; Hellwig 1905; Schefold and Werner 1912: 6; Seyfarth 1913: 286–91).

However, with a general shift towards a biological model of the origin of criminality at the turn of the century (Gibson 2002; Horn 2003; Neye 1976; Wetzell 2000), this explanation for man-eating was reinterpreted. A key role in this debate was played by Cesare Lombroso's *L'huomo delinquente* (*Criminal Man*), first published in Germany in 1887.[8] From his point of view, savages, children and the insane shared the same characteristics: they were considered to lack moral principles, to be unable to control their own (sexual) desires, and to possess a tendency towards cruelty and violence. Lombroso's central argument was that criminals were in fact atavistic beings, whose corporeal and hence moral evolutionary status was that of a 'savage'. He considered the criminal to be 'an atavistic being who reproduces in his person the ferocious instincts of primitive humanity and the inferior animals' (Lombroso 1910: 345).

His argument relied on the idea that the history of humankind was a continuous progress of 'civilisation'. It was, in fact, a combination of several existing theories, which in turn connected easily to juridical, medical and criminological discourses. The first part was Auguste Comte's argument that all human societies developed along the same lines: proceeding from so-called primitive cultures to complex modern societies. According to Comte, the history of humankind was comparable to the individual development of a white bourgeois (and, we might add, healthy) male. Societies grew from childhood (theological stage), to puberty and youth (metaphysical or abstract stage), and finally to adult manhood (positive stage, modern Western societies). History, progress and 'civilisation', were identified with the development of bourgeois norms and values, in a theory often referred to as the law of three stages (Comte 2000: 27). This notion of an interconnectedness of evolutionary and moral development was also the underlying principle of Charles Darwin's study on the *The Descent of Man, and Selection in Relation to Sex* (Bowler 1992: 144–5; Darwin 1906: 99, 117, 146–7). Combined with his ideas of the 'survival of the fittest' and of 'natural selection', this underlying assumption of civilisation and progress was the gateway for racist and Social Darwinist interpretations of Darwin's theories (Crook 1996: 270; Maasen and Weingart 2000: 41–62; Weingart 1995: 127;). This formed the second part of Lombroso's model while the third element derived from Ernst Haeckel's theory on the interconnectedness of the individual development (ontogeny) of any single organism and the evolution of its species (phylogeny)[9] – he theorised that the former would recapitulate the latter. Whereas Haeckel had thought about the morpho-logical characteristics of biological organisms in devising his theory, Lombroso applied Haeckel's concepts to the bodily and moral develop-ment of human individuals. The central rhetorical figure in his argument was the analogy of criminals being like children or like 'savages', all of them representing earlier stages of human civilisatory development on a moral and bodily level (Gibson 2002: 18–19; Horn 2003: 29–57; Wetzell 2000: 28–31). As such, according to Lombroso, children needed a strict education enforcing discipline and obedience, since they were especially vulnerable to criminal influences (Lombroso 1887, 99–109). To demon-strate his point, he quoted the daughter of a Scottish brigand who was allegedly brought up on human flesh: 'And why should we be sickened by human flesh? – If people only knew how delicious it tastes, everybody would eat their own children' (Lombroso 1887: 112).

However, the German doctors, criminologists and legal experts did not accept Lombroso's theories unanimously, though the majority of them finally conceded the concept of 'degeneration' (or 'Entartung'), which stressed the interdependence of exogenous factors such as familial and social environment, education, individual conduct, unhealthy influences on the embryo and endogenous hereditary disposition (Birnbaum 1930a: 116–20; Wetzell 2000: 63–8). Individuals of a 'degenerative disposition' were considered to be 'psychopaths', unable to adjust to the challenges of normal life, and were deemed to be prone to deviant behaviour because they presumably lacked the necessary will power to withstand the seductions of criminality. Most frequently, and this was the shared conviction of medical and criminological experts, psychopathy prevailed among members of the 'lower classes' and in families of a hereditary neu-ropathic disposition (Birnbaum 1911: 56). Psychopathy was not consid-ered to be a pathological condition clearly distinct from normality, but the result of a creeping process of gradual changes of personality traits (Birnbaum 1930b: 437–8, 442; Kahn 1928: 472–7; Kraepelin 1904: 815–41, 825–30). Physicians and psychiatrists identified 'psychopathic crises' which every individual went through: adolescence and old age. For women, this list was extended to include pregnancy and menstruation (Birnbaum 1930b: 440; Kahn 1928: 466–77). Thus, medical and psy-chiatric experts devised a continuum of (ab)normality rather than a clear-cut distinction between insanity and normality. From this point view, cannibalism (much as any other form of criminality) was contagious: inspired by bad example and unable to restrain their tendency towards deviant behaviour because of their degenerative disposition, psychopaths would succumb to criminal influences in their familial and social environment. Thus, cannibals were produced by infection, either corporeal (hereditary) or social (practices).

From a methodological perspective, it is important to register that although not completely in unison with Lombroso's ideas German experts nevertheless shared his underlying assumptions on the interconnectedness of the development of morality or 'civilisation' and human evolution. This model, especially when we keep its basis in Comte's argument on the development of societies in mind, strangely echoes Deleuze's and Guattari's theory on the history of desire in *Anti-Oedipus*. Here, they argue that desire, the flow of life, takes three different forms according to the different modes of synthesis regulating and ordering this flow. Each mode is realised in a distinct historical and political formation: 'the tribal/primitive, the barbarian/despotic, and capitalist'. (Colebrook 2002: 121–2; Deleuze and Guattari 1983, 153–300). Whereas primitive or tribal societies are characterised by the cruelty and pain with which bodies are marked and connections of membership are established among them, despotic or barbarian societies operate on the basis of a hierarchical order that governs and regulates the flow of desire between its members. In capitalist societies, this hierarchical order is abandoned again and the flow of capital itself becomes the transcendental aim of all social action (Deleuze and Guattari 1983: 215–67). They assume that desire is transformed from the pure flow of intensities into a regulated pulse between assemblages such as subjects, tribes or states. They are, however, operating with a radically different concept of history and evolution than did the authors of the sources involved in the historical case study examined here. To Deleuze and Guattari, history is not progressing but is a set of contingent events (Deleuze and Guattari 1983: 154). Similarly, for them, 'evolution does not proceed in order to achieve the creation of species or beings; it is not governed by actual goals or already present organisms. Evolution is itself a virtual power: a capacity or potential for change and becoming which passes through organisms' (Colebrook 2002: 2). Consequently, Deleuze and Guattari do not assume that the different lines of the history of desire, resulting in either the primitive, the barbarian or the capitalist formation, are distinct phases in the evolutionary development of humankind and therefore mutually exclusive. On the contrary, they conceive of them as overlapping and intersecting geological strata that rely on and transform each other (Deleuze and Guattari, 1983: 211–13).

Other scholars have elaborated at length on the notion of evolution and its relation to biological evolutionary theory from a Deleuzian perspective (Grosz 2004: 17–63), a line of argument which we cannot pursue in further detail here. In the context of my analysis, it must suffice to note that *although* Deleuze and Guattari conceptualise history and evolution differently, their theory of the history of desire still operates on the basis of the same principle: that of culture or 'civilisation' as a restraint of affect and desire. This becomes most apparent when we consider their reliance on Nietzsche's *On the Genealogy of Morals* to support their argument (Deleuze and Guattari 1983: 158–9, 207–8). Nietzsche, himself a contemporary of Krafft-Ebing and Lombroso, developed a critique of 'civilisation' and cultural progress by a radical inversion: he advocated the re-evalution of affects, instincts and desires to disrupt the rule of bourgeois norms and values. According to him, culture and civilisation deformed and crippled the natural beauty of the beast every human being was (Nietzsche 1969: 93, 140–2). He did not, however, question the model as such nor its implications within colonial discourse: he re-polarised it (Holub 1998: 43). In the German debate on cannibal sex killers at the beginning of the twentieth century, Nietzsche's 'beast' was identified with the violent urges lurking within every male body, waiting for a chance to break out and wreak havoc: 'in the hidden ground – that is in the subconscious soul – of every civilised man [Kulturmenschen] hides a beast of prey' which has 'to run wild from time to time' (Herbertz 1932: 123).

Along with the critical repolarisation of the notion of 'civilisation', Deleuze and Guattari embrace Nietzsche's ambivalent perspective on violence. On the one hand, they regard violence as an inherent part of the creation of both tribal and despotic societies, just as Nietzsche considered the imposition of cultural norms and moral values on the 'beast' to be an act of violence. On the other hand, they regard 'becoming', the dissolution of identities and of molar structures in general, to be a destructive and violent process. In *A Thousand Plateaus* they describe it as 'a war machine or criminal machine, which can reach the point of self-destruction' in which 'there is a circulation of impersonal affects, an alternate current that disrupts signifying projects as well as subjective feelings, and constitutes a nonhuman sexuality' (Deleuze and Guattari 1987: 257).

Sperm

The dominant medico-psychiatric argument on the origins of homosexuality ran along similar lines to the one on psychopathy. As demonstrated by a number of studies on the history of (homo)sexuality, the end of the nineteenth century saw a general shift towards a biological explanatory model as did the explanation for criminality in general (Somerville 1994: 247; Terry 1995, 130–1). Within this framework, homosexual desire was perceived to be the consequence of a pathological constitution, which allegedly went along with an inclination towards general criminal deviance. The 'homosexual body' emerged (Somerville 1994: 243). Yet, whereas the difference between homosexuals and 'healthy' heterosexuals seems to be clear-cut from this general perspective, a closer look at the arguments of leading psychiatrists and sexologists of the time presents a more complex picture. Typically, the fear of contagion was crucial to the argument. In his seminal study *Psychopathia Sexualis*, Krafft-Ebing divided the 'antipathic sexual instinct' according to its alleged origination from 'acquired' or 'congenital' homosexuality (Krafft-Ebing 1998: 186–8). Sexual sentiments towards a member of the same sex arose most frequently, according to him, in exceptional circumstances in which no heterosexual partners were available: in prisons, on ships, among the military, in bagnios or in boarding-schools (Krafft-Ebing 1998: 188). In most cases, Krafft-Ebing stated, the individuals resumed heterosexual intercourse as soon as they returned to normal life.

His main concern in this context was the influence of masturbation, which allegedly ruined the nervous system and spoiled – or worse annihilated – the 'healthy' sexual instinct completely (Krafft-Ebing 1998: 188–9). Weakened by its devastating influences, looking for new ways to satisfy his titillated sensuality and unable to perform 'normal' intercourse, the masturbator would either associate feelings towards a friend of the same sex with homosexual desire or (if he came into contact with 'a seducer') would turn into a 'cultivated pederast', a term which referred to those who practised anal sex actively, or passively would as a male prostitute (Krafft-Ebing 1998: 190, 392, 404). This infectious contact was even more dangerous for youngsters, who were considered to have inherited a 'tainted' physiology. Lacking the will power to resist temptation because of their degenerative neuropathic disposition, their latent homosexual desire would be awakened:

> Gradually, in contact with persons of the same sex, sexual excitation by them is induced. Related ideas are coloured with lustful feelings, and awaken corresponding desires. This decidedly degenerate reaction is the beginning of a process of physical and mental transformation. (Krafft-Ebing 1998: 190)

The final stage of this transformative process, according to Krafft-Ebing, was the fully evolved psychic and physical 'sexual inversion'. He considered this form of homosexual desire to be 'a functional sign of degeneration', and 'a partial manifestation of a neuro- (psycho-)pathic state, in most cases hereditary' (Krafft-Ebing 1998: 188, 223). Thus, he considered homosexuality to be a learned behaviour ('perversity') as well as a manifestation of degeneration ('perversion') (Krafft-Ebing 1998: 190). Contagion, that is infection by bad example or seduction, was considered to be the decisive element for both. And seducing young males was exactly what Haarmann had allegedly done.

During the Haarmaan trial the argument of the prosecutor proceeded along the lines of the medico-psychiatric discourse: to prove his 'homosexual predisposition', the bill of indictment against Haarmann listed a number of incidents which suggested that he had seduced, or at least had tried to seduce, boys or young men long before the killings. Among the examples was the story of him (in 1913) inviting a thirteen-year-old boy to his home where he suggested mutual masturbation.[10] This was the very same scenario Krafft-Ebing and his colleagues were most concerned about: seduction by a 'degenerate', by a 'true' homosexual, during the crisis of adolescence in which youngsters, still insecure and unstable in their sexual identities, were believed to be most vulnerable and receptive to degenerative influences. This scenario was repeated by the prosecutor in his descriptions of Haarmann's attempts to find sexual partners and potential victims: picking up young, good looking males at the central station, inviting them to his home, entertaining them with food and drink and seducing them into same-sex practices.[11] Moreover, as the prosecutor pointed out, Haarmann's sexual partners often belonged to a group that was thought to be of 'tainted' disposition in the first place: the runaway inmates of youth welfare homes (or so-called 'Fürsorgezöglinge').[12] These youths were themselves thought to be psychopaths: maladjusted petty criminals, the majority of them from working-class backgrounds, whose families could not provide the level of childcare and attention that bourgeois norms demanded, and who had been put under the supervision of public welfare.[13]

A closer look at Haarmann's biography reveals that he had spent several years of in the very same 'total institutions' (Goffman 1990), which according to medico-psyciatric experts were breeding grounds for homosexuality.[14] At the age of sixteen, his parents sent him to the military school of the garrison Neubreisach. In 1895, he was discharged from service because the military physicians believed him to suffer from 'epileptic insanity'. After being accused of the attempted rape of a five-year-old girl and having oral sex ('unnatural fornication') with two boys in 1896, Haarmann was confined to a mental asylum from which he fled in 1897.[15] From 1900 to 1903 he served in the military, from which he was discharged because he had collapsed repeatedly after physically challenging marches. The physicians' diagnosis was hebephrenia, feeble-mindedness and former insanity. Between 1905 and 1922, he spent several terms in prison, his first sentence in 1905 at the age of twenty-seven. The crimes he was convicted for included theft, repeated theft, malicious mischief, fraud, begging, assault and battery. The longest sentence Haarmann served was five years and two months of penal service from 1913 to 1918.[16]

As demonstrated by sociological studies, sexualised violence is used among the inmates of total institutions to establish a hierarchical order among those present. In the absence of females to refer to or to contrast against, a form of hypermasculinity is established that relies on subordinating other masculinities by enforced same-sex practices or rape, while simultaneously devaluating homosexual desires (Bereswill 2004: 103–4; Smaus 2003: 105–18). Haarmann, for his part, did not speak about experiences of sexual violence in the institutions in which he had been confined. Yet the statements of other convicted criminals who had been in prison at the same time suggest that enforced sexual contacts indeed must have been part of those practices, which (re)produced the masculinities and the hierarchical order among them.[17] Thus, from a biographical perspective, homosexuality was part and parcel of the male corporealities (re)produced by the disciplinary regime of the carceral system as described by Michel Foucault in his study *Discipline and Punish* (Foucault 1991: 231–56). Generally, confinement to some sort of total institution, most often a boarding school or the military, was considered to be an integral part of every 'normal' male biography in Imperial Germany (Frevert 2004: 170–82, 196–9).

Haarmann, for his part, denied having engaged in any kind of same-sex practices such as fellatio or anal sex, but willingly confessed to having mutually masturbated with other men on a regular basis. His denial persisted even in the interviews conducted by Dr Ernst Schultze, director of the mental asylum Haarmann had been transferred to, and who examined Haarmann to determine his moral and legal accountability. Haarmann's lack of shame and sense of guilt outraged the psychiatric expert Schultze to a level that provoked him to distance himself from Haarmann's behaviour and his attitude. Schultze even used a swear word ('Schweinerei': swinish behaviour), which was not to be expected from an educated man of his social position:

[Do you think mutual masturbation is] *Decent?*
They all do it – all the boys.
Not me!
Well – everybody does it, I think.

This is swinish behaviour!
No, it's not swinish.
It's punishable.
No, it's not punishable.
But it is![18]

Strictly speaking, Haarmann was right. The German penal code prohibited same-sex practices between men if they were mimicking heterosexual intercourse: anal sex and fellatio were therefore illegal but
not mutual masturbation, as regulated in §175 'Reichsstrafgesetzbuch'
(dating from 1871) under the term of 'unnatural fornication'. Until
1935, the punishment was six months imprisonment and possible loss
of civil rights (Sommer 1998: 43–57). On the basis of this regulation,
Haarmann had been sent to prison after having mutual fellatio with
two sixteen-year-old youths in 1918.[19] Often, contemporaries used the
term 'pederasty' to describe the indictable practices, not necessarily
referring to sexual acts with children but to anal intercourse, regardless of the object (Krafft-Ebing 1998: 397, 404).[20] Male homosexual
desire was defined in terms of 'natural' male heterosexuality, which was
thought to be inherently aggressive in order to overcome the 'obstacles'
man would meet in courtship. This aggressiveness was seen as part of
the corporeal heritage of man's evolutionary development. During
the process of 'civilisation' these violent impulses had been restrained
by moral sentiments and learned manly self-control: taking women by
brute force had been replaced by bourgeois, 'civilised' norms and
manners (Krafft-Ebing 1998: 1–2, 56). Again, we find an evolutionary
argument that identified restraint of natural impulses and the development of moral values and norms with 'civilisation'. An argument
which resonates, as we have seen above, with the history of the restraint
and transformation of desire Deleuze and Guattari outline in *Anti-
Oedipus*.

According to Krafft-Ebing, male individuals who practised extreme
sexual violence against women demonstrated 'associations between lust
and cruelty' which had to be attributed to a degenerative disposition.
Whereas in the healthy and 'civilized man of to-day' these associations
were to be found only 'in a weak and rather rudimentary degree', hereditarily incriminated psychopaths suffered from a pathological enhance-
ment of these destructive impulses referred to generally as 'sadism'
(Krafft-Ebing 1998: 54, 56). In extreme cases, this could express itself in
destruction, murder and even cannibalism (Krafft-Ebing 1998: 62). This
concept was adopted by criminological experts and by legal practition-
ers alike: a murder to satisfy destructive sexual desires was termed

'Lustmörd'. Erich Wulffen, in his influential guide for judges, police officers, civil servants, physicians and pedagogues, defined the 'Lustmörd' accordingly and finally warned his readers: 'The mere act of cohabitation with its physiologically inherent violence and lust can induce the sadistic feelings and make him kill his victim' (Wulffen 1928: 458). In accord with this idea of an inherent connection between killing and male sexual violence, Haarmann was charged not with unnatural (homosexual) intercourse but with murder: this was because, according to the prosecutor, he had tried 'to satisfy his sadistic-perverted desires'.[21] In his medical opinion of Fritz Haarmann, the psychiatrist Ernst Schultze characterised him as a 'pathological personality' and argued that he should have kept himself apart from the homosexual community. Being well aware of his urge to kill, he should have exercised manly self-control.[22] Haarmann was found guilty of having murdered twenty-four young men and was sentenced to death on the 19 December 1924. He was executed on 16 April of the following year.[23]

Infection

In *A Thousand Plateaus*, Deleuze und Guattari develop 'becoming' as a strategy to subvert or exit capitalist, phallogocentric structures of domination, presenting 'becoming-woman' as the privileged way to dissolve fixed identities. The other main line of flight they speak about is 'becoming-animal'. These lines are established by unnatural participations in which one term turns into the other and vice versa. Deleuze and Guattari introduce the werewolf as the typical example of a demonic animal that propagates not by filiation but by infection, transforming others into themselves, into a part of the pack, a part of the multiplicity. As mentioned above, the contempories of Fritz Haarmann often described him in similar terms. He was called wolf or beast, even 'werewolf'. Moreover, according to medico-psychiatric discourse, Haarmann represented a contagious threat. First, because he transformed ordinary citizens into cannibals by introducing human flesh into the commodity sphere. Considering the depraved condition of society's morality in general, Haarmann was believed to have both contributed to this degeneration and to be a symptom of it at the same time. Second, he seduced young males into homosexuality. Once infected, they would transform into homosexual 'inverts' themselves, indulging in sex with young men and thereby spreading homosexuality even further. As the 'true invert' he allegedly was, Haarmann acted upon his hereditarily perverted disposition: 'it' was in his nature.

All these aspects correspond with a rather modern concept of the were-wolf, figured most prominently in today's neo-gothic fantasy films or television series such as *Van Helsing* (USA, 2004) or *Buffy, the Vampire Slayer* (USA, 1997–2003) which in fact merges the werewolf with the idea of the vampire, who kills to survive, and who feeds upon his prey thereby transforming his victims into his kindred. It is this concept of the werewolf that Deleuze and Guattari refer to when they present it as the demonic animal, which reproduces by contagion instead of (hetero)sexual reproduction. Moreover, they allude to this modern concept by stating that both vampires and werewolves form bands and 'transform themselves into one another'. Deleuze and Guattari conclude that the werewolf, just like the vampire, 'does not filiate, it infects' (Deleuze and Guattari 1987: 266). Yet, this transformation is most likely not what Haarmann's contemporaries had in mind when they spoke of him as the 'Werewolf of Hanover'. In one of the leading German ency-clopaedias, the *Brockhaus Konversations-Lexikon*, the werewolf was described as a man who is temporarily transformed into a wolf by using a magic device. Putting on either a ring or a shirt (sometimes a belt) made from wolfs-hide, he obtained not only the animal's appearance but also its thirst for blood and savagery. While under the spell the werewolf mutilated corpses and robbed little children ('Werwolf' 1895: 649). The article also contained a reference to the disease 'lycanthrophy'. It was described as a related condition, but stemming from a pathologically dis-torted fantasy. Bearing in mind the psychopath's lack of control over his or her own desires and imagination, a second connection between the werewolf and Haarmann appears: insanity.[24] Although they feared the infectious corporeal links connecting him to them, by referring to Haarmann as the (in)famous pack animal or mythological figure, his neighbours and fellow-citizens emphasised not his contagious state but the excess of violence he exerted while killing.

However, as I have demonstrated, violence was perceived to be an inherent part of a 'normal' and 'healthy' male sexuality, object of choice not withstanding. If not carefully and permanently controlled, these atavistic violent urges would break out. The ability to keep desires and violent drives in check was a central part of white, male, bourgeois and hegemonic masculinity. Hereditarily 'tainted' individuals, such as homo-sexuals or psychopaths, as well as indigenous people, were thought to lack this capacity. Therefore, as a number of scholars have noted, the 'Lustmörder', the sexual killer, defined *ex negativo* what was consid-ered to be normal male sexuality and the amount of violence that men could exert legitimately (McLaren 1997: 9; Siebenpfeiffer 2005: 191).

My re-evaluation of the historical material suggests a more differentiated picture. The distinction between norm and pathological aberrance was not a simple binary opposition: instead, experts devised a continuum of (ab)normality in which every single male individual was to be located. White male sexual identity was messy, multi-layered and imbued with allegedly atavistic and perverted desires. As such, the body of the 'Lustmörder', from the perspective of German medico-psychiatric experts in the 1920s, embodied atavistic impulses that had to be controlled and regulated by manly will power. Thus, the violent evolutionary past was part of every male corporeality, a concept that resonates in the simultaneity of historical and political formations of desire that Deleuze and Guattari argue for in their *Anti-Oedipus*, and in their description of the criminal 'war-machine' that violently destablises existing formations and identities in *A Thousand Plateaus*.

Becoming-man

To conclude: from an historical perspective, several aspects of Deleuze and Guattari's denial of the possibility of 'becoming-man' are to be noted. First, the monolithic masculinity Deleuze and Guattari speak about dissolves into multiple lines of flight, into a multiplicity of connections and relations. The (homo)sexual cannibal killer was not the abject other of white male identity but its precondition, determining the relations and connections which established it in the first place. Accordingly, the sex-killer can be considered to be the Anomalous that triggered transformative lines of flight, a becoming that undermined dominant phallocentric molar structures of social and individual identities. Far from being a peaceful process, this becoming was violent, disruptive and bloody. As we have seen above, this interpretation corresponds with Deleuze's and Guattari's own notion of becoming as 'a war machine or criminal machine' that violently 'disrupts signifying projects' (Deleuze and Guattari 1987: 257). Second, my enquiries demonstrate the historicity of Deleuze's and Guattari's concept. Far from suggesting that they actually shared the racist and misogynist assumptions of Lombroso or Krafft-Ebing, we can register the intellectual heritage they continued: the tradition of post-Enlightenment Western thinking in which it was assumed that history, or culture and 'civilisation', is the result of the control and regulation of a desire that at one time was roaming free. In contrast to the historical texts I have analysed here, Deleuze and Guattari do not assume an evolutionary progression but argue for the simultaneity of the different lines of the history of desire and call for an emancipatory disruption of the structures established by it. Third, we can identify Deleuze and Guattari's praise of violence and primitiveness, as well as its identification with masculinity, as being embedded in an historical discourse that was part of establishing hegemonic white male masculinity in Germany at the beginning of the twentieth century. Moreover, by mapping the historical location of this masculinity and reconstructing the lines of flight through which it was realised, we can locate the starting point of a becoming-man, which Deleuze and Guattari denied existed in the first place. This becoming, though, has its own historical specificity and is embedded in specific power relations and discourses. It is one way of 'responding to constraint', just like the molar identity man, the 'specific orbit' from which it starts (Massumi 1992: 95, 103). As a consequence, we will have to rethink becoming as a 'sex-specific' process, as Rosi Braidotti has argued, a process that will 'take different forms according to different gendered positions' (Braidotti 1994: 121). Finally, bearing this last point in mind, the political potential of 'becoming' as a strategy to exit the phallocentric mode must be reconsidered.

References

Archival Sources

NHStA (=Hauptstaatsarchiv Hannover)
Bill of indictment against Friedrich Haarmann, 4 November 1924, Hann. 173 Acc. 30/87, No. 80a: 3–106.
Death Certificate Haarmann, Kl. Erwerb. A 401: 12.
Medical Opinion on Friedrich Haarmann by Dr Ernst Schultze, 1 October 1924, Hann. 155 Göttingen No. 864a: 106–30.
Proceedings of the interviews conducted by Dr Schulze, 26 July to 9 August 1924, Hann. 155 Göttingen No. 864a: 676/1–734.
Testimony of police officer Müller, 7 July 1924, Hann. 155 Göttingen No. 864a: 4–5.
Verdict against Friedrich Haarmann and Hans Grans, 19 December 1924, Hann. 173 Acc. 30/87, No. 80: 107–55.
HSA (=Hauptstaatsarchiv Düsseldorf)
Testimony of Wilhelm Hofer, 26 November 1929, 17/531: 5–6.

Other Works Cited
'Anthropophagie' (1902), in *Meyers Großes Konversations-Lexikon: Ein Nachschlagewerk des allgemeinen Wissens*, Vol. 1, Leipzig: Bibliographisches Institut.
'Der Werwolf von Düsseldorf' (1931), in *Vossische Zeitung*, 12 April.
'Kannibalen' (1924), in *Vorwärts*, 31 December.
'Werwolf' (1895), in *Brockhaus' Konversations-Lexikon*, Vol. 16, Leipzig: Brockhaus.

Andree, R. (1887), *Die Anthropophagie. Eine ethnographische Studie*, Leipzig: Veit.
Arens, W. (1987), *The Man-Eating Myth: Anthropology and Anthropophagy*, Oxford: Oxford University Press.
Bereswill, M. (2004), '"The Society of Captives" – Formierungen von Männlichkeit im Gefängnis. Aktuelle Bezüge zur Gefängnisforschung von Gresham M. Sykes', *Kriminologisches Journal*, 36(2): 92–108.
Birnbaum, K. (1911), *Die krankhafte Willensschwäche und ihre Erscheinungsformen. Eine psychopathologische Studie für Ärzte, Pädagogen und gebildete Laien*, Grenzfragen des Nerven- und Seelenlebens, Vol. 79, Wiesbaden: Bergmann.
Birnbaum, K. (1930a), 'Entartung', in K. Birnbaum (ed.), *Handwörterbuch der medizinischen Psychologie*, Leipzig: Thieme.
Birnbaum, K. (1930b), 'Psychopathen', in K. Birnbaum (ed.), *Handwörterbuch der medizinischen Psychologie*, Leipzig: Thieme.
Bowler, P. J. (1992), *The Non-Darwinian Revolution: Reinterpreting a Historical Myth*, Baltimore: Johns Hopkins University Press.
Braidotti, R. (1994), *Nomadic Subjects: Embodiment and Sexual Difference in Contemporary Feminist Theory*, New York: Columbia University Press.
Brückweh, K. (2006), *Mordlust. Serienmorde, Gewalt und Emotionen im 20. Jahrhundert*, Frankfurt: Campus.
Colebrook, C. (2002), *Understanding Deleuze*, Crows Nest, NSW: Allen & Unwin.
Comte, A. (2000), *The Positive Philosophy of Auguste Comte*, Vol. 1, trans. Harriet Martineau, Kitchener: Batoche Books.
Connell, R. (1995), *Masculinities*, Cambridge: Polity.
Crook, P. (1996), 'Social Darwinism, The Concept', *History of European Ideas*, 22: 261–74.
Darwin, C. (1906), *The Descent of Man and Selection in Relation to Sex*, London: Murray.
Deleuze, G. and F. Guattari (1983), *Anti-Oedipus*, trans. Robert Hurley et al., London: Continuum.
Deleuze, G. and F. Guattari (1987), *A Thousand Plateaus: Capitalism and Schizophrenia*, trans. Brian Massumi, London: Continuum.
Foucault, M. (1991), *Discipline and Punish: The Birth of the Prison*, trans. Alan Sheridan, London: Penguin Books.
Frevert, U. (2004), *A Nation in Barracks: Modern Germany, Military Conscription and Civil Society*, trans. Andrew Boreham with Daniel Brueckenhaus, Oxford: Berg.
Frey, E. (1959), *Ich beantrage Freispruch. Aus den Erinnerungen des Strafverteidigers Prof. Dr. Erich Frey*, Hamburg: Blüchert.
Gibson, Mary (2002), *Born to Crime: Cesare Lombroso and the Origins of Biological Criminology*, Westport, CT: Praeger.
Goffman, I. (1990), *Asylums: Essays on the Social Situation of Mental Patients and Other Inmates*, New York: Doubleday.
Gould, S. J. (1977), *Ontogeny and Phylogeny*, Cambridge, MA: Belknap Press.
Groß, H. (1903), 'Zur Frage vom psychopathischen Aberglauben', *Archiv für Kriminologie*, 12(4): 334–40.
Grosz, E. (2004), *The Nick of Time: Politics, Evolution, and the Untimely*, Durham: Duke University Press.
Grosz, E. and E. Probyn (1995), 'Introduction', in E. Grosz and E. Probyn (eds), *Sexy bodies. The Strange Carnalities of Feminism*, London: Routledge.
Halberstam, J. (1998), *Female Masculinity*, Durham: Duke University Press.
Hellwig, A. (1905–6), 'Aberglaube beim Meineid', *Monatsschrift für Kriminalpsychologie und Strafrechtsreform*, 2: 511–12.
Herbertz, R. (1932), *Die Psychologie des Unbewußten*, Leipzig: Quelle & Meyer.

Holub, R. C. (1998), 'Nietzsche's Colonialist Imagination: Nueva Germania, Good Europeanism, and Great Politics', in S. Friedrichsmeyer, S. Lennox and S. Zantop (eds), *The Imperialist Imagination. German Colonialism and Its Legacy*, Ann Arbor: University of Michigan Press.

Horn, D. G. (2003), *The Criminal Body: Lombroso and the Anatomy of Deviance*, London: Routledge.

Kahn, E. (1928), 'Die psychopathischen Persönlichkeiten', in O. Bumke (ed.), *Handbuch der Geisteskrankheiten*, Vol. 5, Spezieller Teil 1: 1: Die psychopathischen Anlagen, Reaktionen und Entwicklungen, Berlin: Springer.

Kilgour, M. (1998), 'The Function of Cannibalism and the Present Time', in F. Barker and P. Hulme and M. Iversen (eds), *Cannibalism and the Colonial World*, Cambridge: Cambridge University Press.

Kraepelin, E. (1904), *Psychiatrie. Ein Lehrbuch für Studierende und Ärzte*, Leipzig: Barth.

Krafft-Ebing, R. von (1998), *Psychopathia Sexualis. With Especial Reference to the Antipathic Sexual Instinct. A Medico-Forensic Study*, translated from the 12th German edition and with an introduction by Franklin S. Klaf, New York: Arcade.

Lessing, T. (1973), *Haarmann. Die Geschichte eines Werwolfs*, München: Rogner & Bernhard (originally published: Berlin: Die Schmiede, 1925).

Lombroso, C. (1887), *Der Verbrecher in anthropologischer, ärztlicher und juristischer Beziehung*, Hamburg: Richter.

Lombroso, C. (1910), 'The Criminal', *Putnam's Magazine*, 7: 793–6 (reprinted in D. M. Horton and K. E. Rich [eds], *The Criminal and Anthropological Writings of Cesare Lombroso Published in the English Language Periodical Literature During the Late 19th and Early 20th Centuries*, Criminology Studies, Vol. 22, Lewiston: Edwin Millen Press, 2004).

Lombroso, C. (2006), *Criminal Man*, trans. M. Gibson and N. Hahn Rafter, Durham: Duke University Press.

Maasen, S. and P. Weingart (2000), *Metaphors and the Dynamics of Knowledge*, London: Routledge.

McLaren, A. (1997), *The Trials of Masculinity: Policing Sexual Boundaries, 1870–1930*, Chicago: University of Chicago Press.

Massumi, B. (1992), *A User's Guide to Capitalism and Schizophrenia: Deviations from Deleuze and Guattari*, Cambridge, MA: MIT Press.

Neye, R. A. (1976), 'Heredity or Milieu: The Foundations of Modern European Criminological Theory', *Isis*, 67: 335–55.

Nietzsche, F. (1969), 'Götzendämmerung oder wie man mit dem Hammer philosphirt', in F. Nietzsche, *Werke: Kritische Gesamtausgabe*, G. Colli and M. Montinari (eds), Berlin: de Gruyter, Section 6, Vol. 3: 49–154 (originally published: Leipzig: Naumann, 1889).

Obeyesekere, G. (2005), *Cannibal Talk. The Man-Eating Myth and Human Sacrifice in the South Seas*, Berkeley: University of California Press.

Schefold, K. and E. Werner (1912), *Der Aberglaube im Rechtsleben*, Juristisch-psychiatrische Grenzfragen Vol. 8: 8, Halle a.S.: Marhold.

Schweinfurth, G. (1918), *Im Herzen von Afrika. Reisen und Entdeckungen im zentralen Äquatorial-Afrika während der Jahre 1868–1871. Ein Beitrag zur Entdeckungsgeschichte von Afrika. Veranstaltet zu Ehren der Vollendung des 80. Lebensjahres des Verfassers am 29. Dezember 1916 von seinen Freunden, mit Abbildungen und Karte*, Leipzig: Brockhaus.

Seyfarth, C. (1913), *Aberglaube und Zauberei in der Volksmedizin Sachsens. Ein Beitrag zur Volkskunde des Königreichs Sachsen*, Leipzig: Heims.

Siebenpfeiffer, H. (2005), *'Böse Lust': Gewaltverbrechen in Diskursen der Weimarer Republik*, Köln: Böhlau.

Smaus, G. (2003), 'Die Mann-von-Mann-Vergewaltigung als Mittel zur Herstellung von Ordnung', in S. Lamnek and M. Boatca (eds), *Geschlecht Gewalt Gesellschaft*, Otto-von-Freising-Tagungen der Katholischen Universität Eichstätt-Ingolstadt, Vol. 4, Opladen: Leske & Budrich.

Somerville, S. (1994), 'Scientific Racism and the Emergence of the Homosexual Body', *Journal of the History of Sexuality*, 5(2): 243–66.

Sommer, K. (1998), *Die Strafbarkeit der Homosexualität von der Kaiserzeit bis zum Nationalsozialismus. Eine Analyse der Straftatbestände im Strafgesetzbuch und in den Reformentwürfen (1871–1945)*, Frankfurt: Lang.

Tatar, M. (1997), *Lustmord: Sexual Murder in Weimar Germany*, Princeton, NJ: Princeton University Press.

Terry, J. (1995), 'Anxious Slippages Between "Us" and "Them". A Brief History of the Scientific Search for Homosexual Bodies', in J. Terry and J. Urla (eds), *Deviant Bodies: Critical Perspectives on Difference in Science and Popular Culture*, Bloomington: Indiana University Press.

Weingart, P. (1995), '"Struggle for Existence": Selection and Retention of a Metaphor', in S. Maasen, E. Mendelsohn and P. Weingart (eds), *Biology as Society. Society as Biology: Metaphors*, Dordrecht: Kluwer Academic Publishers.

Wetzell, R. F. (2000), *Inventing the Criminal. A History of German Criminology, 1880–1945*, Chapel Hill: University of North Carolina Press.

Wulffen, E. (1928), *Der Sexualverbrecher: Ein Handbuch für Juristen, Polizei- und Verwaltungsbeamte, Mediziner und Pädagogen. Mit zahlreichen kriminalistischen Originalaufnahmen*, Berlin: Langenscheidt.

Films and Television Series

Buffy, the Vampire Slayer, created by Joss Whedon, USA: Twentieth Century Fox, 1997– 2003.

Van Helsing, directed by Stephen Sommers, USA: Universal Studios, 2004.

Werewolf of London, directed by Stuart Walker, USA: Universal Pictures, 1935.

Notes

1. See for example the liberal *Vossische Zeitung*, reporting on Peter Kürten: 'Der Werwolf von Düsseldorf' (12 April 1931) or Lessing 1973: 51.
2. For the concept of hegemonic masculinity see for example: Connell 1995: 76–7. I will speak of male masculinities, referring to Judith Halberstam's argument (Halberstam 1998: 1–16) on the significance of embodiment of masculinity.
3. Verdict against Friedrich Haarmann and Hans Grans, 19 December 1924, NHStA Hannover, Hann. 173 Acc. 30/87, No. 80: 107–55, 111–12.
4. Verdict against Haarmann and Grans: 111 and 117–18.
5. Bill of Indictment against Friedrich Haarmann, 4 November 1924, NHStA Hannover, Hann. 173 Acc. 30/87, No. 80a: 11.
6. See Testimony of police officer Müller, 7 July 1924, NHStA Hannover, Hann. 155 Göttingen No. 864a: 4–5 and the Verdict against Haarmann: 510.
7. His study was influential far beyond his lifetime. For example, the entry on anthropophagy in one of the prominent German encyclopaedias, the *Meyers Großes Konversations-Lexikon*, relied heavily on his work as did articles on cannibals on the occasion of Haarmann trial (Anthropophagie 1902 and Kannibalen 1924)
8. This first German edition was the translation of the third Italian edition, published in 1884. There is an excellent new English translation of *L'huomo delinquente* available, which comprises abridged versions of the first to fifth Italian editions (Lombroso 2006). Unfortunately, some parts of the third edition which

are crucial to my argument have been omitted here. To keep the references unequivocal, all quotations in this essay will follow the first German edition, all translations into English will be my own.

9. Ernst Haeckel (1834–1919) was the most influential supporter of Darwin's theories in Germany at the end of the nineteenth century. Haeckel's own theories relied on the work of Karl Ernst von Baer (1792–1876), who theorised that the development of the embryo proceeded from general to specific forms ('Baer's law'). Both theories had been dismissed in biology and zoology in the 1920s. Their influence on criminology and psychiatry, however, was not impaired (Gould 1977: 115–66 and 202–6).

10. Bill of Indictment against Haarmann: 9.

11. Bill of Indictment against Haarmann: 11.

12. Bill of Indictment against Haarmann: 27–8.

13. The majority of his victims were in fact apprentices, pupils, unemployed workers or artisans. Some of them had left their families following a dispute or to seek employment or entertainment in the city (Verdict against Haarmann and Grans: 128–50).

14. The term 'total institution' was coined by Irving Goffman to designate social institutions that are strictly hierarchical and closely control or regulate every part of the lives of the individuals involved, e.g. mental institutions, prisons or monasteries. Foucault refers to the same kind of institutions as 'complete institutions' (Foucault 1991: 235).

15. Verdict against Haarmann and Grans: 108.

16. Verdict against Haarmann and Grans: 110–12.

17. See for example the testimony of Wilhelm Hofer on the behaviour of Peter Kürten during his time in prison (26 November 1929, HSA Düsseldorf, 17/ 531: 5–6). Kürten was another of the infamous sex-killers of the 1920s in Germany. On sex-killers in Weimar Germany in general see Tatar 1997, Siebenpfeiffer 2005 and Brückweh 2006.

18. Proceedings of the interviews conducted by Dr Schulze, 26 July to 9 August 1924 in Hannover, NHStA Hannover, Hann. 155 Goettingen 864a: 708.

19. Bill of Indictment against Haarmann: 12.

20. As the paragraph spoke of 'male persons' only, lesbian love was not persecuted, although experts described lesbianism along the lines of male homosexuality. Yet, in contrast to male homosexuals, Krafft-Ebing assumed, the 'majority of female homosexuals do not act in obedience to an innate impulse' but displayed so-called cultivated homosexuality. Moreover, because women's sexuality was allegedly passive by nature, they would not pursue their perverted desires as actively as male homosexuals presumingly did (Krafft-Ebing 1998: 262–91, 405–8).

21. Bill of Indictment against Haarmann: 94. The second motive the prosecutor mentioned was Haarmann's aim to enrich himself by robbing his victims and selling their clothes.

22. Medical Opinion on Friedrich Haarmann by Dr Ernst Schultze, 1 October 1924, NHStA Hannover, Hann. 155 Göttingen No. 864a: 130.

23. Death Certificate Haarmann, NHStA Hannover, Kl. Erwerb. A 401: 12 and Verdict against Haarmann and Grans: 107.

24. The first depiction of a werewolf as a contagious animal was most likely the film *Werewolf of London* (1935). The story revolves around an English scientist who was bitten by a werewolf during his field research in Tibet.

Chapter 7

Ageing, Perpetual Perishing and the Event as Pure Novelty: Péguy, Whitehead and Deleuze on Time and History

James Williams

On History as Ageing

'But I know there is ageing.' Are these wise words designed to mine the unconscious of believers in the eternal supply of new events, or a false counsel of despair? Is this sensitivity to the ever-presence of ageing an experienced brake on unconditional confidence in absolute novelty, or a conservative rearguard action against change? Or maybe it's just a resigned reflection in reaction to particular times (the First World War is, after all, just round the corner and the author of these words has accurately presaged his death, aged forty, leading his troops in the opening exchanges of the conflict)? Perhaps, then, it is a view on time that we moderns can safely ignore with our perspective on history as a source of ever stronger hope.

The words come from Charles Péguy's *Clio*, his rich and poetic essay on history in relation to life. The book is lauded by Gilles Deleuze as a great work on the event, yet he overlooks Péguy's refrain on ageing, either by interpreting Péguy's examples of repetition as consistent with his own (Deleuze 1968: 8–17), or by selecting passages for their closeness to his own definition of the event as aleatory, emergent and inclusive of a moment of pure novelty (Deleuze 1969: 68). However, if Péguy is right – or at least if Clio, the muse of history, is confirmed in her dialogue with Péguy as it runs through the book, first focusing on her sadness at carrying the woe of ageing, thereafter transferring it to him, before finally waving his eyes shut, tired and short of glory in a cool forecast of the event of his death – then Deleuze's masterly and many-jewelled time-machine cannot run as freely as he lets us believe. It cannot run on the eternal return of pure difference and instead must accept another of the tropes of Péguy's verse. Everything acquires a patina of age. Even the new must bend to this law, because the new carries the law; it is how we experience loss of sheen and of purity. The new is the return of ageing, but even more, it is its inflation. History is a bloated and slowing cycle: its subjects grow evermore tired on their way to final collapse. According to Péguy's reading of historical cycles, the rejuvenating circle of time at the heart of Deleuze's philosophy cannot function as a machine for the production of pure novelty, because the circle itself runs according to a process of ageing. In *Cinema 2*, Deleuze describes film as such a machine where filmmakers like Rossellini attempt to give us back a belief in this world against the modern 'fact' of loss of belief (Deleuze 1985: 223). The key is to affirm a belief in the world and our relation to it without promising a better world. Péguy's counter-claim is that even this attempt can only deepen the loss when it too comes to fail, because it is not belief in a better world that is at fault, but rather that no gesture can renovate our relation to the world without betraying or ageing earlier beliefs.

Against this ageing world, obliterating the drag of its historical memory and the necessary slowing implied by its filling, the eternal return of the new is Deleuze's metaphysical gift to modernism. It frees the modern world of the error of hope, dependent on shackling the new to particular time-bound and treacherous figures, while retaining the life-affirming power of novel events. Yet, counter to hopeful self-deceivers or innocents, Péguy describes revolutions as betrayed when we seek either to preserve them or to repeat them against a necessary fading not only back into their time, but also in our blunt readings which cover it with layers of distorting sediment. No doubt Deleuze would agree with this denunciation of false repetitions. He borrows Péguy's account of the fall of the Bastille and his study of Monet's Nymphéas from *Clio*, as two of the first entrances into repetition for itself in *Difference and Repetition* (Deleuze 1968: 8). Yet he also elides Péguy's sense of the tragedy hovering and waiting to descend later in history, as even good repetitions or good revolutions become tangled with terrible reckonings.[1]

Péguy's book is haunted by the battle of Waterloo, where the true heart of the revolution, the revolutionary people, was led to sacrifice:

> It was then that it was this people sensing that nothing would resist it, this people that could not restrain itself from involvement, that felt its blood rushing, that felt itself called towards those first windmills on that mound and through twenty-three years of the greatest epic ever played in the world towards that last farm on the edge of that wood towards that plane on the heights of Hougoumont.
>
> From that cannonade where everything was to begin, to that nightfall where everything was to end. (Péguy 1932: 115)[2]

Having invoked *Clio*, Deleuze pays homage with one of his most simple lines on repetition: 'The head is the organ of exchanges, but the heart, the loving organ of repetition' (Deleuze 1968: 8). Péguy, though, fears for this heart and sees the remnants of the revolution hurtling with enthusiasm towards the farm attacked at the start of the battle of Waterloo and then on to the failed charges against British, Dutch and Prussian lines where thousands would die and a retreat would begin, ending with the restoration of monarchy. Following Hugo in *Les misérables*,[3] Péguy alternates between individual suffering and an external objective account of losses and disaster in battle. This dialectic is in stark contrast with Deleuze's multiple view of battles in *Logic of Sense* and *A Thousand Plateaus*, where the battle is a paradoxical relation between the event for an individual and an event for all (Deleuze 1969: 178). Here, the battle is neither personal nor collective, but rather a series of individual events that communicate without ever being reducible to one another. This negates the grand historical undoing found in Hugo and Péguy, but perhaps at the cost of a wishful or unrealistic refusal to see the battle grinding down individual and communal repetitions alike.

With Heraclitus, Péguy and Deleuze know that the actual side of events can only happen once, but Péguy also claims, or Clio and history do, that the reasons for these tarnishing processes implicate the engine of the new. Things cannot return because they age. They age because new events occur. These are only new because they age what has already taken place. Once new events land, they pass without pause into history, as pile upon pile of once glittering novelties amass and lose their differences. Time and history run on ageing. As the treasury grows, each new jewel becomes smaller and fades faster, each one fails in its destiny to equal or even outdo the old, serving instead only to crowd their space, to turn gems into baubles, thereby feeding a special kind of forgetfulness, not the liberating affirmation of Nietzschean forgetting, but forgetting as the wearing down, confusion and loss of even the possibility of truly novel events: 'It is not surprising that the waves press. Countless shadows, an enormous mass of shadows wish to drink this blood on the edge of the tomb. Yet they can only drink one at a time. It is not surprising that the shadows crowd around' (Péguy 1932: 137).

Péguy followed Bergson's lectures at the Collège de France and *Clio* is one of the first works to take up and work with Bergsonian *durée* or duration, the lived stretch of time that resists the infinite divisibility of the instant and the mathematical equivalences of the single continuous line of time from past to future. The book also adopts Bergson's cone of time as memory, pointing towards the future and carrying an increasing base behind it, like a soap bubble inflated through a tiny hoop. Deleuze does the same with his concept of the second synthesis of time as the pure past (Deleuze 1968: 110–12). But Péguy sees duration and the cone as processes of ageing. Nothing endures as a living thing without fading in all its durations:

> But I know that there is ageing. The ageing of every man and the ageing of the whole world. Real duration, my friend, the one that will always be called Bergsonian duration, organic duration, the duration of the event and of reality essentially implies ageing. Ageing is essentially organic. Ageing is incorporated at the very heart of the organism. To be born, to grow, to age, to become and to die, to grow and to decline, are all one; it is the same movement; the same organic gesture; it is what the ancients excellently call the domain of corruption. (Péguy 1932: 53)

Clio's argument rests on history, on its events and greatest works, rather than on metaphysical deductions. It is a challenge of empirical memory: show me something that does not fade. Péguy names the greatest glories – ancient poetry (Homer), modern theatre (Beaumarchais), revolution (1789), divine revelation (Jeanne d'Arc), struggles for justice (Dreyfus), truthful song (in Hugo), the greatest paintings (Monet's Nymphéas) – but Clio returns each one to its time as the beginning of decline and to our time as an acceleration of betrayal. She does so by listening to what is living and intense in each event, then showing its life draining away or distorting through inept modern receptions:

> Thus is the common historical measure, the common historical and even mechanical misfortune, the common temporal misfortune of the work or the temporal event, of the historical work and event, that is, of the recorded work and event. Briseis is in our hands. It is a great danger for her. It is a great danger for Achilles. It is exactly from that interior contrariety that the entire temporal is wormy, my poor friend, the historic, everything historic is wormy, the event is wormy, the work, that integrating part of the event, is wormy. Thus is my deep wound, my temporal wound, my eternally temporal wound. (Péguy 1932: 32)

Péguy's gloomy and necrotic argument is, then, not that there cannot be novelty. It is rather that all novelty is born fading because its intensity comes from life as duration and not from an eternal quality or substance. Homer's Briseis and Achilles are set organically into their time, never fully to return and only to be misinterpreted and misunderstood. Their living intensity requires this inscription, but one that must always betray it through material wasting. It also requires a reception, but one that must always bury the work and its intensities through a necessary ignorance and blunted senses.[4]

Péguy subverts the progressive potential of Bergson's cone in its advance towards an open future by counter-balancing it with another cone, tip to tip, with the second base directed towards the future. Bergson discusses the process of ageing in *Creative Evolution* in the context of the examples of the embryo, menopause and puberty. Against Péguy's diversion of creative evolution, Bergson can be read as claiming that ageing depends on a deeper process of changing form: 'In short, what is properly vital in ageing is an unfelt and infinitely divided continuation of change in form' (Bergson 1959: 510). The recording of *duration* as becoming is the ultimate creative process behind ageing, rather than the recording of what has aged. Péguy's response rests on an even deeper historical process understood as a prior condition for change. It lies in two questions. How can there be change in form if formal change is not related to what any thing has changed from? Is not history the necessary record of all those things we have changed from and therefore aged by departing from them? History is then an inflating tube throttled in its middle. Two cones expand around the middle knot with new memories, not only the 'past' one, but the future one too. As the past fills so does the future, because each novel event struggles for novelty against a growing archive. This archive itself wears away, because the growing past returns in the future as worn and as competing with any possible novelty. There is therefore a two-way process of ageing along the cones: the past ages and so does the future, and caught between them the present becomes ever smaller and less capable of true novelty. Counterbalancing Deleuze's synthesis of the pure past, we have a concurrent synthesis of the pure future; they grow old together. To age in the past is to become tarnished; to age in the future is lose even the possibility of acquiring lustre. Not only must any field necessarily become crowded, but wherever an event is situated on the two facing cones, it is subject to a process of ageing as a becoming smaller and as a loss of significance. We moderns experience this in terms of our growing individual worthlessness and the many psychic commotions caused by the struggle to satisfy an ambition that grows stronger because it is thwarted, paradoxically, in a world where fame has become a benchmark and a commodity. Péguy sees this as a problem of generations. Each successive generation is a lesser part of a growing tree and less able to find glory. His reasoning again depends on the necessity of a reception, in this case, of judges capable of esteeming and preserving our actions. Trapped in the past, each generation finds itself pleading to too few future judges among too many past appellants (the first cone with its leading point). As present, each generation is not only falling away into a growing field of future appellants but also looking into a future of lesser judges struggling for worth against the growing past (the second cone, leading with its expanding base). When past generations age and multiply, future ones lose all opportunity for discerning judges and thereby become poor judges for the past. Every generation is betrayed in this process:

> On the very day of its death, it enters into competition with every effaced generation, with every fallen generation, with every appellant generation: with every dead generation. But not only that: soon, tomorrow, it enters into competition, as appellant generation, with more new appellant generations, with ceaselessly new appellant generations, that is, with those very generations, those generations that one took for judges and that will tomorrow die. (Péguy 1932: 166–7)

The call for judges is a need for memory and commemoration. Memory carries Péguy's argument, since it is memory that transports ageing from the past and into the future. For him, there can be no movement of time as duration without memory, but this very faculty is one of dustiness and fading. Duration requires recording, but recording ages past durations and new ones alike by yoking them together. History is essentially ageing, because it depends on memory. Its agony is not of the dusty irrelevant archive, but rather of the significant event ineluctably losing heirs to its significance, not by rarity or ignorance, but by a necessary superabundance of predestined mediocrity. Should we need a contemporary sign of these processes, they lie in the ever-increasing energies devoted to publicity rather than creation, in the struggle to pass from private originality to recognised excellence.

Below the paragraph from *Clio* quoted at length by Deleuze in *Difference and Repetition* and in *Logic of Sense* (Deleuze 1968: 245; Deleuze 1969: 68) we therefore find a severe counter to his account of the eternal return of pure difference, but also to his interpretation of that key passage. Deleuzian metaphysicians could have engineered their way around the problem of ageing with the formula 'only difference returns and never the same'. When challenged about the implied lack of continuity needed for meaningful history, they could then retort that the same returns, but as different, offering a continuity of change. But Péguy's argument troubles this ingenuity with acute questions: What records the difference? What is the measure of difference, if not some memory of what has faded? Is not memory itself this gauge and ever-changing archive? It is conceded that the same never returns, or rather necessarily returns as different, but it is how it is different that marks the split between believers in novelty and those who see the ageing of the world in the return of difference. Péguy's argument is sophisticated and knowing, for it addresses the purity sought by Deleuze in the return of difference to show that purity itself is a concept that ages and that depends on ageing its surroundings. This difference over the significance of purity is played out in the examples they give of purity. For Péguy, Sleeping Beauty is a pure but doomed beauty with the fate of keeping perfection against ageing but at the cost of a cut away from the world. For Deleuze, Alice's perfection is one of multiple becomings, rather than ultimate stasis. He is attracted to Alice for her multiple changes in direction and scale, spreading confusion in linear motion. For Péguy the perverse attraction of Sleeping Beauty is in the terrible message she brings to those who look upon her or seek to compete, but more terribly still in her own tragic inner fallibility: when perfect she is detached from her world, when brought back to it, she begins ageing and losing her perfection. The signs of novelty and novelty itself are not the purest returnees, because they break on the nonsense of this relative purity. If pure becoming occurs, if its emergence as charted by Deleuze in his reading of Péguy is validated, it is at the cost of a memory verifying and therefore disproving that purity. This is pure ageing:

> So long as the interior articulations of the event are marked by external articulations, by articulations of relief, by political articulations, by historical articulations that draw them, that are supposed to represent them and that represent them more or less faithfully, so long as we see those surface breaks, those mountains formed by folding, those contractions, we can give ourselves the pleasure of believing that we still understand something of it. But when there is nothing left to grasp, we feel that we are in ageing itself, and in pure ageing.

Nothing comes to disguise the surface of that irreversible river (Péguy 1932: 269–70).

Deleuze selected his passage from *Clio* for its description of emergence in historical crisis points, where history passes through an event that changes everything, affirming chance and novelty and cancelling established patterns: 'the critical points of the event' (Péguy 1932: 269). He stopped his reading before the lesson, or rather he stuck with the first, apparently affirmative lesson, when it was only a step in a longer and more dispiriting one. There are two ways of reading the lines that immediately follow those quoted by Deleuze. These ways describe different experiences of novel emergent events, experienced not exactly as they occur, but just after they have passed, where we are no longer caught in their sensations, but rather linger in the subplot of unconscious effects hidden behind the only apparently more vivid sensual ones (*What happened?*).[5]

Does novelty wash through the world as a liberating force, or as a tarnishing agent? Péguy stages this question within a search for meaning in historical struggles. At the critical point where we expect a conflict to lead somewhere, not necessarily to a better place, but to one where our actions are resolved in some way, something happens that undoes all expectations. Nothing happens: 'Nothing happened. And a problem we could see no end to, a problem with no way out, a problem everyone was up against suddenly exists no more and we wonder what we were talking about' (Péguy 1932: 269). The difference between the two thinkers is played in the sense of the 'nothing'. Here, in accordance with both their views on sense, we should not look for meaning in the occurrence but for effects, such as sensations, actual material effects and, most importantly, effects on the reserve of potential significances for future events. The 'nothing' that happens is therefore an event not only in its unpredictability and discontinuity – as implied by the concept of emergence, both borrow more or less accurately from the physical sciences – but also in its essential character as what Deleuze calls an haecceity, a novel flash of material effects and passionate affects determining an event as singular and therefore as new, in harmony with a series of communicating individuals, where communication is not meaningful but sensual, a communion of differential touches. For Péguy, the mystery of the event is that this novel wash must be attached to the expectation it confounds. A great effort and search for glory is cut down by a novelty that is therefore doubly implicated in history as ageing. It devalues problems that pass away, and its new problems are faded by the memory of what happened to the old. Deleuze could claim that this overturning of what he would call questions, in favour of the transforming renewal of problems, is consistent with the eternal return of pure novelty:

> Nothing is as mysterious, she said, as these points of deep conversion, as these upheavals, as these profound renewals. It is the very secret of the event. We were struggling with this problem. And we were getting nowhere. And it maddened us . . . And it aged us. And then all of a sudden nothing has happened and we are a new people, in a new world, with a new mankind. (Péguy 1932: 269)

This would again be to overlook Péguy's further step and query. What comes after this mysterious renewal, if not a deep awareness and memory of what the transformation has done to the past, of what therefore will be done to it in future, and of how it carried these twin effects in a merely apparent purity? If we are history *and* this mysterious event, then the event must carry a pure ageing into history, because there are no new events free of ageing effects on history and there is no memory of those events that does not age them.

On Time as Perpetual Perishing

Another reader of Bergson, Alfred North Whitehead, suggests a way to preserve Deleuze's eternal return of pure novelty from Péguy's historical pessimism.[6] He does this by introducing the concept of perpetual perishing – much transformed – from Locke and then responding to it by inflecting the role of memory, shearing it away from ageing and from the process of passing away into history. There is indeed a perpetual perishing of 'actual occasions', but there is also their novel return in a process of becoming. Organic process is never one without the other and, most importantly, becoming outweighs perishing. Locke uses the concept of perpetual perishing to describe the fate of the instant in time. The essence of the instant is to perpetually perish or to vanish. In his description of duration, far removed from Bergson, indeed a target for Bergson's view of duration as lived and stretched in multiple ways, Locke seeks to give definitions for different ideas of time independent of space; these are time, eternity, succession and the instant. Our idea of the instant, he claims, is of a 'perpetually perishing part of succession' and we only acquire an idea of duration through the succession of ideas (Locke 1985: 89). The drama of perpetual perishing is rendered in the *Essay Concerning Human Understanding* through moments of sleep or unconsciousness, where ideas perish for want of succession:

> When that succession of *ideas* ceases, our perception of duration ceases with it; which everyone clearly experiments in himself, while he sleeps soundly, whether an hour or a day, a month or a year; of which duration of things, while he sleeps or thinks not, he has no perception at all, but it is quite lost to him; and the moment wherein he leaves off to think, till the moment he begins to think again, seems to have no distance. (Locke 1985: 90)

Locke's arguments here are of no use against Péguy, since the perpetual perishing of ideas where they become 'quite lost' is not the problem of history. Instead, ageing is a problem of the deep connection of ideas rather than their independent succession. Therefore, Locke's thought experiment has created the wrong image for understanding this process, since ageing effects duration in Bergson's sense: that is, not successive ideas, but inseparable lived durations that ideas, imagined as instants or in succession, cannot capture. Locke's time is a fiction that resists a more original duration and ageing through a theatrical representation of sleep and perishing where immersed bodily continuity is bracketed off from a point-like consciousness. Ideas are then nodes connected by relations, such as 'A successor of B'. It is true that if ideas have a miraculous life of instantaneous appearance and perishing, alongside external connections to one another, then perishing cannot have the pervasive effect described by Péguy. However, if these connections are internal, then the perishing of one becomes a dismal organic memory in the appearance of others.

In *Adventures of Ideas* and *Process and Reality*, Whitehead develops the concept of perpetual perishing away from the instant and its oblivion and towards the dual process of perishing and becoming, understood as a novel transforming return. His study turns on two important intuitions against Locke: first, perishing is not of ideal instants, but of actual components in wider processes; second, perishing cannot be total oblivion because no whole process perishes, but only a state. A beautiful phrase from *Adventures of Ideas* puts this succinctly: 'Thus perishing is the initiation of becoming. How the past perishes is how the future becomes' (Whitehead 1948: 176). However, this bald statement cannot of itself refute Péguy's pessimism. On the contrary, it is consistent with Péguy's model, and both Whitehead and Péguy side with Bergson against Locke's overly simplistic and still geometric model (where the perishing idea resembles a point that vanishes). So though the shift to manifold connected processes over independent elements avoids dread of complete death or total disappearance, it is not the case that this argument refutes Péguy's bias towards ageing in the relation between the two processes: 'Thus each actual thing is only to be understood in terms of its becoming and perishing. There is no halt in which the actuality is just its static self, accidentally played upon by qualifications derived from the shift in circumstances' (Whitehead 1948: 316). In fact, in the simple version of Whitehead's process philosophy as set out in *Adventures of Ideas*, Péguy's main point is confirmed because Whitehead's process depends on the return of ideas, a return Péguy would rightly see as insipid and sad because the idea returns bereft of the original physical and emotional durations that gave it its singular and glorious role at a particular time. Moreover, Péguy's point on the crowding of ideas and the attendant devaluation of physical and sensual attainment seems to hold firm against Whitehead's apparent idealism: 'This process involves a physical side which is the perishing of the past as it transforms itself into a new creation. It also involves a mental side which is the Soul entertaining ideas' (Whitehead 1948: 317). Does this not imply an indifferent growth in the number of ideas and therefore a diminishment of the perished, alongside a gradual loss of lived intensity?

It matters that it is real relations of different kinds that return. According to Whitehead's model, as applied to Péguy's example of Monet's Nymphéas, nexūs or series of 'prehending' relations perish. These prehensions, or positive feelings and co-dependencies, pass away when taken within particular limits. This audience, that garden, this artist, that connection of textures and colours, this light, this art-world, this society, all grow and achieve satisfaction together, then pass away, in the way worlds are said to pass away in 'great events' (*La Belle Époque passed away in the First World War*). Yet, this only takes place as a final perishing if we falsely abstract from ongoing prehensions and the capacity of ideas to store and reset the bygone relations in new prehensions and actual occasions. Though the previous passage quoted on the role of ideas in becoming could lead to the conclusion that the return depends on individual mental memories and novel ideas, this does not fully capture Whitehead's position; it distorts it. Prehensions and ideas are not mind dependent, but rather describe the way different processes depend upon others. For such a process to take place there does not have to be a particular idea from the past taken up in a particular mind in the future. So the 'idea' of the relation between greens and blues in Monet's work is taken up in later paintings and sets them in relation to different lights and environments, irrespective of whether the idea of such a transfer has been entertained in the mind of a new artist, or indeed Monet himself. When Whitehead refers to a creative Eros, this is not the creativity of a human mind – a model in danger of perpetuating Locke's externalist and point-like version of consciousness. There are no real independent actual entities, only processes of different kinds related in different ways according to perishing and becoming. The creative push in any novel process is there merely through the fact of its novelty and not any creating intellect. The deduction of the presence of a past 'idea' follows from a dependent process-based connection to a perished occasion, rather than a particular mental memory:

> The process is itself the actuality and requires no antecedent static cabinet. Also, the processes of the past, in their perishing, are themselves energising as the complex origin of each novel occasion. The past is the reality at the base of each new actuality. The process is its absorption into a new unity with ideals and with anticipation, by the operation of the creative Eros. (Whitehead 1948: 318)

The unnecessary cabinet described here is that of prior unchanging substances supposedly underpinning concrete reality. There is process and nothing but process, and substance only leads to the fallacy of misplaced concreteness where unchanging metaphysical substance is taken as concrete as opposed to processes of becoming: '. . . the accidental error of mistaking the abstract for the concrete' (Whitehead 1927: 64). Any abstraction is an error if it leads to the conclusion that it allows us to reach a self-sufficient entity. Therefore a statement such as 'what is past is past' is necessarily false for Whitehead, because the past is also in the process of future becoming as creative of novelty.

These conclusions are not simply metaphysical positions in *Adventures of Ideas*; they take on profound historical and moral roles. The two are hard to distinguish in Whitehead, since his approach to history is in terms of moral progress and decline. His argument is that due to perpetual perishing historical moments *must* pass away: that is, they cannot be preserved as abstract entities as the basis for any conservatism. He is therefore profoundly progressive. Given the necessary passing, and given its form as the impossibility of returning as the same, the future necessarily recreates the past it prehends or is in process with. History is then a process of decline and renewal. This latter creative moment is the adventure from the title of his book: 'Without adventure civilization is in full decay' (Whitehead 1948: 321). But again this does nothing to refute Péguy's claim which, translated into Whitehead's terminology, is that adventure itself is a process of ageing because the weight and extent of process increases in cycles of perishing and becoming, squeezing out the potential for novelty in the creative moment. Péguy's *Clio* trains us to detect the latent signs of the discouragement of ageing, even in Whitehead's profoundly hopeful book: 'Also let us hope that our present epoch is to be viewed as a period of change to a new direction of civilization, involving in its dislocations a minimum of human misery. And yet surely the misery of the Great War was sufficient for any change of epoch' (Whitehead 1948: 320).[7] The Great War was a change in epoch, but not a halt in the terrible inflation of misery.

Whitehead is aware of this danger. *Adventures of Ideas* closes with a chapter entitled 'Peace' which seeks to draw together four virtues of the cycle of perishing and becoming (truth, beauty, adventure and art) through a fifth (peace). Peace inoculates the others from the kinds of 'turbulence' that bring them to turn on each other or on themselves in a tragic sense of futility even in the highest virtues. The following paragraph presents Whitehead's version of the problem of ageing. It replaces *Clio*'s romantic flourish, intricate artistic examples and repetitive poetic style with Whitehead's precise vocabulary, everyday metaphors and peculiarly hermetic syntax. A simpler yet still poetic mode of insight:

> We have seen that there can be no real halt of civilization in the indefinite repetition of a perfected ideal. Staleness sets in. And this fatigue is nothing other than the creeping growth of anaesthesia, whereby that social group is gradually sinking towards nothingness. The defining characteristics are losing their importance. There may be no pain or conscious loss. There is

merely a slow paralysis of surprise. And apart from surprise, intensity of feeling collapses. (Whitehead 1948: 328)

Confronting this staleness and collapse full face, peace does not deny them, but rather maintains a confidence in novelty despite them through a sense of the harmony between loss and creation. This harmony is achieved through the belief that creation can counter-balance tragedy, rather than eliminate it. This is not a hope in perpetual progress, nor is it the belief in the impossibility of the return of decay. It is rather the conclusion that novelty can live up to the task of moving beyond each tragic event and the growing reserve of all tragedies:

> Amid the passing of so much beauty, so much heroism, so much daring, Peace is then the intuition of permanence. It keeps vivid the sensitiveness to the tragedy; and it sees the tragedy as a living agent persuading the world to aim at fineness beyond the faded level of surrounding fact. Each tragedy is the disclosure of an ideal – What might have been and was not: What can be. (Whitehead 1948: 329)

In *Adventures of Ideas*, this argument does not rise to the detail of why that which has perished can become again and not perish in the same way or worse in the form of cycle feared and charted by Péguy. We are therefore left with an emotive claim that without doubt conveys great nobility and wisdom. It also has some basis in historical examples as rotting states find new potential or give way to novel ones. The claim therefore has inductive strength, but it will depend greatly on contemporary moods and historical selection and interpretation. It is not enough to counter the logic of Péguy's arguments on history and time.

Such counters may be available in *Process and Reality*. This much more rigorous development of Whitehead's process philosophy gives a similar prominence to the idea of perpetual perishing and introduces an important and useful distinction from the outset. Perishing has a dual quality whereby the actual and ideal aspects of process pass away differently. If we accept that real process involves actual physical prehensions, alongside real ideal ones, such as the ideas and values running alongside physical situations, then we can see that while actual physical relations perish, the ideas, though also changing with that passing, are available to be taken up in new ideas in a different way. For example, ideas about laws and about social goods can connect to, make possible and give impetus or critical resistance to new technical changes, even though the physical manifestations of technology continually pass into dust. Despite the startling changes that take place in industrial landscapes as they are redeveloped, ideas and values associated with these forms of industry are ready for novel contexts, in a nostalgic reworking, say, or in progressive vows never to return to past horrors, or in new interpretations of original models. For Whitehead, real process necessarily involves ideas and actual occasions. To concentrate on one or the other is then an abstraction which, though perhaps necessary for the representation of ideas and actual occasions, only ever gives an incomplete account of process.

Whitehead bases his distinction on the difference in determination between the two sides of the process. The actual physical occasion is fully determined by its prehensions, that is, the physical relations of dependency in processes of transformation of one occasion by another (for instance, in the way one being takes another as food). All of these pass with the occasions. But the ideas are much less determined and can be taken up in new nexūs (loosely, networks of processes):

> Actual occasions in their 'formal' constitutions are devoid of all indetermination. Potentiality has passed into realization. They are complete and determinate matter of fact, devoid of all indecision. They form the ground of obligation. But eternal objects, and propositions, and some complex forms of contrast, involve in their own nature indecision. They are, like all entities, potentials for the process of becoming. (Whitehead 1978: 29)

The argument is quite subtle here, because Whitehead is careful not to separate fully actual occasions and ideas, or more precisely, eternal objects, as necessarily connected sides to any process. Instead, they are distinguished in a more graded way through their potential for becoming, as grounded in the nature of their determination. This means that Péguy's point about the abstraction of ideas without historical location does not apply; eternal objects are in sensual processes which do perish, but they also carry forward to new actual occasions in new nexūs. Whitehead shares Péguy's suspicion of abstraction. Moreover, in associating novelty with the combination of novel actual occasions and of new forms for continuing eternal objects, *Process and Reality* escapes the problem of tarnishing, since though any actual occasion becomes tarnished or fades even in its ongoing historical relations, this is not the way it becomes at all, since novelty is a matter for the idea in process and not the actual occasion. Whitehead sums up this point through the phrase 'objective immortality' which means immortality in the becoming of the idea or eternal object necessarily associated with perishing and novel occasions: 'The "perpetual perishing" of individual absoluteness is thus foredoomed. But the "perishing" of absoluteness is the attainment of "objective immortality"' (Whitehead 1978: 60). Yet, if Whitehead mitigates the process of ageing in actual things through their ideal continuity, Péguy's points still apply to the eternal objects and their vulnerability to the following fork. Either, eternal objects carry no trace of the actual occasions and processes they participated in, in which case they cannot support the idea of progress developed against perishing. Or, eternal objects carry a trace of that ageing, in which case Péguy is right and the trace of past perishing is also the seed for future and ever-increasing ageing.

Paradox and Resistance to the Vices of Forward Momentum

Péguy and Whitehead maintain a direction in time and this characterises not only their views of time but also any ethos dependent on the views. Their theories of time involve different levels of time and different entities, yet for the former the idea of ageing depends on a directedness to the future – albeit one where the intensity of novelty in the future is always subject to an increasing effect of ageing. For the latter, as Isabelle Stengers has pointed out, God underwrites novelty as resistance to ageing, not as an external agent, nor as a final cause, but as an immanent process whereby eternal objects return in new occasions free of the perishing they were attached to in earlier events (Stengers 2002: 497–528).[8] Whereas actual occurrences perish, eternal ideas return in novel events and God is this process of return. As I have argued, this confidence in return as novelty depends greatly on our confidence in the absence of traces of ageing in the eternal objects and in the novel events in which they participate. If we are situated in an epoch dominated by diminishing and repeated historical events, Péguy is more convincing than Stengers and Whitehead on the role of memory in time and through duration; and this role supports his view that the novel event tarnishes the present and past that it happens to, thereby also tarnishing itself. Can Deleuze provide us with an alternative view of time that responds to Péguy's arguments and thereby supports the eternal return of difference free of an increasing effect of ageing?

A first indication of an answer occurs towards the beginning of *Difference and Repetition* where Deleuze discusses Péguy's examples of the commemoration of the taking of the Bastille and Monet's Nymphéas (Deleuze 1968: 7–8). Deleuze's most important insight against ageing is that novel events act back in time and alter prior members in the series, taking them to 'nth degrees' and reinvigorating them in the past. Thus he is more radical than Péguy or Whitehead in his approach to time by ridding us of any priority for forward movement into the future. Novelty is then nothing to do with the new as a separation from the past. So the problem of ageing and the question of whether eternal objects really rid themselves of a trail of perpetually perishing actual occurrences are overtaken by the thesis that what we age from and that which perishes are reinvigorated, not as memories, but as participants in novelty. This is because past occurrences are incomplete without the eternally returning and transforming intensities they expressed and dramatised. These intensities are not ideas or eternal objects in the Whiteheadian mode, nor are they spiritual and aesthetic qualities, as in Péguy's account. Instead, they are the variations in relations that give significance to occurrences as events; that is, they determine them as different, in terms not of qualities or predicates but of sensual variations with effects both in other actual things and in accompanying ideal relations of variations. The past is never left behind in Deleuze's metaphysics, so it neither ages, nor ages us, nor passes away in favour of a better future. Instead, it is reassembled in a way that resists its identification with *general* movements of fading or amplification. There are such changes in intensity, but they are always dependent on the *singular* reassembly achieved by a singular replaying of the past with novelty. In *Difference and Repetition*, the retroactive effects of novel events and their intensities is shown through the way in which the third synthesis of time – loosely the process of the future – is a condition for the first (the synthesis of the present) and second (the synthesis of the past). I have argued for this at length elsewhere (Williams 2003: 86–110), so to conclude this essay I shall show similar arguments as set out in *Logic of Sense* through the paradoxes relating two times charted throughout that book: Aion and Chronos.

The first thing to note about Aion and Chronos is their paradoxical *relation* and the role this relation plays with respect to a different kind of *logical* paradox. The logical paradox is a very familiar one. It seems that Deleuze commits us to a view of time involving reverse time-travel, or causal action back through time, with all the attendant contradictions such as killing one's forebears or stopping an event said to be world-constituting (*In a skilful martial arts move learned from Kill Bill, Volume 2, he removed the gun from Princip's sweaty grasp*). The awareness of the necessity of an irreversible forward momentum is an important factor in Whitehead's metaphysical drive from past to future: 'This passage of the cause into the effect is the cumulative character of time. The irreversibility of time depends on this character' (Whitehead 1978: 237). Deleuze's solution to this paradox is a split in time between a time focused on the present and on physical wounds and mixtures, Chronos, and a time focused on the past and on the future, and on fluctuations in intensity and significance, Aion (Deleuze 1969: 190–8). The relation between the two times is paradoxical because they interact with one another, but cannot be reduced to shared laws – causal laws, for example. We therefore have a time where the past and the future are drawn into the present and subject to the effects it has as it passes away and moves into the future, for example, in an archduke's wound and death. We also, though, have a time where the significance of that wound is always open to being replayed in terms of its intensity and therefore its effects, for instance in a historical work robbing the death of its privileged position in explanation of the causal processes leading up to mass mobilisation in 1914. With Péguy and Whitehead, Deleuze refuses to accept a simple linear time associated with a simplistic materialism – at least in *Logic of Sense* and assuming that he does not substitute this materialism with a more complex one based on contemporary science. Against Péguy and Whitehead, Deleuze does not seek a consistent model of time where an actual and an ideal realm are reconciled in a shared process of forward movement. Instead, there is a genetic and creative paradoxical relation between two times which allows reverse effects through time in terms of the effects of sense on actual events (the significance of actual events changes back in time) and in terms of the effects of actual events on sense (actual events alter the relations of values and intensities in sense).

An event is therefore two-sided: the physical, dominated by the present; and sense, dominated by the past and the future. Intensity is a factor on both sides and connects them through two non-causal relations of mutual determination: changes in the intensity of sense determine which events and individuals come to the fore in the actual (for example, through which wounds are taken as the significant causes for identifying which present actual events are focused on in terms of future actual causes); relations between actual causes determine which relations in sense come to the fore and which slide into the background. Echoing his interpretation of Spinoza's parallelism, Deleuze therefore engineers a time where networks of related actual causes run on one side of the event and networks of related sense-effects run on the other. This is without doubt a complex model, surprising in its refusal of simple causality and in its much more open and aleatory model of series of disjunctive events. Disjunction means that each event splits series forward and back on the side of sense and on the side of actual occurrences. A simple example can illustrate this complex structure and its resistance to Péguy's ageing and Whitehead's redeemed perishing. Take your most familiar walk and change it at a random point. The event at the change alters the causal capacity of the prior and later actual points. What they can do changes because their relation to other points has changed (you'll never see the later points and earlier ones lose, for example, their soothing quality because they now prepare for the change). The event also alters relations of significance and value associated with the points on the walk (the thrill of birdsong or the reassurance of a diesel-fuelled hubbub might be replaced by the soothing of running water or the irritation of silence). The apparently innocuous change in a walk alters conditions back in time, but is also itself conditioned by past times. There is therefore never a pure ageing, since the present is a form of novelty that can change what it ages from. Neither though is there a pure perishing of actual events saved by the return of eternal objects in new events, because the relation of the eternal to past occurrences is set in play again in each novel event – forward and back in time.

References

Bergson, H. (1959), *Oeuvres completes*, Paris: PUF.
Deleuze, G. (1968), *Différence et répétition*, Paris: PUF.
Deleuze, G. (1969), *Logique du sens*, Paris: Minuit.
Deleuze, G. (1985), *Cinéma 2: l'image-temps*, Paris: Minuit.
Halévy, É. (1937), *A History of the English People in 1815*, London: Penguin.
Hugo, V. (1999), *Les misérables*, Paris: Folio.
Locke, J. (1985), *An Essay Concerning Human Understanding*, London: Dent.
Péguy, C. (1932), *Clio*, Paris: Gallimard.
Price, L. (2001), *Dialogues of Alfred North Whitehead*, New Hampshire: Nonpareil.
Stengers, I. (2002), *Penser avec Whitehead: une libre et sauvage création de concepts*, Paris: Seuil.
Whitehead, A. N. (1927), *Science and the Modern World*, Cambridge: Cambridge University Press.
Whitehead, A. N. (1948), *Adventures of Ideas*, Harmondsworth: Penguin.
Whitehead, A. N. (1978), *Process and Reality: An Essay in Cosmology*, ed. David Ray Griffin and Donald W. Sherburne, New York: Free Press.
Williams, J. (2003), *Gilles Deleuze's Difference and Repetition: A Critical Introduction and Guide*, Edinburgh: Edinburgh University Press.

Notes

I am grateful to the British Academy for a grant towards research on Deleuze and Charles Péguy in spring 2007. My thanks go to Claire Colebrook and to Jeff Bell for their valuable suggestions greatly improving this essay. Of course, all the remaining errors remain my burden; they cannot fail to age their author even or especially in new attempts to correct them.

1. Deleuze acknowledges the importance of ageing for Péguy, in relation to his style and its dependence on repetition. However, even where the importance of ageing is noted, it is countered with the chance of a saving repetition against the one that concatenates. See Deleuze 1968: 34.
2. My translation. Note the technique of repetition used throughout *Clio* to create a physical sense of tiredness and change, as central figures and ideas become surrounded by new events.

3. Victor Hugo, 1999, esp. Chapter XVI. Umberto Eco discusses Hugo's presentation of the battle in 'Vegetal and Mineral Memory: The Future of Books', *Al-Ahram Weekly* Online, No. 655, 20–26 November 2003; http://weekly.ahram.org.eg/2003/665/bo3.htm (accessed 17/09/2007).
4. '"The young men of Troy were devastated when Briseis chose the virgin robes." *Briseis's cheeks turn bright red*', in *Troy*, dir. Wolfgang Peterson, 2004
5. For Deleuze's account of the effects around the question 'What happened?' see his discussion of Scott Fitzgerald in Deleuze 1969: 181–9.
6. There is an interesting connection back to Péguy and through history and historians via Élie Halévy, whose historical work on Britain in the nineteenth century (Halévy 1937) influences Whitehead's *Adventures of Ideas* (see Whitehead 1948: 33 and the related discussion of history at 318–22). Halévy's brother, Daniel, also an historian, worked with (and sometimes against) Charles Péguy in his *Cahiers de la Quinzaine* and the Halévy brothers were active in the political, publishing and academic worlds set around the École normale in Paris. It is also worth noting that in *Adventures of Ideas* Whitehead writes movingly about Péguy's beloved Chartres, site of his annual pilgrimages after his son's survival of a grave illness.
7. Whitehead suffered great personal loss and grief in the death of one of his sons in the First World War: 'The Whiteheads' two sons, North and Eric, were in the first world war and the younger, Eric, an aviator, was killed. Their daughter, Jessie, entered the Foreign Office. Only as one came to know them gradually year after year did one even remotely understand how Eric's loss was felt. Finally they could talk of him eagerly and with laughter, but Whitehead once said that the most vivid wordings of grief or attempts at consolation by those masters of speech, the English poets, to him "only trivialized the actual emotions"' (Price 2001: 7).
8. Note that according to Stengers, Whitehead's immanent God is secular rather than an external source of religious values, paradigms or laws.

Chapter 8

Cinema, Chronos/Cronos: Becoming an Accomplice to the Impasse of History

David Deamer

'This book does not set out to produce a history of the cinema' writes Deleuze in the Preface to the English edition of *Cinema 1* (Deleuze 2002: ix). Yet despite such a declaration, a (necessarily incomplete but cogent) history of cinema does arise from the pages of the cinema books, even if only as a by-product of his real project, the 'practice of . . . concepts that cinema gives rise to' (Deleuze 2001: 280). Similarly, the cinema books do not seemingly set out to explore the relationship between film and history in general. Yet, once again, this is exactly (inevitably) what happens. Further, Deleuze makes explicit claims about this relationship. While commentators of the cinema books have acknowledged the part the history of cinema plays in his work (Kovács, 2000), the nexus of film and history in general has yet to recognised. This is the endeavour of this essay.

In 1983 and 1985 Gilles Deleuze published two related volumes: *Cinéma 1, L'Image-mouvement* and *Cinéma 2, L'Image-temps* (hereafter *C1* and *C2*; they appeared in translation in English in 1986 and 1989 respectively). In these books Deleuze's fundamental move is to assemble the philosophy of Henri Bergson's *Matter and Memory* with cinema. Bergson's text, published in 1896 (the same year as the first cinema exhibition), acknowledges the world of matter and the world of spirit as different in kind, neither one being reducible to the other, yet they interact, they are inseparable. The world of matter acts upon the human and creates a sensori-motor response: *I see, I feel, I react*. The world of the spirit (or memory, but also time and thought) unlocks the sensori-motor situation . . . *how should I perceive? how should I feel? how should I react?* or even, *can I react, can I feel, can I perceive?* Crucial in his formulation is that the human is a 'centre of indetermination' where matter and memory collide – and the collision of matter and memory is the very possibility of freedom (Bergson 1991: 36).

Deleuze sees a correspondence in Bergson's distinction between the world of matter and the world of memory in the cinematic medium. On the one hand, some movies tend to organise themselves around the sensori-motor response: a character sees, feels and reacts and the act changes the world of the film. Deleuze calls this the cinema of the movement-image and explores this in his first cinema book, *C1*. On the other hand, his second cinema book, *C2*, explores how some films tend to problematise such an organisation: characters cease to function, or function not as expected, and the world is opaque, ambiguous and unrectifiable. In extreme cases, the film can even fail – deliberately – to extract a coherent character to centre upon. For Deleuze, this is not simply a question of narration in-and-of-itself. Rather, narration is a secondary effect arising from the philosophy of the capture, selection and organisation of visual and audio images. Movement-images attempt to present a world situation that is recognisable to the spectator and which can put coherent subjects to work to re-order that world. Time-images, by contrast, attempt to defamiliarise the world and resist the formation of the subject, thus – one might say – allowing the spectator a certain freedom to think for themselves. From such broad co-ordinates Deleuze produces two semiotics which explore, in turn, a vast taxonomy of movement-images and time-images. Deleuze provides two theses for the transformation between the two semiotics.

First Thesis of the Transformation of the Movement-Image to the Time-Image

In consideration of the movement-image a number of initial observations can be delineated. One: in any moment of a movement-image film the image is – at one and the same time – a perception-image, affection-image and action-image. Conversely, any single image in-and-of-itself tends towards one aspect having dominion over the others. Two: as Deleuze puts it, the film in its entirety 'is never made up of a single kind of image' (Deleuze, 2002: 70). Rather, any film of the movement-image is a combination of perception-, affection- and action-images. This combination is achieved through montage: the editing together of different images. Yet once again, 'a film [in its entirety] always has one type of image which is dominant', meaning that 'each of these movement-images is a point of view on the whole film' (Deleuze, 2002: 70). Three: Deleuze, implicitly adds a final observation. If a component dominates a shot, if a film is dominated by one component, so too is it possible that the entire oeuvre of a director can be said to be dominated by a tendency of preference for an image. Therefore we have directors that organise their films around the perception-image, around the affection-image and – most commonly – around the action-image.[1]

Deleuze does not restrict himself to simply decomposing the movement-image into these three categories. And this is where the real fun starts. Rather, he extends the number of images from three to ten then divides each image into three sub-categories he calls signs. In this way the movement-image is composed of thirty-three signs.[2] The extension of images is generated by Deleuze overlaying Bergson's sensori-motor schema with the semiotics of Charles Sanders Peirce. Deleuze describes Peirce's sign system in this way: firstly the image affects us (firstness); secondly, we act upon the image (secondness); thirdly, the image is thought about (thirdness). Now, it is clear that this schema, while bearing a resemblance to that of Bergson, does not completely fit. On the one hand, Peirce's topography begins with how an image affects, whereas this is not the first category in Bergson, which is perception. On the other hand, Peirce's system passes beyond action, seemingly the final category in Bergson. In order to reconcile the differences between the two schemas Deleuze invents corresponding terms for each of the other's categories. He labels Bergsonian perception as having 'zeroness' in reference to Peirce, in this way the perception-image disappears into the other avatars of the movement-image (this will become important in the generation of the sub-categories or signs).[3] Peircian thirdness, by contrast, is described as 'relation' in reference to Bergson and can be thought of as 'the closure of deduction' (Deleuze 2001: 32). In Bergsonian terms this is the 'habitual memory' which underpins the sensori-motor schema causing recognition and invoking an automatic response (Bergson 1991: 85). Simply put, our bodies obey habitual laws based upon a repetition of the perception–affection–action chain. This is thought as a component of the movement-image, which Deleuze names the relation-image.

While the avatar of the relation-image constitutes the first outcome of the generative process of mapping Peirce and Bergson, this simple manoeuvre puts in motion the creation of a number of other categories. There is a second version of the action-image, which Deleuze specifies as the AS form in distinction to the 'original' SA form: the latter describes the way in which the situation spirals down to engender a character's actions; while in the former it is actions which reveal the situation.[4] Prior to this, there is the impulse-image, which is a kind of proto-action-image, where characters act upon pre-individual drives. Then there is a process of transformation which puts the two forms of the action-image into relationship, and so we have the attraction-image, inversion-image and discourse-image.[5] Finally, Deleuze passes beyond the relation-image to describe recollection-images and dream-images, both of which fall within the domain of habitual memory and explore memories (through flashbacks) and represent dreams.[6] Thus the ten images of the movement-image.

As well as this extension, Deleuze also describes how each image can be decomposed into three signs. Initially inspired by Bergson – 'we have no reason . . . for representing the atom to ourselves as a solid, rather than liquid or gaseous' (Bergson 1991: 199) – Deleuze subjects the perception-image to a triadic decomposition: the signs of which are the solid, the liquid and the gaseous. As Deleuze puts it 'we start out from a solid state, where molecules are not free to move about (molar or human perception)', then 'we move next to a liquid state, where the molecules move about and merge into one another', and finally 'we . . . reach a gaseous state, defined by the free movement of each molecule' (Deleuze 2002: 84).[7] The gaseous aspect of the perception-image forms the genetic sign, a 'camera-consciousness' rather than a human one, while the liquid and the solid are signs of composition, increasingly organising the chaos and centring upon the human and constructing the subject (Deleuze 2002: 85). Finally, if the perception-image is 'zeroness', is 'identical to every image', each of the nine other images will also have this triadic decomposition (Deleuze 2001: 31). Thus, the thirty-three signs of the movement-image.

In the transformation of the movement-image into the time-image it is not that the movement-image is replaced, rather it is as if it has been overcome, becoming a 'first dimension' (Deleuze 2001: 22). For Deleuze, what constitutes a 'beyond' of the movement-image emerges through what he calls a 'triple reversal' (Deleuze 2001: 22). First, the link between situations and actions breaks down and the sensori-motor link becomes disconnected. Consequently, perception-, affection- and action-images lose their specificity and become pure optical and pure sound situations: opsigns and sonsigns. Second, these opsigns and sonsigns become relinked creating hyalosigns, complex images which are combined as narratives resulting in the emergence of chronosigns. Chronosigns operate by creating non-linear or serial narratives and go on to 'constitute a new image of thought', which is the third reversal (Deleuze 2001: 215). This new image of thought Deleuze names the noosign which tears thinking away from habitual/automatic memory images (relation-, recollection- and dream-images) and so must be engaged with as lectosigns, images that must be read rather than simply seen. This third reversal is the cinematic parallel of Bergsonian pure memory.

The radical difference between the sensori-motor schema and pure memory is captured by Bergson in the statement that while the sensori-motor schema occupies the body, pure memory does not (Bergson 1991: 139). This is, without doubt, the most difficult aspect of Bergson's work in *Matter and Memory*. If pure memory is not of the body/brain, where is it? What is it? Bergson is elusive, to say the least. One might say that for Bergson pure memory is nowhere. Further, one might say that pure memory is the future as well as the past, including pasts that have never happened, or pasts that are contradictory. To ask where or what this nowhere/nothing is, is to attempt to speak of memory in a restricted, physical, spatial sense – like data on a hard drive. This is not what Bergson means by pure memory. Pure memory is the past in general and a universal becoming – possibilities. Pure memory can be called the soul, the spirit, true thought and time. Pure memory is also referred to by Deleuze as the *virtual*. The centre of indetermination (the human) calls upon this virtual pure memory to provide recognition in perception, and choice in affection and action. The moment pure memory is brought into the service of the body, it is no longer virtual, but *actual*.

Returning to Deleuze and the cinema, these time-images undermine the linear chronology of past, present and future. If the past and the present are undermined both in themselves as coherent events as well as a single linear pathway, the future can only be produced from material that is without a necessary founding truth. The future literally becomes a 'power of the false' (Deleuze 2001: 126). To acknowledge this is to live unfettered (but not disconnected) from the present and the past, to open oneself up to Bergson's 'becoming', an orientation towards a future and the possibility of freedom and choice. Powers of the false 'will have destroyed every model of the truth so as to become creator and producer of truth' (Deleuze 2001: 151). Crucially, it is not that these time-images are somehow more true than images of a linear flow. The difference is exactly the opposite, the time-image abandons truth. It is the movement-image that aspires to the truth. The time-image problematises truth, setting free the virtual productive forces that emerge from such a problematisation.

While the taxonomy of the movement-image receives its co-ordinates from the nexus of the philosophy of Bergson and the semiotics of Peirce, these new elements of the time-image have a more diverse set of philosophical parallels, including Gilbert Simondon, Martin Heidegger and Friedrich Nietzsche.[8] Further, Deleuze will decompose hyalosigns, chronosigns and noosigns into triads just as he did with the movement-image. In consequence (and in distinction to the ten images and thirty-three signs of the movement-image) the five images of the time-image result in nine signs.[9] In 'The Brain is the Screen' Deleuze says 'there's nothing more fun than classifications . . . they're like the outline of a book . . . an indispensable work of preparation' (Deleuze 2000: 367). In itself, however, the categorisation of a film as a certain type of image has little value. Consequently, Deleuze adds to his statement on classifications that 'it's not the essential thing, which comes next' (Deleuze 2000: 367). The delineation of images and signs is a process that will only find value in a certain specificity, and so it is the way in which cinema gives birth to the avatars of the movement-image and the time-image that concerns Deleuze.

Second Thesis of the Transformation of the Movement-Image to the Time-Image

As described above, Deleuze's images and signs of the cinema – emerging as they do from the philosophy of Bergson's *Matter and Memory* – are ahistorical. However, throughout both books Deleuze continuously points to an event in history which underpins the divergent taxonomies: the Second World War. 'The timing is something like: around 1948, Italy; about 1958, France; about 1968, Germany' (Deleuze 2001: 211). This timeline charts the emergence of Italian neorealism and the subsequent New Wave film movements. For Deleuze, what marks this emergence is an explosion of the action-image which coheres the co-ordinates of the movement-image and – as a consequence – delinks the affection-image, the perception-image and the relation-image. This delinkage is achieved through the reintroduction of aberrations which the movement-image (from the early days of cinema) continually attempted to annul (through an integrated soundtrack, naturalistic colour, invisible montage, etc). In the time-image there is the move away from the dependency on the controlled set to shooting in the street, natural lighting is used, professional actors are replaced by professional non-actors, and there is a re-theorisation of the frame, shot, montage, colour and sound. This reintroduction of aberrations is not a return to what Tom Gunning calls the cinema of attractions, to what is essentially pre-movement-image cinema (Gunning 1990: 56–62). Rather, in the delinkage of the movement-image these filmmakers discovered opsigns and sonsigns: pure optical and sound situations. Deleuze asks the question: 'why is the Second World War taken as a break?' His answer is that 'the post-war period has greatly increased the situations which we no longer know how to react to, in spaces we no longer know how to describe' (Deleuze 2001: xi). Situations where we can no longer act (no longer be the heroine/hero, no longer resolve the chaos), in landscapes destroyed by war. Cities laid waste by mortar fire, aerial assaults and the A-bomb. The movement-image gives way to but – crucially – is not eclipsed by the time-image (Deleuze 2002: 211, 215). From then on, both exist in parallel, oppose each other and interact. In this thesis the movement-image and the time-image have a direct relationship with history in general: the devastation of the human subject, its cities and landscapes, economies and infra-structures that resulted from the Second World War.

However, a trend exists in what might be called the Deleuzian com-munity with regards to the cinema books. This is the attempt to pass over, avoid or downplay Deleuze's claim that the Second World War can be seen as the founding division between the movement-image and the time-image. Indeed, this account of the emergence of the time-image seems to be something of an embarrassment to Deleuzians if the way in which it has been consistently sidestepped is considered. This is perhaps because Deleuze is considered a philosopher of the event: he challenges 'the notion that reality ought to be understood in terms of the determinate state of things', rather events 'subsist over and above the spatio-temporal world' (Stagoll 2005: 87–8). Thankfully, as already outlined, Deleuze provides an ahistorical model for the emergence of the time-image whereby the Second World War is not a determinate factor. Ronald Bogue, for instance, who produced the first sustained account in English of Deleuze's cinema books, does not mention the Second World War until over a hundred pages into his book, and then only in passing. He writes: 'after World War II, Deleuze observes, indications of a collapse of the sensori-motor schema' appear, and that 'the earliest instances of the time-image in Western cinema Deleuze finds in Italian neorealism' – though as we will see, this is not entirely accurate (Bogue 2003: 108–9). However, Bogue does not investigate this claim in depth, nor – interestingly – critique it. David Rodowick, who produced the second sustained engage-ment in English, follows Bogue's preference for the ahistorical model, writing that 'the time-image appears neither suddenly nor as a decisive break with the cinematic movement-image' (Rodowick 1997: 73). Again, like Bogue, Rodowick briefly acknowledges the second, competing explanation: 'alternatively, a number of postwar cinemas . . . open the path toward direct images of time' (Rodowick 1997: 73). In the last analysis, however, despite this balanced approach to the actual problem of the two models (the historical and the ahistorical), Rodowick explores only the philosophical (ahistorical) model in depth.

Is this sidestepping an unconscious attempt amongst academics in the Anglophone world to attempt a reconciliation of Deleuzian film theory with the historical materialist and psychoanalytical models of film criticism? What I mean by this is that the movement-image is generally taken as an instance of cinema's sway to the dominant ideology and the psychoanalytic subject of desire (co-opting Deleuze into a negative criticism of cinema). The time-image, on the other hand, is viewed as being of a different nature, linked to the radical revolutionary cinema of modernism that exposes the movement-image for what it is. This, on the face of it, seems fair enough. However, in this approach there is an implicit tendency to hierarchy that, I contend, is not there in the cinema books. For instance, Constantine Verevis reads Roman Polanski's *Chinatown* (1973) as 'a perfectly realised . . . Hollywood genre film' but one that 'exhibits an ability to *exceed* itself [as a] symbolic text . . . and Oedipal drama' (Verevis 2005: 46). Verevis believes a film should be lauded if it can be proved not to be of the movement-image. In this way *C1* is seen as essentially being a prelude to *C2*, where the real work is done. *C1* describes a cinema somehow worse than that of its successor. No doubt some see the inscription of a cinematic hierarchy through the physical division of *C1* and *C2*, two separately published books. Yet Deleuze is explicit on this matter, there are both good *and* bad films of the movement-image *and* the time-image: 'it is not a matter of saying that the modern cinema of the time-image is "more valuable" than the classical cinema of the movement-image. We are talking only of masterpieces to which no hierarchy of value applies' (Deleuze 2002: x).

The crucial point is this, that in downplaying the historical model of the relationship between the movement-image and the time-image in the domain of the history of cinema, both baby and bathwater go down the swanney. Deleuze is also concerned with the relationship between cinema and history in general. If the transformation of the movement-image into the time-image as a consequence of the Second World War is ignored, Deleuze's exploration of the way in which historical forces come to bear on cinema – particularly in the movement-image – is lost. For, if narration is a secondary effect of the philosophy of the frame, the shot, montage, sound and colour, history could be said to be a tertiary effect. Thus, the question should be, what happens if we take Deleuze at his word?

Chronos and Cronos (Aion): Equilibrium and Impasse

Giovanna Giorgia Gioli in 'Towards a Theory of History in Gilles Deleuze' writes that while Deleuze 'does not provide a theory of History', and while his thought has a 'profound anti-historical development' this 'does not mean that history is not a philosophical problem for him' (Gioli 2005). Gioli cites this through glossing Victor Goldschmidt, writing that there is a 'co-existence of two antithetical sentences inside the Stoic theory of time *"any Time is completely present"* and *"Only present exists"*'(Gioli 2005). Gioli puts the distinction between these two times thus: '*grosso modo* we can say that Chronos is the chronological succession made of encased presents, while Aion is the endless division into an infinite past and an infinite future' (Gioli 2005). Deleuze uses the terms Aion and Chronos throughout his writing from *Logic of Sense* to his collaborations with Guattari and, as Gioli figures it, for Deleuze, the problem 'should not be posed as historical or anti-historical, but should be focused in the possibility of affirming and creating something new' (Gioli 2005).

This resolution of the two antithetical positions of the Stoics with regards to time has its most clear enunciation in Nietzsche. In 'On the Uses and Disadvantages of History for Life' Nietzsche extracts and analyses three aspects of what he calls universal history: the 'monumental', the 'antiquarian' and the 'critical' (Nietzsche 2006: 69). Nietzsche states that with monumental history man 'learns from it that the greatness that once existed was in any event once possible and may thus be possible again' (Nietzsche 2006: 69). Crucially, then, it 'makes what is dissimilar look similar', and 'it will always have to diminish the differences of motives and instigations so as to exhibit the *effectus*' (Nietzsche 2006: 70). Antiquarian history essentially venerates the past to conserve it. In this way it constructs the nation and national identity. For Nietzsche 'by tending with care that which has existed from of old, he wants to preserve for those who shall come into existence after him the conditions under which he himself came into existence' (Nietzsche 2006: 73). Thus, the town, the city, the land takes on a special meaning: locality and nationhood arise. The critical or ethical avatar, however, analyses the past 'bringing it before a tribunal, scrupulously examining it and finally condemning it' (Nietzsche 2006: 76). It designates, from the position of the present, the good and the bad with regards to past events. This critical evaluation is, of course, in the service of the future: how we should live from this point forwards.

For Nietzsche, history as a nexus of the monumental, the antiquarian and the critical can result in 'oversaturation' which can cause a number of 'ill' outcomes ranging from a total inability to act, to never-ending repetitious acts (Nietzsche 2006: 83). The only way to avoid this is through a network of balances. Not only must the monumental, antiquarian and the critical balance out, but these in turn must be balanced with the ahistorical. For Nietzsche, the ahistorical is exemplified by 'cattle, grazing'; he writes: 'they do not know what is meant by yesterday or today . . . [they are] fettered to the moment' (Nietzsche 2006: 60). The ahistorical may be the animal and be directed towards a pure forgetting, but without an element of this, history will simply ossify life. Reciprocally, living totally in the moment without a sense of the historical will condemn us to being animals. Nietzsche's project is to describe how human life needs a double perspective, a nexus of both the historical and ahistorical. In a rigidly historical culture mapped out by monumental, antiquarian and critical history 'no one', for Nietzsche, 'dares venture to fulfil the philosophical law in himself, no one lives philosophically' (Nietzsche 2006: 85). To live philosophically is to balance the historical perspective with the ahistorical, to subject the past to active forgetting. For Nietzsche, this attitude to life is exemplified by the Stoics. Nietzsche's modern man should 'bear himself as a Stoic, wherever he was, whatever he did' (Nietzsche 2006: 85).

It is the Stoic theory of time that can be seen ultimately to underpin Deleuze's division of the movement-image and the time-image in cinema with respect to history. The movement-image is time as Chronos, the time-image is time as Aion. Further, it would also seem that in the cinema books Deleuze adopts the Giolian reading of the Nietzschean position with regards to history more clearly than anywhere else in his writing, for he marks the distinction between chronological and unchronological time differently. For instance, he writes of the time-image as 'non-chronological time, Cronos and not Chronos' (Deleuze 2001: 81). The difference is marked by the absence of a single consonant: 'h'. Deleuze specifically chooses to use these similar terms in C2. As Revilo P. Oliver puts it, in his discussion of Zoroastrian sects: the 'primordial god, Zurvan, later Zervan, was commonly called, in Greek and Latin, Aeon or Cronos (i.e., Saturn, but the name was confused with Chronos)' (Oliver 2007). Deleuze's use of these often confused terms would seem to be indicative of the way in which the movement-image and time-image are at once fundamentally different but at the same time open to resolution: the Giolian perspective of a Nietzschean balance between the historical and the ahistorical.

This approach to Deleuze and history is taken by David Martin-Jones in a recent book on the cinema (Martin-Jones 2006). On the one hand, Martin-Jones sees the division as being one of typage, the movement-image being that which is 'based upon the continuity editing rules established by the Hollywood studio system' and the time-image as 'the new waves which experimented with discontinuous narrative time' (Martin-

Jones 2006: 2). On the other hand, Martin-Jones also acknowledges that 'time-images were first identifiable in postwar Europe' (Martin-Jones 2006: 9). Indeed, for Martin-Jones, it is only after the Second World War that the movement-image achieves its 'dominance' and 'triumphal position'. Further, he goes on to assert that the time-image is 'just as likely to emerge in any nation at a time of crisis' (Martin-Jones 2006: 8). Finally, he discusses how in contemporary cinema films tend to traverse the polarity of the movement-image or the time-image: some films become a mixture of both. However – and here is the crucial point – Martin-Jones, as with Bogue, Rodowick and Verevis, once again inscribes a hierarchy. While those films which tend towards the time-image are to be lauded, films which tend towards the movement-image are seen as problematic. This perspective can be seen as consequence of the attempt to resolve the two antithetical models of time as presented by the Stoics through a Giolian Nietzsche. To return to Gioli, to focus on 'the possibility of affirming and creating something new' rather than 'getting caught up in the antithetical positions of the historical or anti-historical' (Gioli 2005).

Yet what if we do pose the problem as an opposition between historical and anti-historical? What if we do allow ourselves to get caught up in these antithetical positions? Perhaps most surprising this is exactly what Slavoj Žižek calls for in his most recent book, *In Defense of Lost Causes*. Žižek foregrounds just this question: 'does Deleuze's conceptual structure not rely on *two* logics, on *two* conceptual oppositions, which co-exist in his work? This insight seems so obvious . . . that one is surprised it has not yet been generally perceived':

> The line of Deleuze proper is that of the great early monographs (. . . *Difference and Repetition* and *The Logic of Sense*) . . . In his late work, it is the two cinema books which mark the return to the topics of *The Logic of Sense*. This series is to be distinguished from the books Deleuze and Guattari co-wrote, and one can only regret that the Anglo-Saxon reception of Deleuze (and, also, the political impact of Deleuze) is predominately that of a 'Guattarized' Deleuze. (Žižek 2008: 367)

For Žižek, it is this ' "Guattarized" Deleuze' that is to blame for the reconciliation of the two antithetical positions in the Stoics' theory of time. He writes: 'was, therefore, Deleuze not pushed towards Guattari because Guattari presented an alibi, an easy escape from the deadlock of his previous position?' (Žižek 2008: 367).

For Žižek the two incompatible logics are that of 'immaterial becoming as the sense-event, as the *effect* of bodily-material processes-causes' and 'becoming as the *production* of Beings' (Žižek 2008: 367). Žižek is right – and nowhere is the confrontation of these two logics more apparent than in the cinema books. Yet at the same time, Žižek is utterly wrong to claim that 'Deleuze himself was unaware' of this deadlock in his work (Žižek 2008: 367). Deleuze was intimately aware of this problem, indeed, I believe that the cinema books are the place where he examines this impasse most thoroughly. First, the migration of the terms Chronos and Aion into Chronos and Cronos, rather than simply performing a Giolian resolution of the terms, can be seen as doing exactly the opposite, foregrounding the way in which the resolution is problematic, confused. Second, the division of the cinema books into two volumes clearly highlights the distinction, the chasm, between the two semiotics – why did Deleuze choose to publish his work on cinema in two books? Third, the two models of the history of cinema and their complete incompatibility are integral. For instance, in András Bálint Kovács coverage of *C1* and *C2* he shouts '*the cinema books are by definition written from the point of view of the modern*' (Kovács 2000: 156). Yet this is simply not the case. The two opposing narratives for the transformation between the movement-image and the time-image are equally important. The first relies upon an almost evolutionary reading of cinema history: cinema of attraction then movement-image then time-image. The second is ahistorical: the time-image is inherent to the movement-image, and certain filmmakers and film movements set these optical and sound powers free. On the one hand the time-image is a reaction to the 'crisis' in the movement-image related to the physical environmental, mental and economic devastation of the Second World War. On the other hand there are precursors who have explored opsigns and sonsigns prior to Italian neorealism (Ozu, Renoir, Welles). Deleuze, contra Kovács, narrates the two theses from *two different positions*. He narrates the historical account of the crisis from the position of the movement-image: from this viewpoint the time-image is constructed as evolutionary. On the other hand, he narrates the second account from the position of the time-image: an ebb and flow of territorialisation and deterritorialisation in the cinematic art form. From this viewpoint the time-image has always been with cinema and can emerge whenever and wherever the circumstances present themselves.

Fourth – and here we must return to the fundamental philosophical model that inspired the trajectory of the cinema books – Deleuze is well aware of Bergson's position with regards to the limitations of pure memory. To put this another way, the world of memory is a chaotic flow that has to be organised in order for the centre of indetermination to function as a human being: perceptions have to be organised in order for actions to occur, and the exchange of these energies centres on the body as affect. Thus, in becoming human, memory is *necessarily* reduced to an habitual response. The sensori-motor organisation *must* win out. For Bergson, there is nothing more impotent than dreaming or thought that is not directed towards action (Bergson 1991: 141).

It is often said that the difference between the cinema of the movement-image and the cinema of the time-image is equivalent to that of the difference between the object of recognition and the object of encounter. As Deleuze puts it 'something in the world forces us to think. This something is an object not of recognition but of a fundamental encounter' (Deleuze 2004a: 139). Simon O'Sullivan glosses this statement from *Difference and Repetition* in *Art Encounters Deleuze and Guattari*. He writes that an object of encounter is radically different from an object of recognition: 'with the latter our knowledge, belief and values are reconfirmed. We, and the world we inhabit, are reconfirmed . . . An object of recognition is then precisely a representation of something always already in place' (O'Sullivan 2006: 1). With regards to the cinema, the movement-image would seem simply to be the object of recognition, whilst the time-image is the object of an encounter: something which does not reconfirm our beliefs, our understandings, our values. In this way the time-image is a cinema that allows for the possibility of new thought to arise, while the movement-image simply limits and constrains thought. Yet Bergson, in *Matter and Memory*, does not delineate two different types of matter, one that makes us directly react, one that makes us explore pure memory. Rather, he attempts to make us aware of the need for a will to thought (and here is the echo of a more radical Nietzsche and – as we will see – Heidegger). What then can account for this seeming discrepancy between the philosophy of Bergson and theoretical programme of Deleuze's cinema books?

Nothing. Perhaps we can therefore look at the cinema books – the relationship between the movement-image and the time-image – in a different way. While C2 may discuss the cinema of encounter, C1 re-encounters the cinema of recognition, taking as it does films that have been securely mapped many times before and breathing new life into them. Conversely, is it not just as true that films of the time-image, of the modernist cinema, have been just as securely mapped? That they are, in their own way, objects of recognition? Rather it is the cinema books themselves that set free powers of thought that have been ignored or restrained by repetitive and familiar readings. In so doing, C1 and C2 turn both the cinema of the movement-image and the cinema of the time-image into objects of encounter.

Finally – and this is the crucial point – the cinema books do not simply explore the Giolian reading of Nietzsche's resolution of the historical and ahistorical, but the fundamental impasse in the two Stoic theories of time. To take an example from cinema, nowhere is this seen more clearly than in the Japanese film after the A-bomb.

The Crisis: Why Are There No Japanese New Wave A-bomb Films?

'What does this state of things signify?' asks Nagisa Oshima – a director of the Japanese New Wave – referring to the return in 1967 of Ito Sueo's 1946 documentary *The Effects of the Atomic Bomb on Hiroshima and Nagasaki* (Oshima 1992: 144). This film – shot on location, displaying in explicit images the devastation wrought by the A-bomb on the people and buildings of the two cities – was confiscated by the Americans in the early days of the occupation of Japan. For Oshima the return of *Effects* is a perverse but inspired piece of propaganda marking a complicity between the US and Japanese governments. The timing is intentional and essential: the Stop the (Vietnam) War movement in Japan is a fly in the ointment of the anti-Communist programme. The return of the A-bomb film is a centre around which the prevalence of war-images can be organised: 'these overflowing images of war – including the tragic, painful and even meaningless ones – are intended to penetrate our consciousness' (Oshima 1992: 145). For Oshima, 'once they have become the stuff of everyday life, we will probably accept the tragic, the painful, and the meaningless', in effect 'make the people of Japan accept war as an everyday matter' (Oshima 1992: 145). *What is there to do?* as a filmmaker in Japan, asks Oshima. He replies, 'almost nothing', answering this statement with a question, 'except to become accomplices in the state of things?' (Oshima 1992: 145).

What kind of accomplice? Why is there almost nothing that can be done? On the one hand, explore war-images and in so doing inescapably exploit the horrors of history. On the other hand, resist making war-images. Yet against such horrors is not this simply a turning away from history? This is the impasse of post-Hiroshima/Nagasaki Japanese cinema. Critical work on the effect of the A-bomb on Japanese cinema is an area of study that is remarkable in its neglect, a correlative of the fact – it might initially be asserted – that there are not that many Japanese films which deal with the A-bomb. This in turn seems to be a consequence of what Abé Mark Nornes in 'The Body at the Centre' calls 'the spectre of impossibility', the problematic of representing such an event

(Nornes 1996: 122). Nornes's phrase is inspired by the confiscation of Sueo's *Effects* and he writes that the film was 'known as the *maboroshi* atomic bomb film', where *maboroshi* 'translates [as] "phantom" and is used for objects whose existence is known but whose location remains a mystery . . . their shadowy presence tugs on the mind' (Nornes 1996: 120–1). The spectre of impossibility thus encompasses, for Nornes, aspects of prohibition as well as representation.

Taking Nornes's definition as inspiration, the co-ordinates of the spectre of impossibility can be mapped and briefly sketched. First, there is the aspect of *prohibition* which sees films representing the A-bomb and its aftermath banned. This political aspect has a far more pervasive politico-economic correlative – the mechanism of *proscription* results in A-bomb films never being made through an unwillingness by the film industry to fund projects they believe will never be released. Second, even if prohibition and proscription can be circumvented, the spectre of impossibility is not necessarily overcome, but returns as the *impossibility of representation*, as a hopelessness in respect of being worthy of the event. As Dorsey and Matsuoka indicate, filmmakers are confronted by complex ethical and technological issues regarding the representation of Hiroshima and Nagasaki in cinema, 'beginning with the basic questions of whether they can do so, and if so, whether they should' (Dorsey and Matsuoka 1996: 203). This negative aspect has, in turn, a positive correlative: the seemingly insurmountable techno-ethical challenges are exactly that which may spur a filmmaker on towards the *possibility of representation*, overcoming the spectre of impossibility. This positive dimension has a spectrum of outcomes which can broadly be classified into three domains. First, *direct representations*: films in which the effects of the atom bomb on the environments and people of Hiroshima and Nagasaki are rendered on-screen in all their horror. This outcome, as mentioned above, faced prohibition during the American Occupation. Second, *indirect representations*: films in which the A-bomb is transposed to another space-time or is reconstituted through genre pictures: sci-fi, samurai and monster-movie cinema. Third, images which have an origin in the A-bomb and its victims can be *appropriated* into films which seemingly have little to do with Hiroshima and Nagasaki. This appropriation of images extends towards the possibility of a *dispersal* of iconography into Japanese cinema in general and as such a *saturation* of the medium. As Peter Schwenger writes, 'the only language adequate to Hiroshima may then be the unconscious as it speaks in texts' (Schwenger 1992: 54). However, this appropriation of images is equally open to the threat of exploitation, broken cityscapes and melting bodies being used simply as horror images.

The final avatar of the spectre of impossibility is that which can be called an *active forgetting*, an unwillingness to contemplate filming events that would seem to be better off forgotten. This aspect is no doubt partly engendered by prohibition, proscription and the techno-ethical issues of the impossibility of representation, but is also due to the wider cultural climate of guilt the Japanese felt for their actions during the Pacific War. Inuhiko Yomata bemoans such a situation, writing that such an active forgetting means that 'Japan as a nation is well on its way to losing, to eradicating, history' (Inuhiko 1991: 74). This active forgetting, however, can also been seen as having a correlative. Paradoxically, the very resistance to exploring the A-bomb and its effects on the environments and people of Hiroshima and Nagasaki can lead to a *virtual re-emergence* of the event through its very absence: the spectre of the A-bomb will somehow come to haunt a film.

This would seem to explain the reason why there are no films of the Japanese New Wave that explore the A-bombing of Hiroshima and Nagasaki. Every film of the Japanese New Wave is about the A-bomb: a virtual re-emergence of the event through its very absence, not on the silver screen, but on the brain-screen of the spectator. The films of the New Wave explore the postwar era where all the secure cultural co-ordinates of the Japanese past have been thrown into disarray, dislocating all linearity – all inevitability – of historical cause and effect.

The Insufficiency of the Movement-Image and What the Time-Image Can Do

In pictorial art movement is pure potential having to be generated by the viewer. In theatre or ballet, movement is generated by bodies. Cinema, by contrast, not only relies upon the potential movement in the *mise-en-scène* and the actual movement of characters, but crucially *images move in themselves*. Cinema *is* movement. For Deleuze this means cinema communicates '*vibrations to the cortex, touching the nervous and cerebral system directly*' producing a 'shock' to thought (Deleuze 2001: 156). Deleuze goes on to invoke the Heideggerian concept of the 'nooshock' and cites as his main example Eisenstein, because 'the dialectical method allows him to decompose the nooshock into particularly well determined moments' (Deleuze 2001: 156).[10] For Eisenstein, filmwork is necessarily composed of two specifics: '*Primo*: photo-fragments of nature are recorded; *secundo*: these fragments are combined in various ways. Thus, the shot (or frame), and thus, montage' (Eisenstein 1977a: 3). This is the famous 'collision' of shots in contradistinction to the invisibility of the edit (Eisenstein 1977c: 49). Invisible editing consists of each frame transition being cut on a movement, and being joined with another shot in movement to hide the compositional nature of film. The 'collision' of shots through editing has an opposite purpose. It is in no way meant to be invisible, but to draw attention to itself, to foreground it as an act of creation. For Eisenstein 'montage is an idea that arises from the collision of independent shots – shots even opposite to one another' (Eisenstein 1977b: 29). This is a dialectical approach to film editing developed as Soviet montage. Eisenstein's purpose is clear, it is to use cinema as a shock to thought. He writes 'what an unexpected intellectual *shock* came to America and Europe with the appearance of films in which social problems were suddenly presented' (Eisenstein 1977d: 179; italics added).

However, as Deleuze writes, 'everyone knows that, if an art necessarily imposed the shock or vibration, the world would have changed long ago, and men would have been thinking for a long time' (Deleuze 2001: 157). The very idea of a shock to thought is, for Deleuze, a ruse. He continues: 'this pretension of the cinema, at least among the greatest pioneers, raises a smile today' (Deleuze 2001: 157). For Heidegger, the problem of the nooshock is clear: 'man can think in the sense that he possesses the possibility to do so. This possibility alone, however, is no guarantee to us that we are capable of thinking' (Deleuze 2001: 157). For Deleuze, the problem of this conception of the nooshock in the movement-image is that it relies upon the sensori-motor situation. The thoughts the action-image can give rise to tend to be only the ones given to the audience as actualised images. In other words, an image that shocks allows the spectator to think about that image, but in that context alone, in the existing co-ordinates. The paradox is that the shock to thought closes down thought rather than opening it up, or rather, limits thought to the response given in the actualised images on-screen. There are thus, as far as Deleuze can see, three shortcomings to the nooshock of the cinema of the movement-image. First, mediocrity; second, propaganda; and third, the absurd. The first two categories are embodied by 'commercial figurative cinema' and the last by 'abstract experimentalism' (Deleuze 2001: 165).

However, it is the third reason Deleuze posits that may be 'oddly capable of restoring hope in a possibility in the thinking of cinema through cinema' (Deleuze 2001: 165). The pathway from 'abstract experimentalism' to the time-image and true thought can be explored through the writings of Antonin Artaud. Deleuze writes that Artaud sees cinema as 'a matter of neuro-physiological vibrations, and that the image must produce a shock, a nerve-wave which gives rise to thought, "for thought is a matron who has not always existed"' (Deleuze 2001: 165). This might seem, at first, similar to the Eisensteinian concept of shock, yet this is not the case. For Artaud, cinema cannot give rise to thought through commercial and propagandist shock-images, thought cannot arise through 'a succession of images' (Artaud 1972: 65). Rather, true thought arises through 'something more imponderable . . . with no inter-positions or representations' (Artaud 1972: 66). For Deleuze, Artaud's formulation amounts to this: 'what [the time-image] cinema advances is not the power of thought but its "impower"' (Deleuze 2001: 166).

To understand what Deleuze is attempting to articulate necessitates a brief return to Heidegger and his 1951 lectures *Was heist Denken?* (*What is Called Thinking?* Or, alternatively, *What Calls for Thinking?*). For Heidegger, thinking is something that must be learned, not simply copied: 'we can learn thinking only if we can radically unlearn what thinking has been traditionally' (Heidegger 1972: 25). Traditionally, then, for Heidegger, thinking has meant relational, law-like activities. We think to act; 'so far man has acted too much, and thought too little' (Heidegger 1972: 25). The reason for this is that what really needs to be thought about are the things that have not yet been thought. Of course, this presents a radical problem in traditional accounts of thought, for thinking requires an initial object or stimulus, the impetus of a percep-tion. As Heidegger puts it: 'the reason why thought has failed to appear . . . [is] because what is to be thought about, what properly gives food for thought, has long been withdrawing' (Heidegger 1972: 25). That which has been withdrawing becomes that which must be thought about: 'this withdrawal is what properly gives food for thought, what is most thought-provoking' (Heidegger 1972: 25). Withdrawing from the mechanical process of traditional thought is what therefore gives rise to true thought. What is most worth thinking about is not that which is already being thought about.

What has this to do with cinema? The cinema of the movement-image asks the spectator to think directly about what is actualised on-screen. In order to do this it must produce images to be thought about. Unfortunately, in so doing, it actually closes down thought, simply giving the spectator the 'answers', so to speak. The time-image, by contrast, operates by providing indeterminate, delinked images, radically com-promising the givens of the movement-image. This is why some specta-tors, critics and theorists believe the modern cinema is that which will 'never be seen' (Myer 2004: 78).[11] For the multiplex spectator, the mod-ernist cinema is boring. The crucial question must be, why do these spec-tators believe time-image cinema is boring? The answer is that they expect cinema to engage them, to lock them in. When it doesn't, they feel that there must be something wrong with them or, far more likely, something wrong with the film. If they are watching a film and they suddenly realise they have not been thinking about the film but have been following their own thoughts, they panic, believe they have betrayed the cinema, or that the cinema has betrayed them. However, this ability to allow the spectator to access the virtual, to leave the actual images behind is – for Deleuze – the very power of the time-image – its impower.

The Insufficiency of the Time-Image and What the Movement-Image Can Do

Yet, and here is the crux, the fact that New Wave, time-image filmmakers allow their actual images to be overpowered by the virtual does not necessitate that this will occur. It is here that Deleuze's discussion of Heidegger must be tempered with his – albeit less explicit – invocation of Pasolini. Conversely, 'abstract experimentalism' is also problematic. This alternative account can be explored through Deleuze's engagement with Pasolini, whom he deeply respects as a cinema theorist. Deleuze explicitly aligns the time-image with Pasolini's 'cinema of poetry', so it is worth remembering that for Pasolini the modernist cinema should be both formally experimental *and* have a strong socio-historico-political program. In an essay from 1970 called 'The Unpopular Cinema', Pasolini focuses upon the threat to the modernist film by the *'underground'* cinema (Pasolini 2005: 267). Pasolini believes that in these pure formal experiments filmmakers 'push themselves beyond the front line of transgressions', they 'go beyond the firing line', and 'find themselves on the other side, in enemy territory' (Pasolini 2005: 274). Pasolini obviously enjoys himself in expanding the metaphor of battle, for once in this enemy territory, the underground cinema with its purely formal experiments forms a 'ghetto' is confined in a 'concentration camp' (Pasolini 2005: 274). The crux for Pasolini is that such pure formal experiments in cinema are reserved for the intellectual few, a cinema for the clique. In films such as these, the transgressions of the film do not take place at the barricades, but in the 'enemy hinterland', 'the enemy . . . is fighting elsewhere' (Pasolini 2005: 274). Thus what may seem as an anomaly in Deleuze's cinema books can be explained – the exclusion of experimental filmmakers such as Snow, Belson, Jacobs and Landow from C2. These filmmakers have gone beyond the barricades.

This analysis has a wider implication for the time-image in general, beyond the possibilities of abstract experimentalism. If we return

momentarily to the Japanese cinema of the New Wave, David Desser in
Eros plus Massacre observes that the New Wave 'represents . . . the last
time that Japanese film stands in fascinating relationship to a unique set
of historical, social, political, and cultural circumstances' (Desser 1988:
12). Yet Desser's excellent account of the rise and fall of this cinema
makes no mention of the A-bomb – *not even as a lacuna* – in the films of
the movement. It goes unnoticed. So much for a virtual re-emergence on
Desser's brain-screen.

So, a certain insufficiency of the time-image that parallels the certain
insufficiency of the movement-image. Yet, of course, despite this, the
movement-image surely still loses out? Let us explore what would seem
the most secure of the movement-images, the action-image. For Deleuze,
the action-image marks out the relationship between the milieu (situation, environment, social setting) and the actions and behaviours of the
characters therein. In this way the action-image is the most powerful
avatar of the movement-image. In other words, the organisation of these
films depends upon the nurturing of the character in their environment
until he or she can act, and when the action is complete a new situation
is made possible. In Deleuzian terms, what we have here is a situation
spiralling down towards an action which, once resolved, instigates an
new situation. Deleuze labels this trajectory from situation to action to
new situation the SAS' action-image. The formal arrangement of images
in the SAS' form action-image can be seen to be organised through five
laws. These are the laws of alternate parallel montage, convergent
montage, the binominal duel, the polynomial duel, and the gap through
which the hero becomes capable of action. This formal organisation
creates the narration; it also, however, creates a specific form of filmic
history. As Deleuze puts it, the action-image emerging from the five laws
can be seen as 'putting forward a strong and coherent conception of universal history' (Deleuze 2002: 151). Deleuze, in citing 'universal history'
is of course invoking Nietzsche's 'On the Uses and Disadvantages of
History for Life', the three 'species' of the 'monumental', the 'antiquarian' and the 'critical' (Nietzsche 2006: 67). For Deleuze, monumental
history is embodied in the first and second laws of the SAS' form of the
action-image. It is as though the narratives constructed by monumental
history are organised through alternate montage. Situations appear initially static but under threat. The threat thus constitutes the beginning of
the monumental narration which will continue until the threat is either
vanquished or triumphant. In this way it marks the passage from situation to restored situation (S?S'). However, this passage is always
described through the deeds of the heroic – the passage from situation to

restored situation is embodied in action. In this way there are two tendencies – first, that historical events chart the collision of two embodied
forces (parallel montage finding resolution in convergence). Second, that
this structure is repetitive: these forces clash continually, form peaks and
describes homogeneous phenomena. It is the third and fourth laws of the
SAS' form of the action-image that can be seen to constitute an antiquarian perspective on history and thus universalise. Duels are taken in
themselves as structuring events. But of course duels are polynomial and
in this way antiquarian history selects events that – no matter how different – form a coherent mapping of a civilisation. These duels are the
archival data of a nation that are essentialised as traditions. Antiquarian
history, then, attempts to venerate the past to conserve it, constructing a
strong national identity. Lastly, for Deleuze 'the monumental and antiquarian conceptions of history would not come together so well without
the ethical image which measures and organises them both' (Deleuze
2002: 150). This organisation equates critical history with the fifth law
of the SAS' form of the action-image where the gap between situation and
restored situation marks the very co-ordinates of the story being told.
This is thus 'a matter of Good and Evil', where 'a strong ethical judgement must condemn the injustice of "things", bring compassion, herald
the new civilisation' (Deleuze 2002: 151).

For Deleuze the SAS' action-image not only generates a specific form
of narration through its five laws but also generates a specific form of
history through the three avatars of universal history. What is clear from
this is that a *specific form of movement-image cinema* gives rise to a *specific form of historical reification*. While the SAS' film corresponds to universal history, Deleuze writes that 'to this is opposed a type of film which
is no less historical – an ASA' film' (Deleuze 2002: 163). Rather than
'starting from . . . a milieu from which the behaviour of men was naturally deduced', as in the large form, the small form starts 'from modes of
behaviour, to infer from them the social situation which was not given as
an in-itself' (Deleuze 2002: 163–4). Deleuze characterises the small form
as describing a 'habitus' (Deleuze 2002: 160), a philosophical concept
reworked in the 1960s by the sociologist Pierre Bourdieu. The ASA' form
enables the filmmaker to use characters to reveal the situation in which
they find themselves and to align with what can be called a peoples'
history, a history from below. (And we should not think of the action-
image as simply an American model: although in the cinema books the
taxonomy of the SAS' and ASA' formulae are discussed primarily in
terms of the Hollywood film, Deleuze clearly indicates that the action-
image can take other forms. For instance, he cites the Soviet filmmakers

Pudovkin and Dovzhenko: Pudovkin has 'indices and vectors . . . but full of dialectics', while Dovzhenko explores 'the dialectic . . . without need of the five laws of the large form' [Deleuze 2002: 180].)

It is not only the action-images which have specific forms of history. The impulse-image – being an embryonic form of action – does not yet create a universal or people's history but the apocalyptic, a form of history that begins to map historical time over a primitive cyclical time. If the impulse-image marks a narrative construction prior to the action-image and independent of the co-ordinates of universal and local history, the genetic signs of the action-image take the SAS' and ASA' forms, take universal history and history from below, and interweave them. These genetic components of the two forms of the action-image transform each other and prepare the way for the transformations of the attraction-, inversion- and discursive-images which constitute a number of complex exchanges between the SAS' and ASA' formulae. In reflecting upon the SA and AS representational systems themselves, these images reveal a second facet: embryonic relation-images, and so move beyond the action-image. In the relation-image (and the recollection- and dream-image) thought becomes the organising principle. Images of thought are, of course, present throughout the whole taxonomy of the movement-image, just in the same way as perception-, affection- and action-images. Thus the movement-image asks the spectator to think about the narrative and history it generates. In this way, it is clear that the movement-image presents no simple, single form of history.

Becoming an Accomplice to the Impasse of History

The consequence of this is that while the certain insufficiency of the movement-image is mirrored by an insufficiency in the time-image, this is to fundamentally miss the point. Rather, the beauty of the time-image is mirrored by a beauty of the movement-image. Let us remind ourselves, once more, how Deleuze sees it: there are both good *and* bad films of the movement-image *and* the time-image – 'it cannot be said that one is more important than the other, whether more beautiful or profound. All that can be said is that the movement-image does not give us a time-image' (Deleuze 2001: 270).

When Oshima and Shohei Imamura (another key director of the Japanese New Wave) wanted to deal explicitly with the Pacific War and the A-bomb, both turned to the co-ordinates of the movement-image. A failure of the New Wave? A failure of the time-image? Or can becoming an accomplice to the impasse of history be understood in another way? It should also be pointed out that Oshima also saw in Sueo's *Effects* a 'resistance' to war, and the return of the film also had a 'positive significance' for Japan (Oshima 1992: 144). You become an accomplice to the impasse of history if you make films of the movement-image or films of the time-image. Neither cinema has all the answers, the problems addressed by one cannot address the problems addressed by the other. What one can do, the other cannot. Or better, what one cannot do, the other can. This is the impasse, the wonder, of exploring Deleuze's philosophical nexus of cinema images, narration and history.

References

Artaud, A. (1972), 'Witchcraft and the Cinema', in *Antonin Artaud Collected Works: Volume Three*, trans. Alastair Hamilton, London: Calder and Boyars.

Bergson, H. (1991), *Matter and Memory*, trans. N. M. Paul and W. S. Palmer, New York: Zone Books.

Bogue, R. (2003), *Deleuze on Cinema*, New York and London: Routledge.

Deleuze, G. (2000), 'The Brain Is the Screen: An Interview with Gilles Deleuze', trans. Marie Therese Guirgis, in Gregory Flaxman (ed.), *The Brain Is the Screen: Deleuze and the Philosophy of Cinema*, Minneapolis and London: University of Minnesota Press.

Deleuze, G. (2001), *Cinema 2: The Time-image*, Minneapolis: University of Minnesota Press.

Deleuze, G. (2002), *Cinema 1: The Movement-image*, London: The Athlone Press.

Deleuze, G. (2004a), *Difference and Repetition*, trans. Paul Patton, London and New York: Continuum.

Deleuze, G. (2004b), 'On Gilbert Simondon', in *Desert Islands and Other Texts, 1953–1974*, trans. Michael Taormina, Los Angeles and New York: Semiotext(e).

Deleuze, G. and F. Guattari (2004), *A Thousand Plateaus: Capitalism and Schizophrenia*, trans. Brian Massumi, London and New York: Continuum.

Desser, D. (1988), *Eros plus Massacre: An Introduction to the Japanese New Wave*, Bloomington and Indianapolis: Indiana University Press.

Dorsey, J. T. and Matsuoka, N. (1996), 'Narrative Strategies of Understatement in Black Rain as a Novel and a Film', in Mick Broderick (ed.), *Hibakusha Cinema: Hiroshima, Nagasaki and the Nuclear Image in Japanese Film*, London and New York: Kegan Paul International.

Eisenstein, S. (1977a), 'Through Theatre to Cinema', trans. Jay Leyda (ed.), *Film Form: Essays in Film Theory*, San Diego, New York and London: Harvest.

Eisenstein, S. (1977b), 'The Cinematographic Principle and the Ideogram', trans. Jay Leyda (ed.), *Film Form: Essays in Film Theory*, San Diego, New York and London: Harvest.

Eisenstein, S. (1977c), 'A Dialectical Approach to Film Form', trans. Jay Leyda (ed.), *Film Form: Essays in Film Theory*, San Diego, New York and London: Harvest.

Eisenstein, S. (1977d), 'Achievement', trans. Jay Leyda (ed.), *Film Form: Essays in Film Theory*, San Diego, New York and London: Harvest.

Gioli, G. (2005), 'Towards a Theory of History in Gilles Deleuze', in *The Third International Conference on New Directions in the Humanities*; http://h05.cgpublisher.com/proposals/839/index_html (accessed 15/12/2006).

Gunning, T. (1990), 'The Cinema of Attractions: Early Film, Its Spectator and the Avant-Garde', in Thomas Elsaesser (ed.), *Early Cinema: Space, Frame, Narrative*, London: BFI.

Heidegger, M. (1972), *What is Called Thinking*, New York and London: Harper Torchbooks.

Inuhiko, Y. (1991), 'Transformation and Stagnation: Japanese Cinema in the 1990s', in *Art & Text*, 40.

Kovács, A. B. (2000), 'The Film History of Thought', trans. Sándor Hervey, in Gregory Flaxman (ed.), *The Brain Is the Screen: Deleuze and the Philosophy of Cinema*, Minneapolis and London: University of Minnesota Press.

Martin-Jones, D. (2006), *Deleuze, Cinema and National Identity: Narrative Time in National Contexts*, Edinburgh: Edinburgh University Press.

Myer, C. (2004), 'Playing with Toys by the Wayside: An Interview with Noel Burch', *Journal of Media Practice*, 5(2): 71–80.

Nietzsche, F. (1967), *The Will to Power*, trans. Walter Kaufmann, New York: Random House.

Nietzsche, F. (2006), 'On the Uses and Disadvantages of History for Life', in Daniel Breazeale (ed.), *Untimely Meditations*, trans. R. J. Hollingdale, Cambridge: Cambridge University Press.

Nornes, A. M. (1996), 'The Body at the Centre – The Effects of the Atomic Bomb on Hiroshima and Nagasaki', in Mick Broderick (ed.), *Hibakusha Cinema: Hiroshima, Nagasaki and the Nuclear Image in Japanese Film*, London and New York: Kegan Paul International.

Oliver, R. P. (2007), 'The Origins of Christianity'; http://www.revilo-oliver.com/rpo/RPO_NewChrist/chap13.htm (accessed 23/05/2007).

O'Sullivan, S. (2006), *Art Encounters Deleuze and Guattari: Thought Beyond Representation*, London: Palgrave Macmillan.

Oshima, N. (1992), 'The Error of Mere Theorization of Technique', in Annette Michelson (ed.), *Cinema, Censorship, and the State: The Writings of Nagisa Oshima, 1956–1978*, trans. Dawn Lawson, Cambridge, MA, and London: MIT Press.

Pasolini, P. P. (2005), 'The Unpopular Cinema', in ed Louise K. Barnett, *Heretical Empiricism*, trans. Ben Lawton and Louise K. Barnett, Washington DC: New Academia Publishing.

Rodowick, D. N. (1997), *Gilles Deleuze's Time Machine*, Durham and London: Duke University Press.

Schwenger, P. (1992), *Letter Bomb: Nuclear Holocaust and the Exploding Word*, Johns Hopkins University Press, Baltimore.

Stagoll, C. (2005), 'Event', in Adrian Parr (ed.), *The Deleuze Dictionary*, Edinburgh: Edinburgh University Press.

Verevis, C. (2005), 'Cinema', in Adrian Parr (ed.) *The Deleuze Dictionary*, Edinburgh: Edinburgh University Press.

Žižek, S. (2008), *In Defense of Lost Causes*, Verso: London and New York.

Notes

1. This 'implicit' observation is quite clear in *C1*. Directors appear in conjunction with a specific component of the movement-image. For example, Kurosawa is covered in and only in the genetic component of the SAS' relation-image (Deleuze 2002: 186–92) and Herzog is covered in and only in relation to the figure of inversion in the (transformation of figures) reflection-image (Deleuze 2002: 184–6). The examples are numerous.

2. The extension of Deleuze's taxonomy of the movement-image raises problematic issues for his account of how the components differ in different iterations. For instance, during the progression of *C1* an initial version of the taxonomy is revealed. However a glossary of signs and images towards the end of the book does not exactly match what comes before (Deleuze 2002: 217–8). Further, in *C2* – by way of a recapitulation – there is a third account, another variation (Deleuze 2001: 32–3). Ronald Bogue, in *Deleuze on Cinema*, was the first to tabulate the three variations (Bogue 2003: 70–1). Bogue writes 'at a minimum, the signs of the movement-image are fourteen . . . at most, they number twenty-three', but, he asserts, 'obviously, the tally is insignificant' (Bogue 2003: 104). This insignificance means he does not attempt to reconcile the three variations. However, the 'tally', while not the most important aspect of Deleuze's work, is far from insignificant in that it provides the very framework with which to approach the critical aspect: generating the differential readings of the movement-image. Understanding the 'tally' is, to my mind, a prerequisite of fully understanding these differentials. Therefore, a reconciliation of the three variations is, I maintain, a necessity. The possibility of such a reconciliation is possible through a thorough reassessment of Deleuze's appropriation of the semiotics of Peirce. I am currently completing a monograph that explores this aspect of the cinema books.

3. For Deleuze, zeroness can be introduced into the Peircian schema because Peirce takes perception for granted. Perception does not really exist in, of- and for-itself, rather 'perception is strictly identical to every image' (Deleuze 2001: 31). Deleuze continues: 'perception will not constitute a first type of image in the movement-image without being extended into the other types . . . perception of action, of affection' (Deleuze 2001: 31).

4. We might think of SA action-image films as epic, grandiose movies where situations become the impetus for a character's actions (the volcano erupts, the monster/meteorite/alien horde threaten humankind), and their actions ultimately – and most often – save the day. The AS film, by contrast, could be seen as a *film noir*, where the central character follows a line of investigation, gradually discovering, revealing (and again, rectifying) the situation.

5. Deleuze has in mind cinematic versions of figures of discourse such as metaphors (attraction), chiasmus (inversion) and argument (the discursive). It is also worth mentioning that these figures of transformation become the reflection-image in *C2*. This aspect of the cinema books requires much reading between the lines. In *C1* Deleuze describes a transformation of figures that can be decomposed into the figures of attraction, inversion and discourse. In each case, figures intervene as images between situation and action of both the SA and AS form, therefore each is essentially doubled forming two signs of composition (and a genetic sign for each can therefore be discovered). See note 2 above.

6. The recollection-image and the dream-image do not appear in *C1*, but rather in early sections of *C2*. It might therefore be thought (and indeed has been) that these images are part of the time-image taxonomy. However, this is clearly not the case, rather, they are ruse time-images, they represent thought in similar ways to the relation-image. See note 2 above.

7. Solid perception is seen in cinema as shot-reverse shot couplings, static objective framing, logical montage where the camera first frames a wide shot, then a medium shot, then a close-up. Liquid perception is where the camera in movement constructs flowing images in long takes continually reframing environments and bodies. Gaseous perception is the (dis)organisation (montage) of images, chaotic and without a human centre (Deleuze 2002: 84).

8. Lectosigns are the process of reading opsigns and sonsigns, from the Latin *lecto* 'to read'. Hyalosigns are inspired by the work of Gilbert Simondon, who uses

the idea of the crystal (from which the prefix *hyal* – meaning 'glass' – is derived) as a metaphor for the process of individuation. For references to Gilbert Simondon see Deleuze and Guattari 2004: 19, 46, 66 fn.11, 573–4); see also Deleuze 2004b: 86–9. Chronosigns are inspired directly by Bergson's descriptions of pure memory. 'Chronosign', however, seems to be a neologism created by Deleuze himself; as a synonym for the time-image the concept can be seen to emerge directly from Bergson (Bergson 1991). Noosigns are inspired by Martin Heidegger and his discussion of the nature of true thought (Heidegger 1972: 3); see also Deleuze 2001: 156, 308 fn. 2.

9. However, the decompositions are not necessarily based upon the philosophical model from which the time-image element gets its name. Hyalosigns seem to be decomposed into avatars which align with properties of crystalline formations found in physics. Deleuze takes the example of the crystal and identifies how filmmakers have reflected the multiplicitous facia of crystals and the growth of the crystal from a pre-crystal. He identifies three broad trends which form the avatars of the hyalosign: 'two mirrors face to face', 'the limpid and the opaque' and 'the seed and the environment'; each perform exchanges between the actual on-screen image and its virtual connections off screen.

The avatars of chronosigns have a more direct relationship with the properties of pure memory discussed by Bergson in *Matter and Memory*, but are also augmented by Nietzsche's concept of the 'will to power' (Nietzsche 1967); see also Deleuze 2001: 141. Deleuze specifies three types of chronosign that correspond to the three aspects of time in-and-for-itself. 'Sheets of the past' explore the way in which memories are 'no longer confused with the space which serves as its place' (Deleuze 2001: 100). Instead memories explore time itself – the recollection no longer functions as a *foundation* of the present, but as a *product* of the present. 'Points [or peaks] of the present' explore the way in which any present moment is fundamentally divided between the present-in-itself, the past and the future (Deleuze 2001: 100). It is this aspect that can make time 'frightening and inexplicable', for the possibility of action is torn between living in the moment, reacting to the influences of the past and acting for future effects (Deleuze 200: 101). Deleuze refers to these two aspects of chronosigns as the 'order of time' in that they undermine the linear chronology of past, present and future (Deleuze 2001: 155).

The third avatar of the chronosign – which is orientated towards the future – is the 'powers of the false' (Deleuze 2001: 126), and he delineates this function as the 'series of time' as opposed to order (Deleuze 2001: 133, 136, 155). A serial organisation disconnects the continuity of time that constructs the character in the film as locked into a narrative where the present is a product of the past and the future a consequence. Rather than this closed circuit, a serial organisation is one in which time is organised into images in-and-for-themselves which while independent have a multiplicitous virtual presence with each other. As in serialism in music, which attempts to overthrow traditional harmonics without descending into chaos, fundamental elements are continuously rearranged, exploring the difference in repetition. Finally, the avatars of the noosigns seem to emerge directly from cinema itself. How does a filmmaker of the time-image capture thought on-screen? To use relation-, recollection- and dream-images (representations of thought) would mean a return to the co-ordinates of the movement-image. Therefore methods other than the representational must be found. Indeed, for Deleuze, the answer seems beguilingly simple. On the one hand, thought appears through the *mise-en-scène*. As Deleuze writes in C2, 'landscapes are mental states', thus the *mise-en-scène* is 'the brain' (Deleuze 2001: 188; 205). On the other hand thought appears through the body of the actor (Deleuze 2001: 205). Deleuze sees the body as having two poles: those of 'attitude' and 'gest' (Deleuze 2001: 188; 205): 'Gest' is a term taken from Brecht to describe the way in which an actor can foreground gesture. Attitude describes a body that no longer attempts to act. These time-image bodies no longer find their co-ordinates through affect and action, but through thought which no longer appears outside the body on-screen as memory images.

10. Deleuze goes on to say: 'the whole of the analysis is valid for classical cinema' (Deleuze 2001: 146).

11. This quote comes from Noel Burch; see Myer 2004: 71–80.

Chapter 9

Deleuze's Untimely: Uses and Abuses in the Appropriation of Nietzsche

Craig Lundy

This chapter studies the expression of Nietzsche's untimely within a Deleuzian philosophy of history. The concepts of immanence and the outside form a relation throughout Deleuze and Guattari's work that leads to their radical conception of the event, and in particular the historical event. As we see in *What is Philosophy?*, in conjunction with Foucault's actual and Péguy's aternal, the Nietzschean untimely provides a touchstone for Deleuze and Guattari's explanation of creativity in the historical event: the unhistorical is located as both the force and the site from which the sedimentations of history emerge. But while Deleuze and Guattari share in Nietzsche's attempt to facilitate creations counter to our historical present, it cannot be said that they explicitly mirror (or indeed faithfully recount) Nietzsche's analysis of history, its terms, and its effects in society. By tracing the various uses of the untimely throughout Deleuze's work, a differential 'becoming/history' materialises that simultaneously enhances aspects of Nietzsche's thoughts on the untimely whilst conflating others.

This conflation can be located on both sides of the differential: while the forces that form Nietzsche's untimely topology – the ahistorical and the suprahistorical – are transformed into synonyms of 'becoming', 'history' also undergoes a transmutation that effectively attaches to it forms of historicism to which Nietzsche was opposed. The result of these conflations is the replacement of Nietzsche's project of developing a *history for the future* with a Deleuzian *philosophy of the future*, and consequently a hostility towards the figure of history. Once the untimely has been removed from a 'history for life' and subsumed by a philosophy of becoming, it is little wonder that a Deleuzian philosophy of history might appear to be an oxymoron. Attention to Deleuze's particular appropriation of Nietzsche's untimely, however, can show us that the creative elements of Nietzsche's historical project still persist in Deleuze, albeit under the guise of an immanent nomadology – a geophilosophy – that incorporates both the virtual and actual manifestations of an historical event. However, before these subsequent interactions and departures can be explained, a treatment of Nietzsche's ideas on history must be given: it is only through an examination of Nietzsche's aims and ambitions for history that a sense of his untimely can be engendered and distinguished from Deleuze's. Deleuze's use of the untimely will then be seen to be not only a departure but a *productive* misappropriation of Nietzsche, and as such a creation that might itself suggest a new time to come.

Nietzsche's Untimely

In a lecture delivered at the University of Bonn in 1830, Barthold Georg Niebuhr declared that 'History as a discipline first attained its importance in our generation. . . . It is the work of the last fifty years' (Niebuhr 1858: 7). By the time Nietzsche wrote his *Unfashionable Observations* in 1874, this discipline had achieved a status and influence unprecedented in German society and culture. But aside from the politico-educational determinations that this historical consciousness exerted over the new German Empire, the discipline of History also sought to subjugate ontology. As Ernst Troeltsch, an eminent historicist of the Prussian School, explained: 'History was no longer seen as merely one side in a consideration of things or as a partial satisfaction in the thirst for knowledge but rather as the basis of the self-reflection of the species concerning its nature, origins, and hopes' (Troeltsch 1902: 4). Consequently, the names of Niebuhr, Ranke, Droysen, Mommsen and Troeltsch among others together produced a culture of history in late nineteenth-century Germany that in turn historicised culture. As Nietzsche acknowledged, this was a development in which his contemporaries justifiably took much pride: scholarship had indeed 'been furthered at an astonishingly quick pace' (Nietzsche 1995: 86 and 136). Nonetheless, it was these apparent gains that served as the target for Nietzsche's untimely meditations. Let us then examine how Nietzsche diagnosed European degradation in the advent of 'modern historical cultivation' and 'history as an objective science', where others found progress and process, before turning to his alternative vision for history: the oracle of the past transmitted through the creative spirit of youth.

As suggested by Niebuhr, the rise of history in Germany was a relatively recent phenomenon. It was also substantially immersed in the political and social debate on the development of the 'German national character'. Due to her perceived late blooming, the German nation and scholarship of the late nineteenth-century sought to employ the services of history not only to address the political concerns of the period, but, more fundamentally, to generate German history itself through the discovery of its origins. These twin motives led to the promotion of a culture that yearned for and coveted historical knowledge. Leading this charge, Ranke and his team of students at Berlin sought to develop and employ a method that was capable of collecting and analysing historical *Fakta*. Exposed to the vastness of history, the human mind was to act as an impartial processor of data constrained by the sieve of *Wissenschaft* – the model of an ordered inquiry. Although the promise of this method appeared unlimited to its proponents, Nietzsche warned that this modern historical culture possessed three debilitating effects: first, the fetishisation of interiority; second, the onset of 'congenital greyness'; and third, the production of neutered spectators of 'weakened personality'.

As a container of knowledge, the energies of historical cultivation were directed towards an *inner cultivation*. True knowledge was considered to be factual and verifiable, and thus collectable within the individual – the individual as walking encyclopedia. The result of this 'blind' obsession with historical content was the onset of what Nietzsche termed 'congenital greyness'. The apparent strength of the modern method of historical cultivation was that it produced a net effect: not only could the astute adherent produce their own historical *Fakta*, they could also dependently share in the research of others. Indeed, in order to be able to produce their own *Fakta*, one would require the knowledge of such previous research. This meant that the student under historical cultivation was forever positioned as an epigone, simultaneously condemned to minutiae and modesty, as well as the biographer (or eulogist) of humanity. A rule of thumb maintains that biography can only be written by someone who is themselves 'of age', yet this was the paradox that Nietzsche located in historical cultivation: how can a life be judged by someone who has not yet lived? And further, how can the past be assessed when it is presented as '*dead* knowledge riven from its vital context' (Bambach 1990: 262)? Such individuals are themselves dead: 'So cold, so icy that one burns one's fingers on him! Every hand is startled when touching him. – And for that reason some think he glows' (Nietzsche 2000a: 272). According to Nietzsche, the pampered idler in the garden of knowledge is not fit to engage with the past, for they are immune to it. They possess 'weakened personalities'. As Oswald Spengler characterised it in his address to mark the anniversary of Nietzsche's eightieth birthday, Nietzsche had an ability to 'peer into the heart of whole cultures', an ability that was precisely due to his strength of personality, his 'superior vision' (Spengler 1967: 190).

The 'strong personality' for Nietzsche was thus not the resolute man of principle who adhered to the rigors of objectivity, but the individual who was able to *engender*. As Nietzsche surmises, from the subjectiveless stance of the historically cultivated eunuch, the sounds of history remain equally inaudible – 'nothing can affect them any longer' – for their ears are too narrow (Nietzsche 1995: 120).

The ability of modern historical cultivation to exert such an impact on the political and intellectual climate of late nineteenth-century Germany was in large part due to its successful emancipation from the disciplines of Philosophy and Literature. In order to achieve this distinction, History aligned itself with an ethos that was perceived to be the antithesis of its previous parents: the objective methodologies of science. By replacing the ephemeral qualities of 'myth-driven' history with scientific method, the new generation of historians hoped to solidify the foundations of their discipline from which moderate-yet-definitive scholastic gains could be made. Nietzsche's critique of this project, however, revealed that the dis-association from philosophy's most ingrained presuppositions (what Deleuze will later critique as the 'image of thought') was not so easily achieved.

To begin with, we can point out how Nietzsche repeatedly attacked such parallel movements in philosophy itself – namely, the faith in knowledge 'that is finally baptized solemnly as "the truth"' (Nietzsche 2000a: 200). But when directed towards a critique of the new historical methodologies, Nietzsche specifically deplored the association between the disinterested method and the universal concept. The scientific method of history is nothing if not binding. This is because it attempts to remove the historian from history, and hence prevent the historian from subjective tampering. But what is it that such a method can produce? As Nietzsche claims: 'Those "servants of truth" who possess neither the will nor the strength to judge, and who set themselves the task of pursuing "pure, ineffective" knowledge', are only capable of generating 'a truth that amounts to nothing' (Nietzsche 1995: 123). In sacrificing thought to the objective universal, history assumes the mantle of God, 'although this God, for his part, is himself only the product of history' (Nietzsche 1995: 143). And as history finds its final causes in itself, it cannot escape a teleological explanation of presentism. History anoints itself as the 'self-realising concept', 'the dialectic of the spirit of nations', and the 'Last Judgment'. Nineteenth-century historicism, in both its Rankean and Hegelian guises, thus forms a higher tribunal to which both life and knowledge must answer. But the dictates that follow only serve to constrain man, not liberate him. The Ass is loaded with the weight of the world-historical, and under this burden the future-possible of man is condemned.[1]

To bow before the 'power of history' is to inaugurate a repeated deference to every power, 'regardless of whether it is a government, a public opinion, or a numerical majority', and as such to replace the activity of life with the pursuit of historical knowledge (Nietzsche 1995: 143–4). But for Nietzsche, life must assume the higher force, for if knowledge does not work towards the preservation of life then they are mutually destroyed (Nietzsche 1995: 164; 2000a: 236–7). Nietzsche is careful to point out, however, that life is still in need of history: 'That life requires the service of history must be comprehended, however, just as clearly as the proposition that will subsequently be proved – that an excess of history is harmful to life' (Nietzsche 1995: 96). History, then, is not only a negative necessity to be resisted or tolerated, it can and must be used if a healthy life is to be achieved. The question is always, how do we create a history as *memento vivere* and escape history as *memento mori*. To illustrate this, Nietzsche describes three types of history that form relations either in the service or disservice of life: monumental history, antiquarian history and critical history. Although these categories of the historical have themselves been tirelessly debated, such questions ('why three. . .?', 'which one accounts for. . .?') are mostly superfluous, insofar as Nietzsche's purpose with the categories is to provide examples of how history can either engender or inhibit life. His discussion of the modes of history (or what we will call, historicals) is thus a contingent and incomplete one, dependent upon prevailing historical practices. Let us then turn to Nietzsche's general response to the suffocating powers of history – a power that, although significantly different than it was in Nietzsche's day, still reigns supreme today.

How is one to escape the suffocating power and attraction of history and historical knowledge? Nietzsche offers two antidotes: the *ahistorical* and *suprahistorical*. As with the historicals, the ahistorical and the suprahistorical can be used either in the service or disservice of life. The determination of this is of course dependent upon the strength of the antidote administered, which can itself become a poison if inappropriately measured. This is made evident through Nietzsche's consideration of life under the extreme forms of each: concerning the ahistorical, Nietzsche describes the life of a cow, one who cannot even remember what it is without; and for the suprahistorical, a being 'damned to see becoming everywhere' to the point of paralysis (Nietzsche 1995: 89).

But while such extreme forms may destroy life, Nietzsche shows that forgetting and fixation are necessary constituents of a healthy life. On the one hand, it is the act of forgetting that contours the horizons of what can be denoted 'life', for one can only give birth to a perspective when one closes off the endless data of history and in this sense forgets the historical. As Henry Miller would later put it: 'All growth is a leap in the dark, a spontaneous unpremeditated act without benefit of experience' (Miller 1947: 93). If the ahistorical mentality forms one bookend on the historical by providing for 'a little *tabula rasa* of the consciousness' (Nietzsche 2000b: 493–4), then it is the suprahistorical impulse of legislation that forms the other. Being above the historical, the suprahistorical encompasses all of history into a unity. Through the intensity of their consciousness, the suprahistorical being forcibly completes the world, ascertaining its singular meaning in every individual moment. The suprahistorical thus serves as an antidote by way of illustrating the legislative confidence that human action requires: 'If in many cases any one person were capable of sniffing out and breathing once again this ahistorical atmosphere in which every great historical event is born, then such a person, as a cognitive being, would be able to elevate himself to a *suprahistorical* standpoint' (Nietzsche 1995: 92).

Correspondingly, these antidotes can then be thought of as the elixirs of innocence and arrogance. And where are such solutions found? – in the figure, or oracle, of *youth*. Lacking a history yet possessing the innocent-ignorant and arrogant-impudent abilities to create new experiences, the figure of youth offers a relation between life and history that serves as Nietzsche's inspirational power. But how is youth to engage with the past? As we have seen, it is clear that Nietzsche is not proposing that youth should deny history. Rather, Nietzsche argues that the creative youth must engage with the past as an oracle – as a message that remains alive in its receiver: 'The voice of the past is always the voice of an oracle; only if you are architects of the future and are familiar with the present will you understand the oracular voice of the past' (Nietzsche 1995: 130). Before maturity sediments in the individual, rendering that individual a 'man of the world', the youth still harbours the boldness required to shape that world. A Nietzschean 'maturity' is therefore a form of immaturity: 'A man's maturity – consists in having found again the seriousness one had as a child, at play' (Nietzsche 2000a: 273). As the world-process encroaches upon this capacity, Nietzsche implores the individual to hear once again the Delphic Oracle: 'Know thyself.'

Through this figure of the oracle of youth, we then begin to see what Nietzsche has in mind for his project of creating a 'history for life'. Although it is true that Nietzsche's 'On the Utility and Liability of History for Life' lacks any formal explication of what he means by 'life', we do already have some clues. From the opening passages concerning the life of a cow, we can immediately discern that the life Nietzsche is after must be one that is not animalistic but indeed human. However, for a life to be human, it must exhibit *inhuman* moments – those of the ahistorical animal and the suprahistorical legislator. It is these moments that disrupt the 'unthinking commitment to those human, all too human "arrangements" that distract and distance me from myself' (Hicks and Rosenberg 2003: 28). And thus it is these moments that ensure a life maintains its actual lived-ness: continuity and disturbance 'are equally necessary for the health of an individual, a people, and a culture' (Nietzsche 1995: 90). We can also see here that for Nietzsche life is not reducible to the biological, but forms an immanent principle that encompasses society and culture. Life in this multivalent sense must then have access to its inhuman capacities in order to discern needs from pseudo-needs, and realise these needs to the fullest expression. History is one such field that must be put towards this use, but it is also a force that can be used against life. Infatuated with the factual and unable to create, the historicisation of nineteenth-century German life required the intervention of an untimely thought that could reassert the requirements of life. A century later and in a foreign land this thought is recast. Deleuze's appropriation of Nietzsche's untimely, however, contains several transformations that reflect the shift in milieu – the sounds of the Delphic Oracle on a different air. Let us then now turn to Deleuze's interaction with Nietzsche's analysis of history and the untimely.

Deleuze's Untimely

In the widely used English translation of Nietzsche's *Untimely Meditations*, R. J. Hollingdale lists the two untimely forces described in Nietzsche's second essay as the 'unhistorical' and the 'suprahistorical'. Richard T. Gray's translation of the *Unfashionable Observations*, however, employs the term 'ahistorical' in place of 'unhistorical'. This term is arguably superior: while the prefix 'un' suggests an against, 'a' implies an absence, and as the example of the cow in the essay proves, the latter is clearly Nietzsche's intention. What is important and novel about the ahistorical is its ability to be without the historical; if the cow can indeed be said to be against the historical (unhistorical), then this is only because it is so utterly lacking in memory and thus without it (ahistorical). Applying this same logic to the suprahistorical being (who is only against history insofar as he or she can fixate it) we can then conclude that Nietzsche presents two unhistoricals: the ahistorical and the suprahistorical.

While this discussion of translation discrepancies may appear some-what academic and inconsequential, it in fact reveals to us exactly how Deleuze will take his departure from the Nietzschean untimely: he will not only fail to make a conceptual distinction between the ahistorical, the suprahistorical and the unhistorical, but these concepts will be further conflated with a raft of other terms. Consider the following passage from *A Thousand Plateaus*:

> History is made only by those who oppose history (not by those who insert themselves into it, or even reshape it). This is not done for provocation but happens because the punctual system they found ready-made, or themselves invented, must have allowed this operation: free the line and the diagonal, draw the line instead of plotting a point, produce an imperceptible diagonal instead of clinging to an even elaborated or reformed vertical or horizontal. When this is done it always goes down in History but never comes from it. History may try to break its ties to memory; it may make the schemas of memory more elaborate, superpose and shift co-ordinates, emphasize con-nections, or deepen breaks. The dividing line, however, is not there. The dividing line passes not between history and memory but between punctual 'history-memory' systems and diagonal or multilinear assemblages, which are in no way eternal: they have to do with becoming; they are a bit of becoming in the pure state; they are transhistorical. There is no act of cre-ation that is not transhistorical and does not come up from behind or proceed by way of a liberated line. Nietzsche opposes history not to the eternal but to the subhistorical or superhistorical: the Untimely, which is another name for haecceity, becoming, the innocence of becoming (in other words, forgetting as opposed to memory, geography as opposed to arbores-cence). 'The unhistorical is like an atmosphere within which alone life can germinate and with the destruction of which it must vanish . . . What deed would man be capable of if he had not first entered into that vaporous region of the unhistorical?' Creations are like mutant abstract lines that have detached themselves from the task of representing a world, precisely because they assemble a new type of reality that history can only recontain or relocate in punctual systems. (Deleuze and Guattari 1989: 295–6)

While there is much to study in this passage, let us first note how Deleuze and Guattari conflate Nietzsche's untimely terms: the untimely is used interchangeably with transhistorical, subhistorical, superhistorical and unhistorical, and further associated with becoming, haecceity, forgetting and geography. But as we have established, in his 'On the Utility and Liability of History of Life' Nietzsche presented only two distinct terms of the untimely: the ahistorical and the suprahistorical. Why and how then this proliferation and conflation? The immediate textual response is clear: Deleuze and Guattari's aim in the above passage is to bring out the movements of becoming – its geography. Nietzsche's terms are thus placed in the service of a cartography of 'abstract lines' and 'imperceptible diagonals'. Appropriately, Deleuze and Guattari's 'multilinear assemblages' therefore have access to all the various movements of across/beyond, under, over and opposite to.[2]

An historical precedent can be traced in Deleuze's earlier writings that provides context for this usage. In 'Conclusions on the Will to Power and the Eternal Return', a summary written of the colloquium Deleuze convened at the Abbey of Royaument in 1964, Deleuze says in reference to the creation of new values:

> Such values alone are trans-historical, supra-historical, and bear witness to a congenial chaos, a creative disorder that is irreducible to any order whatsoever. It is this chaos of which Nietzsche spoke when he said it was not the contrary of the eternal return, but the eternal return in person. The great creations depart from this supra-historical stratum, this 'untimely' chaos, at the extreme limit of what is livable. (Deleuze 2004c: 125–6)

But is the suprahistorical for Nietzsche, as Deleuze claims, 'irreducible to any order whatsoever'? To the contrary, it is that which *produces an order* – it is the active force necessary for a legislator to engender an order of existence. It would appear then that Deleuze has in fact lost Nietzsche's suprahistorical. Take the most frequently used description of the untimely in Deleuze: the untimely as that which is in opposition to the historical and the eternal (Deleuze 1983: 107; 2005: 72; 2004a: xix, 166; 1995: 170; 2004c: 126, 129; Deleuze and Guattari 1994: 111–13). What does Deleuze mean by this description? Consider this suggestion: if history is an act of localising, the rigid re-presenting of a creative process, while the eternal is an end to this process, or the final fixation, then the untimely for Deleuze is the moving space between a static-small and a static-large. Evidence for this reading can be found in his *Nietzsche and Philosophy*, where Deleuze describes how the broken succession of untimely comets form a 'discontinuity and repetition [that does not] amount to the eternity of the sky which they cross, nor the historicity of the earth which they fly over' (Deleuze 1983: 107). This imagery clearly articulates an untimely that transgresses two types of fixation (by flying *between* them), one human and the other divine. But it is also an untimely that evades Nietzsche's suprahistorical – that untimely antidote capable of lending 'existence the character of something eternal and stable in meaning' (Nietzsche 1995: 163). Deleuze's topology of the untimely thus consistently fails to respect Nietzsche's suprahistorical – Nietzsche's legislative and eternal-untimely – simply turning it into a synonym of the ahistorical.

This is not to say that Deleuze loses a philosophical conception of the eternal altogether, for Nietzsche's Eternal Return will no doubt occupy a most important role in Deleuze's philosophy. Nietzsche's Eternal Return, however, is not the eternal which Deleuze criticises in the passages referenced above. In fact, Deleuze himself explicitly distinguishes between these two concepts of the eternal.[3] As the Nietzschean form is often correlated by Deleuze with the universal, we can even go so far as to claim that Deleuze maintains a conceptual distinction between the eternal and the universal, whereby the former refers to that 'negative' term often described in opposition to the untimely and the latter pertains to Nietzsche's concept of the Eternal Return of difference (giving us concepts such as the universal history of contingency). At any rate, what these two Deleuzian uses of the eternal are precisely not is the eternal-untimely as found in Nietzsche's suprahistorical.[4]

One could potentially save Deleuze here by claiming that as Nietzsche develops his suprahistorical concept into the Eternal Return, so we can in turn locate Nietzsche's suprahistorical as eternal-untimely within Deleuze's use of the universal. This line of thought, however, is as tenuous as the link between the suprahistorical and the Eternal Return in Nietzsche. While Nietzsche's two unhistoricals may indeed be proto-considerations on the problem of eternal becoming, exactly how they relate is debatable. For example, while Thomas Brobjer claims that Nietzsche abandoned the unhistorical concepts after their publication in the *Unfashionable Observations* (Brobjer 2004: 301), Carl Pletsch aligns the suprahistorical with the induced nausea of the 'Vision and the Riddle'. Pletsch goes on to conjecture that this 'great disgust', first exposed by the suprahistorical, was something Nietzsche was already aware of in 1874 yet not ready to confront (Pletsch 1977: 34). Accordingly, this association leads Pletsch to understate the positive/antidotal functions of the suprahistorical in favour of the poisonous, and promote the Dwarf or Buffoon as latter instantiations of the suprahistorical figure. In contrast to Pletsch, Deleuze offers an inverse association of the suprahistorical to the Eternal Return, courtesy of his reading the Eternal Return as a return of 'difference' rather than 'the same'. This reading subsequently demands that the suprahistorical be matched not to the Dwarf or Buffoon, but to the figure of the Overhuman: 'To nihilism [Nietzsche] opposed transmutation, that is the becoming which is simultaneously the only action of force and the only affirmation of power, the transhistoric element of man, the Overman (and not the superman)' (Deleuze 1983: xiii).

Of these three interpretations of the relation between the suprahistorical and the Eternal Return, it may be that we find Deleuze's position preferable, but even if we grant this it will arguably still not be sufficient in recovering Nietzsche's suprahistorical as eternal-untimely in Deleuze's untimely topology. As we see in the above quotation, Deleuze stipulates a preference for the Overman rather than the Superman. It is, however, Nietzsche's higher men who offer the appropriate correspondence to the suprahistorical. As with the higher men, a suprahistorical human is one who puts themselves in the place of God – who forcibly completes the world and finds *their* meaning in all things. This overdetermining meaning could be the 'knowledge' of 'The Man with the Leech', the 'happiness' of the 'Voluntary Beggar', or the 'deathdrive' of the 'man who wants to die'. In each case the higher men formulate a principle of evaluation that remains the same and banishes transmutation. Just as their collected act of power alludes to the Overhuman to come, so the suprahistorical forms a guiding marker for the 'youthful' historian of life to draw from without mimicking. Deleuze, however, indicates a desire to circumvent this process. His direct association of the unhistorical with the Overhuman indicates not only a disregard for the unhistorical-as-poison, but also shows his eagerness to transmute the higher men through collation into their successor – the Overhuman – and as such immediately radicalise the suprahistorical-eternal into the Eternal Return of difference. Therefore, even if we allow for a Deleuzian connection of the unhistoricals to Nietzsche's later concepts of the Eternal Return and the Overhuman, we are still left without the Nietzschean suprahistorical as eternal-untimely. We can then conclude that just as Deleuze collates the higher men into the 'blazing comet' that is the Overhuman, so he binds all the various *affirmative* movements of the unhistorical together, collapsing the a-, non-, supra-, trans- and sub-historical together, in order to achieve the pure tendency of eternal becoming. As this pure tendency will require an opposing force of equal stature, it should then come as no surprise that Deleuze generates the assemblage, or differential, '*becoming/history*', where history comes to embody everything that becoming is not. But as we will see, the intelligibility of this differential comes at a price: the conversion of Nietzsche's *history for the future* into a *philosophy of the future*.

From History to Philosophy

Our discussion thus far of Deleuze's transmutation of terms indicates a pattern of purpose in Deleuze that is tangential to Nietzsche's original problem/project. Nietzsche's historical arrow, a weapon previously named the oracular *historian* of youth, has been relaunched as a *philoso-*

pher of the future. While the philosopher of the future is indeed a significant figure throughout Nietzsche's work, the contention here is (a) that Nietzsche nevertheless maintained a capacity for history itself to have access to becomings (via the oracle and youth, for example), and (b) that Deleuze ignores this capacity of history insofar as he subsumes it within his own philosophy of becoming; in Deleuze, if a Nietzschean 'history for life' is to exist (or better yet, to become), then it must do so *as philosophy*.

This transmutation in fact masks a subtle inversion of the burden of proof that operates in Nietzsche's project. Nietzsche felt compelled to show that for a life to be called truly human, it required those inhuman elements of the ahistorical and suprahistorical. The development of a 'history for life' thus ensued, describing how *history* must be effected by and guided between the two beacons of the unhistorical. But for Deleuze, the objective is not so much to develop a history for life as it is to release life from the grip of history; history forms the boundaries of striation, in opposition to which the movements of life form a war-machine. As lines of flight move through the fixating elements of history in rhizomatic style, the critical question no longer concerns what use the unhistoricals might be for a 'history for life', but in what way the striating powers of history can be complementary to the creative powers of becoming. If Nietzsche's aim was to deride the current fashion of historicising life by emphasising the necessities of becoming for history (that is, to make becoming relevant to history) then Deleuze's posture is the inverse: he is principally concerned with the expression of irreducible becomings, and history is only reluctantly acknowledged as a necessary constituent of this.

As evidence, take the following passages from *What is Philosophy?* and from an interview with Antonio Negri:

> History today still designates only the set of conditions, however recent they may be, from which one turns away in order to become, that is to say, in order to create something new. The Greeks did it, but no turning away is valid once and for all. Philosophy cannot be reduced to its own history, because it continually wrests itself from this history in order to create new concepts that fall back into history but do not come from it. How could something come from history? Without history, becoming would remain indeterminate and unconditioned, but becoming is not history. Psychosocial types belong to history, but conceptual personae belong to becoming. The event itself needs becoming as an unhistorical element. The unhistorical, Nietzsche says, 'is like an atmosphere within which alone life can germinate and with the destruction of which it must vanish'. It is like a moment of

grace; and what 'deed would man be capable of if he had not first entered into that vaporous region of the unhistorical?' Philosophy appears in Greece as a result of contingency rather than necessity, as a result of an ambiance or milieu rather than an origin, of a becoming rather than a history, of a geography rather than a historiography, of a grace rather than a nature. (Deleuze and Guattari 1994: 95–7)[5]

The thing is, I became more and more aware of the possibility of distinguishing between becoming and history. It was Nietzsche who said that nothing important is ever free from a 'nonhistorical cloud'. This isn't to oppose eternal and historical, or contemplation and action: Nietzsche is talking about the way things happen, about events themselves or becoming. What history grasps in an event is the way it's actualized in particular circumstances; the event's becoming is beyond the scope of history. . . . [H]istory amounts only to the set of preconditions, however recent, that one leaves behind in order to 'become', that is, to create something new. This is precisely what Nietzsche calls the Untimely. (Deleuze 1995: 170–1)

Is it actually the case that Nietzsche claims history cannot be experimental, that becoming is not a part of history in Nietzsche, and that Nietzsche calls this creation the untimely? This is so only if one is to read 'history' as 'history against life', and interpret the development of a history that is attuned to the oracular needs of youth, or, a *history* for the future, as a *philosophy* of the future. An examination of Deleuze's use of Nietzsche's concepts of the untimely has shown that Deleuze consistently strips the nuance of Nietzsche's historical analyses and puts them in the services of a philosophy of becoming. We can then say that in the above passages Deleuze is using a facile conception of history as a tool of explanation for the geography of becoming. How could something come from history under such a transmuted conception? Nietzsche had already shown us how: as a critical history for the future. The title of the second essay in *Unfashionable Observations* cannot be any clearer: 'On the Utility and Liability of History for Life'. History must be used in order to serve life, in order to activate the healthy life of a person, a people and culture. The closing of the same essay provides a further explanation in the form of a practical model: Greece. Although Deleuze follows Nietzsche in adopting the Greek example, the burning question is not so much 'why Greece?', but 'what can a model of the past do for us?' The answer to these two questions is the same, but the latter formulation indicates how *history* is active in the creation of life. For Nietzsche, the (Greek) model of the past is to function as an historical example of how history must be overcome. Henk de Jong describes this situation most capably:

But we should never forget that when Nietzsche so vehemently attacked historicism he did so *in the name of history*. When advocating the unhistorical and the transhistorical [note: read ahistorical and suprahistorical according to our terms], when condemning historicism from this double perspective, it was *history* that made him do so. . . . [Nietzsche] wanted to imprint on his readers that the past was of the greatest importance to us, precisely because it helped us see how in the past individuals succeeded in transcending their own past. To put it in a paradoxical tautology, the past could liberate us from the past because only the past showed us how to liberate ourselves from it. In this strange way Nietzsche can be said to have been even more of a historical thinker, to have been even more an advocate of the ultimate significance of history, than most of his historicist opponents. His later *Zur Genealogie der Moral* is perhaps the best proof of all this. (Jong 1997: 273)

If the *Genealogy of Morals* is indeed the best example, then perhaps *Beyond Good and Evil* is a close second: when Nietzsche turns his history/genealogy towards the future, he invokes various models or comets that align with the 'paradoxical tautology' de Jong has identified (see Nietzsche 2000a, Ch. 5: 'Natural History of Morals'). What is it that the figures of Caesar, Cesare Borgia, Kaiser Friedrich II and Napoleon are supposed to *do* for *us*? As we know, they must certainly not act as 'monumental' idols to be mimicked and worshipped. If such (historical) figures, from their strength of personality, were indeed able to break beyond good and evil, then in a sense we already live in the world that they have engendered; no new creation can arise as long as we remain their disciples. Deleuze is well aware of this – Zarathustra's solitary return to the mountain plays heavily in his thought. But he has nevertheless forgotten Nietzsche's target or aim in the critique of historicism (an aspect that is for Nietzsche always necessary if one is to gauge the trajectory of a thought). For Deleuze, Nietzsche's attack of historicism is made in the name of the unhistorical, the untimely, becoming, and finally philosophy, but not history. This is evident from an early stage in Deleuze's writing:

History thus appears as the act by which reactive forces take possession of culture or divert its course in their favour. The triumph of reactive forces is not an accident in history but the principle and meaning of 'universal history'. This idea of a historical degeneration of culture occupies a prominent place in Nietzsche's work: it is an argument in Nietzsche's struggle against the philosophy of history and the dialectic. (Deleuze 1983: 139)

The struggle identified here is precisely that of Nietzsche's 'On the Utility and Liability of History for Life' – the struggle against historicism and the historicisation of culture. But as Deleuze joins in this struggle, he attacks not a particular type of history, as Nietzsche did, but History itself. Thus Deleuze effects a conflation on both sides of his 'becoming/ history' differential. Not only are the various forms of the untimely collapsed together, but history is rendered synonymous with the various forms of historicism and 'history against life'.

The extent of these correlations is quite evident from the various instances in which Deleuze appeals to the following phrase from Nietzsche: 'But I have to concede this much to myself as someone who by occupation is a classical philologist, for I have no idea what the significance of classical philology would be in our age, if not to have an unfashionable effect – that is, to work against the time and thereby have an effect upon it, hopefully for the benefit of a future time' (Nietzsche 1995: 86–7).[6] Deleuze repeatedly fails to reproduce the first half of this quotation, quite simply ignoring the fact that Nietzsche is here referring to the impact *philology* or *history* must have on life, and reading in its place 'philosophy' at every instance. That Nietzsche's work on the untimely is philosophical is unquestionable. But Deleuze's appropriation of Nietzsche's concepts of history has nevertheless been used to make inaccurate extrapolations of not only Nietzsche's position on the ontology of history, but the possibilities and responsibilities Nietzsche holds for History as a discipline. For Nietzsche, if becoming is to be distinguished from history, it is only in order that they become integrated in a 'history for life'; if 'history isn't experimental', then it must be made so under the guidance of the oracle of youth; and if the untimely is the leaving behind of history 'in order to become', then what it must become is a *history for the future.*

Two objections to this thesis immediately call for consideration: first, could it be said that the dispute here is merely terminological and that Deleuze is simply referring to Nietzsche's youthful historian as a philosopher of the future? If so, then Deleuze's critique of history is only intelligible insofar as the creative powers of Nietzsche's 'history for life' have been consumed in Deleuze's definition of philosophy as the discipline that involves creating untimely concepts. We would consequently be justified in seeking an historical creativity (that is, history as *itself* creative), as defined by Nietzsche, in the *philosophical* work of Deleuze, despite the repeated claims in Deleuze's later career that history creates nothing.[7] This would also resolve the apparent contradiction that arises from the fact that Deleuze appeals extensively to historical examples when explicating philosophical concepts in those very works where he most severely criticises history (most notably in his writings with Guattari).

As a second objection, it could be argued that Deleuze has only 'forgotten' aspects of Nietzsche's project insofar as he himself has a new target: Nietzsche's arrow unleashed in a new direction. One could then legitimately claim that Deleuze's 'forgetting' is nothing less than what Nietzsche called for. While this chapter is more than willing to concede this position, it is nonetheless appropriate to locate where and how this distinction arises so that the differing trajectories/diagonals can indeed be properly drawn, for what is at issue is precisely the reconciliation of Nietzschean 'forgetting' with Nietzschean 'history', as well as the avoidance of overly emphasising the unhistorical at the expense of the historical (as is prevalent in Deleuze studies). Only once this marriage is made can Nietzsche's paradoxical project of using history in order to liberate us from it be realised. The critical task of analysing Deleuze's misappropriation of Nietzsche is therefore entirely consistent (and indeed simultaneous) with a promotion of its productive uses. Within the same breath, we can say that Deleuze both 'forgets' aspects of Nietzsche and recasts them, just as Nietzsche did with the Greeks.

This is perhaps Deleuze's great 'abuse' of Nietzsche – the arrogation of Nietzsche's work within a new conceptual creation of his own. Combining our responses to the above objections, we can then say that while Nietzsche calls on the Greeks as an *historical* example of exceeding-history, Deleuze frames the questions: 'Who are today's Nietzscheans?' and 'Will Genghis Khan come back from the dead?' strictly from within a *philosophical* apparatus: 'the plane of immanence' and 'conceptual personae'. Nietzsche's concept of 'history for life' is then replaced with 'philosophical time' as the antagonist to a history that 'conforms to the ordinary laws of succession' (Deleuze and Guattari 1994: 58–9). In flaunting such linear laws, Deleuze is able to construct a Nietzschean philosophy of sense and force that spans from the plural yet singular capacities of 'youthful history' to the aphorism '*I am every name in history*' (Nietzsche 1976: 686). From the early *Unfashionable Observations* to his final letters, 'Nietzsche' emerges as the proper name of a concept (as a figure) in Deleuze's oeuvre.[8] Thus when Deleuze claims in the name of Nietzsche, 'if you want to know what I mean, then find the force that gives a new sense to what I say, and hang the text upon it' (Deleuze 1997: 145), it is nothing if not a re-sounding of the Delphic Oracle, and as such an appropriation of Nietzsche's *history for the future* – unhistoricals and historicals – within a *philosophy of the future*. In accounting for this transmutation of Nietzsche's untimely, we must then follow Deleuze's differential 'becoming/history' back into his wider philosophical discourse. There it will appear with many masks and be put to many uses, and there a philosophy of history should emerge in Deleuze that is not only more than a critique of facile historicism but also a crucial part of his general philosophy of time.

References

Bambach, C. R. (1990), 'History and Ontology: A Reading Of Nietzsche's Second "Untimely Meditation"', *Philosophy Today*, Fall: 259–72.

Brobjer, T. H. (2004), 'Nietzsche's View of the Value of Historical Studies and Methods', *Journal of History of Ideas*, 65(2): 301–22.

Deleuze, G. (1983), *Nietzsche and Philosophy*, trans. H. Tomlinson, London and New York: Continuum.

Deleuze, G. (1995), *Negotiations: 1972–1990*, trans. M. Joughin, New York: Columbia University Press.

Deleuze, G. (1997), 'Nomad Thought', in D. Allison (trans. and ed.), *The New Nietzsche*, Cambridge, MA: MIT Press.

Deleuze, G. (2004a), *Difference and Repetition*, trans. P. Patton, London: Continuum.

Deleuze, G. (2004b), *The Logic of Sense*, trans. M. Lester with C. Stivale, ed. C.V. Boundas, London: Continuum.

Deleuze, G. (2004c), *Desert Islands and Other Texts*, New York and Los Angeles: Semiotext(e).

Deleuze, G. (2005), 'Nietzsche', in *Pure Immanence*, trans. Anne Boyman, New York: Zone Books.

Deleuze, G. and F. Guattari (1983), *Anti-Oedipus: Capitalism and Schizophrenia*, trans. R. Hurley, M. Seem and H. R. Lane, Minneapolis: University of Minnesota Press.

Deleuze, G. and F. Guattari (1989), *A Thousand Plateaus: Capitalism and Schizophrenia*, trans. B. Massumi, Minneapolis: University of Minnesota Press.

Deleuze, G. and F. Guattari (1994), *What is Philosophy?*, trans. G. Burchell and H. Tomlinson, New York: Columbia University Press.

Hicks, S. V. and A. Rosenberg (2003), 'Nietzsche and Untimeliness: The "Philosopher of the Future" as the Figure of Disruptive Wisdom', *The Journal of Nietzsche Studies*, 25: 1–34.

Jong, H. D. (1997), 'Review: Historical Orientation: Jorn Rusen's Answer to Nietzsche and His Followers', *History and Theory*, 36(2): 270–88.

Miller, H. (1947), *Wisdom of the Heart*, London: Editions Poetry.

Niebuhr, B. G. (1858), *Vorträge über römische Alterthümer*, Berlin.

Nietzsche, F. (1976[1889]), 'Letter to Jakob Burckhardt', in F. Nietzsche, *The Portable Nietzsche*, trans. and ed. W. Kaufmann, New York: Penguin Books.

Nietzsche, F. (1995[1874]), *Unfashionable Observations*, trans. R. T. Gray, Stanford, CA: Stanford University Press.

Nietzsche, F. (2000a[1886]), 'Beyond Good and Evil', in F. Nietzsche, *Basic Writings of Nietzsche*, trans. and ed. W. Kaufmann, New York: Modern Library.

Nietzsche, F. (2000b[1887]), 'On the Genealogy of Morals', in F. Nietzsche, *Basic Writings of Nietzsche*, trans. and ed. W. Kaufmann, New York: Modern Library.

Nietzsche, F. (2005[1883–5]), *Thus Spoke Zarathustra*, trans. G. Parkes, Oxford and New York: Oxford University Press.

Pletsch, C. E. (1977), 'History and Friedrich Nietzsche's Philosophy of Time', *History and Theory*, 16(1): 30–9.

Spengler, O. (1967[1937]), 'Nietzsche and His Century', trans. D. O. White, Chicago Il.: H. Regnery Co.

Troeltsch, E. (1902), *Die Absolutheit des Christentums und die Religionsgeschichte*, Tübingen: J. C. B. Mohr.

Notes

I would like to thank Paul Patton and Kylie Benton-Connell for their invaluable assistance throughout the writing of this chapter.

1. Where Hegel would cry out 'World, World, World' Nietzsche responds 'Man, Man, Man' (Nietzsche 1995: 146–7).
2. In a strange coincidence, Deleuze's use of Nietzsche's concept of the ahistorical is consistent with the Hollingdale translation. Deleuze is each time employing a Nietzsche passage on the ahistorical to refer to the more general unhistoricals (according to our schema of concepts outlined above). Paradoxically, therefore, the Hollingdale (as opposed to Gray) translation is better suited to conveying both Deleuze's textual meaning and his conflation of terms.
3. Deleuze and Guattari repeatedly describe becoming as not eternal yet conclude by equating it with the 'Eternity of becoming according to Nietzsche' (Deleuze and Guattari 1994: 111–13).
4. For further evidence of this see Deleuze 1983: 139–40. In his only reference to Nietzsche's unhistorical terms, Deleuze fails to establish any critical difference between the 'non-historical' and the 'supra-historical'.
5. It should be noted that the Nietzsche translations contained here, as in the quotation from *A Thousand Plateaus* above, are Hollingdale's.
6. For Deleuze's uses of this phrase, see Deleuze 1968/2004a: xix; Deleuze 2004b: 302; Deleuze 1983: 107 (although this is actually a parallel reference of *Unfashionable Observations III* [Nietzsche 1995: 173]).
7. For example, see Deleuze 1995: 170–1; Deleuze and Guattari 1989: 295–6; Deleuze and Guattari 1994: 95–7, 110–13.
8. This position, of course, necessarily removes Deleuze from the debates over excluding portions of Nietzsche's corpus from analysis – debates such as 'are the early works of youth contradicted by the mature Nietzsche?', or 'must we disregard his later writings as works of insanity?'

Chapter 10

Is *Anti-Oedipus* a May '68 book?

Ian Buchanan

Everything begins with Marx, continues on with Lenin, and ends with the refrain, 'Welcome, Mr Brezhnev.'

Gilles Deleuze and Félix Guattari, *Anti-Oedipus*

When Gilles met Félix

Gilles Deleuze and Félix Guattari met in the summer of 1969. Deleuze says of their meeting that Guattari was the one who sought him out, that at the time he didn't even know who he was. Evidently their meeting went well because Deleuze suggested they work together (Nadaud 2006: 12). A lot of ink has been spilled speculating about how their collaboration worked in practice, all too often with the nefarious motive of sorting out who wrote what. It seems to me, however, that Deleuze says it all when he says that they each thought that the other had gone further than they had and therefore they could learn from each other. In conversation with Claire Parnet, Deleuze described his way of working with Guattari as a 'pick-up' method, but then qualifies it by saying 'method' is not the right word and suggests 'double-theft' and 'a-parallel evolution' as perhaps better alternatives. (Deleuze and Parnet 2002: 18)

> It started off with letters. And then we began to meet from time to time to listen to what the other had to say. It was great fun. But it could be really tedious too. One of us always talked too much. Often one of us would put forward some notion, and the other just didn't see it, wouldn't be able to make anything of it until months later, in a different context. . . . And then we wrote a lot. Félix sees writing as a schizoid flow drawing in all sorts of things. I'm interested in the way a page of writing flies off in all directions and at the same time closes right up on itself like an egg. And in the reticences, the resonances, the lurches, and all the larvae you can find in a book. Then we really started writing together, it wasn't a problem. We took turns at rewriting things. (Deleuze 1995: 14)

In 1969 Gilles Deleuze was 44 and having just completed his Doctorat D'Etat he was the very epitome of a respectable professor. This was indeed how even his friends regarded him. 'Deleuze was a delightful character,' Antonio Negri would say later, 'but he was a professor, an intellectual!' (Negri 2004: 46). Similarly, Guattari informs us that he had hoped his collaboration with Deleuze would mean that Deleuze would get out more and get more involved in political action, yet it seemed to have the opposite effect (Guattari 1995: 28).[1] This should not be taken to mean that Deleuze was inactive or uninvolved politically.[2] It simply acknowledges that his preference was to conduct politics through his writing by promulgating new forms of thought via the invention of new concepts. Deleuze more or less affirms this himself when he declares that one shouldn't travel around too much because it interferes with one's becoming (Deleuze 1995: 138). Yet in spite of his aloofness, this extremely scholarly professor clearly exerted a powerful intellectual magnetism in his seminars and in his books. Viewers of *L'Abécédaire de Gilles Deleuze* – a remarkable eight-hour dialogue (Deleuze explicitly refused to do an interview) between Deleuze and Claire Parnet recorded for French television, but only screened after his death – can see this clearly.[3] Prefacing the interview there is a tantalisingly brief glimpse, in grainy, poorly lit black and white footage, of one of Deleuze's seminars at the University of Vincennes in 1980, which shows a relatively small room filled to capacity with evidently spellbound students.[4] The plain, functional table at which Deleuze is seated is covered with an array of tape recorders and microphones, the desiring-machines of a new generation of students. Richard Pinhas, experimental musician and dedicated Deleuzian, was one of those new kinds of students with a tape recorder. He made recordings of dozens of Deleuze's seminars, which he has now made available on the web at webdeleuze.com. In the process he has inaugurated an incredible, spontaneous collective archival project aimed at making Deleuze's teaching as accessible as possible: the recordings have been transcribed and translated into several languages, thus providing Deleuze scholars with an invaluable resource.[5]

Intellectually Deleuze defined himself against the generation that came before him – he respected and admired his teachers, but nonetheless rejected their teaching very firmly. 'I could not stand Descartes, the dualisms and the Cogito, or Hegel, the triad and the operation of the negation' (Deleuze and Parnet 2002: 14). The one exception was Sartre.[6] In his early student days, he saw Sartre as a breath of fresh air, but did not feel drawn to existentialism or phenomenology (Deleuze and Parnet 2002: 12). Novelist Michel Tournier recalled that even then as an undergraduate Deleuze was already a powerful innovator:

> We soon came to fear his talent for seizing upon a single one of our words
> and using it to expose our banality, stupidity, or failure of intelligence. He
> possessed extraordinary powers of translation and rearrangement: all the
> tired philosophy of the curriculum passed through him and emerged
> unrecognisable but rejuvenated, with a fresh, undigested, bitter taste of
> newness that we weaker, lazier minds found disconcerting and repulsive.
> (Tournier 1988: 128)

In his own description of his student days, Deleuze said he belonged to a
generation 'that was more or less bludgeoned to death with the history
of philosophy' (Deleuze 1995: 5). What Deleuze objected to was the
repressive way this history of philosophy was used to wrap thought in
the straightjacket of the imperative injunction 'you can't do this until
you've read that' which all students are familiar with. His way of escaping this was to think of 'the history of philosophy as a sort of buggery or
(it comes to the same thing) immaculate conception. I saw myself as
taking an author from behind and giving him a child that would be his
own offspring, yet monstrous' (Deleuze 1995: 6). His monographs on
Hume, Bergson, Nietzsche and Spinoza, written in the early part of his
career, do not put words into the mouths of their subjects, but are
nonetheless able to make them say something quite different to the
received view of them. But more importantly, these books enabled
Deleuze to think differently; they were his lines of flight, or 'witch's
brooms' (Deleuze and Parnet 2002: 15), that took him outside and
beyond the confines of his situation, giving him the freedom to do philosophy for himself. By his own estimation, he did not really begin to do
philosophy for himself until he wrote *Différence et répétition*, the major
thesis for his Doctorat D'Etat. It was this book, according to Deleuze –
particularly Chapter 3: 'The Image of Thought', which concerns precisely the conditions of possibility for producing radically new thought –
that paved the way for his collaborative work with Guattari (Deleuze and
Parnet 2002: xvii).

A few years younger than Deleuze, Félix Guattari was only 37 in 1969.
At this point in his career he had neither a degree nor a book to his name.
Again, Negri provides a vivid portrait highlighting the contrasting personalities of the two future collaborators. Speaking of Deleuze, Negri
says:

> We talked about many things, but I couldn't tell him that I was depressed,
> that I was tired, that I had problems. I couldn't ask him to do anything for
> me. It was difficult to explain to him what was happening in Italy. With Félix
> I could. Very soon we began to come up with ideas together – and not only
> from the theoretical point of view. (Negri 2004: 46)[7]

Guattari had a gift for organising people, for bringing them together and engineering a creative spark between them. It was almost as if he was the living embodiment of 'transversality', the concept he invented to describe relations between subjects and objects, or subjects and subjects, which is neither unifying nor totalising. Before he met Deleuze, Guattari had already gained notoriety in France as a political activist. He was known in the French press as 'Mr Anti-' for his public campaigning on a range of causes from the decolonisation of Algeria, the improved treatment of prisoners in French prisons (he was a member of Michel Foucault's Groupe d'Information sur les Prisons), the improved treatment of the mentally ill in French insane asylums, the establishment of free radio, to Gay rights and Green politics. In 1973 he outraged national sensibilities by publishing a special issue of the journal *Recherches*, edited by Guy Hocquenghem and René Schérer, and provocatively entitled 'Three Billion Perverts: An Encyclopaedia of Homosexualities'.[8] French courts banned it and ordered all copies destroyed. Guattari was also fined, but he proudly never paid. More controversially, he collaborated with Negri, who was arrested in 1977 on charges of terrorism for his association with the Red Brigades. Guattari also spoke out against the extradition from Germany to France of Klaus Croissant, a German lawyer sympathetic to the Baader-Meinhof Group; and in the late 1950s and early 1960s he carried cash for the Front de libération nationale algérien (Algerian National Liberation Front), the guerrilla army fighting for independence from French rule in Algeria.

Guattari's activism was informed by his clinical practice as a psychotherapist in the private psychiatric clinic La Borde, founded in 1953 by Jean Oury with the aim of providing a radically new form of care which 'de-institutionalised the institution'. At La Borde all staff, including cooks and cleaners, participated in providing therapy for the patients, many of whom were psychotic, and all staff, including doctors and nurses, participated in the maintenance of the hospital. 'What we're trying to do', Guattari explained in a note to Deleuze, is 'upset the caste imaginary that marks these patients, nurses and doctors (not to mention all the numerous subcastes!)' (Guattari 2006: 144). Guattari was enlisted by Oury because of his ability to organise collective action and thus help break down the barriers between staff and patients. Guattari received formal training in psychoanalysis from France's most important interpreter of Freud, Jacques Lacan, achieving the status of *analyste membre* in 1969. Although he remained a member of Lacan's school, the École freudienne de Paris, until its dissolution in 1980 shortly before the master's death, Guattari's relationship to Lacan and Lacanian psychoanalysis was at best ambivalent. The publication of Guattari's notebooks, *The Anti-Oedipus Papers*, has made it clear just how strained relations were between them, especially after the publication of *Anti-Oedipus* (even though that work was, in the words of its authors, designed to save Lacan from the Lacanians). Indeed, even before it was published Lacan was distressed by its possible contents and according to Guattari's journal put pressure on him to give him a copy of the manuscript. Guattari had to refuse because Deleuze, whose relation with Lacan wasn't as personal, only wanted to show Lacan the text when it was finished.[9] Deleuze and Lacan clearly regarded each other as rivals, as is evident in the fact that they deliberately scheduled their seminars at the same time, compelling students to choose between them. That Deleuze saw himself as the clear winner in their struggles can be seen in his tart remark that in writing *Anti-Oedipus* they'd tried to give Lacan some 'schizophrenic help'. By which he meant eliminating Lacan's signature conceptual innovations, his notions of structure, the symbolic order, the signifier, and so on, which in Deleuze's unequivocal phrase are 'thoroughly misguided' (Deleuze 1995: 14).

The collaboration between Deleuze and Guattari is often described as a meeting of opposites, a love story between a wasp and an orchid as one writer has put it (Nadaud 2006). But despite superficialities, this is clearly false inasmuch as it implies the one completes or complements the other. Moreover this myth, for that is clearly what it is, has had a rather pernicious effect. Guattari is variously treated as the junior partner and his contribution either downplayed or ignored altogether (and almost all commentators on Deleuze, myself included, have been guilty at one time or another of writing 'Deleuze' when really they meant 'Deleuze and Guattari'), or worse, as the corruptor of Deleuze, and condemned to take the fall for all that is strange, disturbing or simply incomprehensible in their writings. I can only agree with Gary Genosko that something must be done to address the confiscation of Guattari's contribution, though I confess I'm at a loss as to what that might be (Genosko 2002: 16).

May '68

It is often said, on the authority of the authors' own words, that *Anti-Oedipus* is a May '68 book. But what does that mean? As Kristin Ross argues in her history of the events of May and its influence on French intellectual life, *May '68 and its Afterlives*, the meaning of May '68, one of the largest mass movements in history, was never straightforward or obvious, even to its participants, who were in any case very far from being uniform in their backgrounds, opinions, politics and motives.[10] Neither Deleuze nor Guattari are included in Ross's pantheon of thinkers, activists and writers whose 'intellectual and political trajectories' can be traced back to May '68 (Ross 2002: 6). At first glance, this might seem an injustice because, after all, it is not as though Deleuze and Guattari did not involve themselves in the events of May – particularly Guattari, who took part in the infamous occupation of the Théâtre de l'Odéon. However, there is more than a grain of truth in Ross's verdict. By their own admission, Deleuze and Guattari were blindsided by May '68; it took them both by surprise and left them floundering for a response.[11] But, having said that, I see no reason to go along with Ross in thinking that Deleuze and Guattari's concepts of desire and becoming cannot be used to account for what happened that May (Ross 2002: 106, 116). The difficulty they had in forming a response can be seen in the very texture of the work they produced together, especially its frequently bemoaned complexity. They were as troubled by the actualities of May '68 as they were excited by its possibilities, and this ambivalence clearly shapes their theory of desire which tries to account for the contradictory currents of political thought and action that events like May '68 bring into stark relief. Deleuze and Guattari were stirred by the possibility for change May '68 seemed to betoken, namely the liberation of desire itself, but they were also highly sceptical of the doctrinal turn that accompanied it, which seemed to them to promise the incarceration of desire all over again. They were particularly opposed to the Left Bank Maoism that blossomed that spring like the proverbial hundred flowers. They rejected the idea that May '68 constituted a first or preliminary stage in a longer struggle that would culminate in the installation of a new state apparatus.[12] 'It would be strange', Guattari remarked, 'to rely on a party or state apparatus for the liberation of desire' (Guattari 1995: 62).

If it is legitimate to say that *Anti-Oedipus* is a May '68 book, however, then it is because it was in a spirit of mutual ambivalence and uncertainty about May '68 that the two thinkers first came together in 1969. '[I]t was as less a question of pooling knowledge than the accumulation of our uncertainties and, even a certain distress in the face of the turn of events after May '68' (Guattari 1995: 93). In other words, it is legitimate to say *Anti-Oedipus* is a May '68 book providing it is understood that Deleuze and Guattari were not 'soixante-huitards' or May '68ers, and that their view of those events was quite different from the students and workers who put up barricades in the streets and tore up pavements in search of the beach underneath. Their reticence regarding May '68 can partially be explained in generational terms inasmuch as Deleuze and Guattari saw themselves as belonging to the generation prior to the actual '68ers (if by that one means the students at the Sorbonne who provided the initial spark of protest that set the politically seismic events in motion). Their intellectual and political formation took shape during the Second World War and its aftermath, and bore the scars of the defeat, occupation and liberation of France in its scepticism towards all forms of organised politics. As Guattari explained in an interview following the publication of *Anti-Oedipus* in France in 1972: 'We are part of a generation whose political consciousness was born in the enthusiasm and naivety of the Liberation, with its conspirational mythology of fascism.' He further qualified this remark by adding that the 'questions left hanging by the other failed revolution that was May '68 were developed for us based on a counterpoint that was all the more troubling because, like many others, we were worried about the future being readied for us, one that could make you miss the fascism of yore' (Guattari 1995: 94). In other words, Deleuze and Guattari were distrustful of the immodest and frequently hubristic claims that were made about what May '68 really meant – i.e., that it had somehow changed everything – though they were not opposed to it in principle as many of their generation in fact were.[13] Ten years later, in *A Thousand Plateaus*, they would lash out at May '68 naysayers like Raymond Aron as follows:

> [T]hose who evaluated things in macropolitical terms understood nothing of the event because something unaccountable was escaping. The politicians, the parties, the unions, many leftists, were utterly vexed; they kept repeating over and again that 'conditions' were not ripe. It was as though they had been temporarily deprived of the entire dualism machine that made them valid spokespeople. (Deleuze and Guattari 2004b: 238)

As is obvious from the stridently anti-capitalist tone of *Anti-Oedipus*, Deleuze and Guattari were highly sympathetic to the utopian (i.e. world-transformative) dimension of the May '68 struggles, but they weren't ready to accept that the solution was an immediate transition to communism.

> Liberated desire means desire that escapes the impasse of private fantasy: it is not a question of adapting it, socialising it, disciplining it, but of plugging it in in such a way that its process not be interrupted in the social body, and that its expression be collective. What counts is not the authoritarian unification, but rather a sort of infinite spreading: desire in the schools, the factories, the neighbourhoods, the nursery schools, the prisons, etc. It is not a question of directing, of totalising, but of plugging into the same plan of oscillation. As long as one alternates between the impotent spontaneity of

anarchy and the bureaucratic and hieratic coding of a party organisation, there is no liberation of desire. (Guattari 1995: 62)

There can be no denying that *Anti-Oedipus* is conceived as a revolutionary book, that is, as a book that wants to open our eyes to the potential for revolution in the realm of everyday life. But as the passage just cited makes clear, its definition of revolution doesn't include taking power.[14] It doesn't mean overturning one regime and then installing another, reforming government from top to bottom, as the Maoists and Leninists demand. It wants no part of such programmes. Revolution for Deleuze and Guattari means schizophrenising the existing power structure, making it vibrate to a new rhythm, making it change from within, without at the same time becoming a schizophrenic. But they don't offer a model for a new society, save that it won't replicate the old repressions. Their argument is that we'll never get to that new society the militants of every persuasion claim their doctrine is leading us towards if we don't first of all shed our old habits, our old love of power, our manifold addictions to the exercise of force, our customary obsequiousness in the face of power, and so on. 'Schizoanalysis as such does not raise the problem of the nature of the socius to come out of the revolution; it does not claim to be identical with the revolution itself' (Deleuze and Guattari 2004a: 415). Its only question is, 'Where will the revolution come from?' From start to finish, *Anti-Oedipus* is dominated by this single question:

> Will it come in the person of a Castro, an Arab, a Black Panther, or a Chinaman on the horizon? A May '68, a home-grown Maoist planted like an anchorite on a factory smoke-stack? Always the addition of an axiom to seal off a breach that has been discovered; fascist colonels start reading Mao, we won't be fooled again; Castro has become impossible, even in relation to himself; vacuoles are isolated, ghettos created; unions are appealed to for help; the most sinister forms of 'dissuasion' are invented; the repression of interest is reinforced – but where will the new irruption of desire come from? (Deleuze and Guattari 2004a: 413)

Deleuze and Guattari's answer to this question is that the new irruption of desire must always come from within desire itself. Desire is revolutionary in itself, Deleuze and Guattari argue, but is constantly being shackled to, or worse converted into, interest, and as interest it is susceptible to capture, domestication and pacification. Their conviction, reiterated throughout *Anti-Oedipus*, is that 'capitalist society can endure many manifestations of interest, but not one manifestation of desire, which would be enough to make its fundamental structures explode, even at the kindergarten level' (Deleuze and Guattari 2004a: 414). But pure manifestations of desire are rare, even in actual revolutionary situations.

> One cannot account for a revolutionary situation by a simple analysis of the interests of the time. In 1903 the Russian Social Democratic Party debated the alliances and organisation of the proletariat, and the role of the avant-garde. While pretending to prepare for the revolution, it was suddenly shaken up by the events of 1905 and had to jump on board a moving train. There was a crystallisation of desire on a wide social scale created by a yet incomprehensible situation. Same thing in 1917. (Guattari 1995: 65)

By the same token, there are always groups in place to capitalise on the disruption to the social order revolution causes.

> Daniel Guérin has said some profound things about the revolution of 1789. The bourgeoisie never had any illusions about who its real enemy was. Its real enemy was not the previous system, but what escaped the previous system's control, and what the bourgeoisie strove to master in its turn. It too owed its power to the ruin of the old system, but this power could only be exercised insofar as it opposed everything else that in rebellion against the old system. The bourgeoisie has never been revolutionary. It simply made sure others pulled off the revolution for it. It manipulated, channelled, and repressed an enormous popular desire. (Guattari 1995: 65)

The point not to be missed here is that one cannot use interest as a way of determining where the revolution will come from, but one must take interest into account when one considers the parallel problem of 'Who will betray the revolution?' And for Deleuze and Guattari, these two questions, 'Where will the revolution come from?' and 'How will it be betrayed?', are ultimately different sides of the same coin.

Algeria, Vietnam, Italy . . .

Apprehending *Anti-Oedipus* as a May '68 book is useful way of focusing the multiple and multivalent impulses that went into writing it, but the limitations of this framing device are obvious.[15] It risks making it seem that *Anti-Oedipus* was a purely local affair, a single-shot response to a single-shot event that took place in Paris three decades ago. It is true to say that many of the debates *Anti-Oedipus* weighs into are patently Parisian in nature. Indeed, it spars more or less overtly with practically every leading light of the intellectual scene in Paris at that time, particularly Louis Althusser, Jacques Lacan and Lévi-Strauss. But having said that, it is also true to say that the debates inspired by the work of Althusser, Lacan and Lévi-Strauss, not to mention the theoretical upheavals provoked by Jean Baudrillard, Hélène Cixous, Jacques Derrida, Michel Foucault, Luce Irigaray, Julia Kristeva and Jean-François Lyotard, reverberated around the world, albeit in the hermetic confines of University English and French departments. Students from all over the world flocked to Paris in the late 1960s and early 1970s to sit at the feet of these master thinkers who in their unwillingness to accept at face value the received wisdom of the past, in any of the disciplines, appeared to offer not only a new way of thinking, but verily a whole new worldview. In the history of theoretical discourse, *Anti-Oedipus* appeared at the dawn of a decade that was, as Fredric Jameson has put it, 'essentially French' (Jameson 1990: 5). However the fact that theory had become or was becoming global in its distribution at this point does not prove that its production was anything other than a purely local affair. For that reason it is worth looking at May '68 itself and asking whether or not it was the purely local affair it appears to be to the untutored eye. Anticipating the discussion to follow, I want to propose the following corollary to my initial claim that it is legitimate to treat *Anti-Oedipus* as May '68 book: it is legitimate to the extent that May '68 itself is treated as a complex, multiply determined event whose place in history is far from settled.

Bernardo Bertolucci's highly stylised film about May '68, *The Dreamers* (2003), is a vivid illustration of the narrow, exclusively Parisian image of the events that has to be overturned if we are to see things in their proper historical light. Bertolucci depicts May '68 as a student protest, which is how it began, but its significance in history derives from the fact that it soon became a nationwide protest involving more than 9 million striking workers. The effects of the strikes are made apparent to us in the film in the form of mounds of uncollected garbage mouldering in stairwells and on street corners, but the striking workers themselves are never shown. Moreover, Bertolucci makes it seem that the student protests began in the privileged cloisters of the Latin Quarter, and not, as was actually the case, in the functionalist towers of the new universities in the outlying immigrant slum areas of Nanterre and Vincennes, where students were provided 'with a direct "lived" lesson in uneven development' (Ross 2002: 95). According to the great Marxist philosopher Henri Lefebvre, it was this daily 'experience' of the callousness of the state that radicalised the students and provided the catalyst for their connection to worker's movements (Ross 2002: 95). Secondly, through the vehicle of its twin brother and sister protagonists, Isabelle (Eva Green) and Theo (Louis Garrel) – both in their late teens or early twenties and still living at home with their relatively well to do parents –

it depicts the students who took part in May '68 as naive, self-absorbed and perverted. Cocooned in their own fantasy world concocted from fragments of movies and books, Isabelle and Theo are a postmodern version of Ulrich and Agathe. They meet an American exchange student, Matthew (Michael Pitt), and invite him to join them. When their parents go away, they are able to indulge their whims uninhibitedly and the scene is set for a clichéd romp through the three staples of 1960s counterculture, namely sex, drugs and rock'n'roll. They take bubble baths together and get stoned on hash; Matthew and Isabelle make love on the kitchen floor while Theo fries an egg and looks on with Brechtian disinterest; they drink papa's fine wine straight from the bottle and debate movies and politics long into the night as though nothing else mattered. They ignore the world outside.

Matthew soon upsets their idyllic universe by accusing them both of being unworldly: Isabelle because she's never been out on a real 'date' and Theo because of his starry-eyed romanticisation of the Chinese Red Guards. It all begins when Isabelle demands that he shave his pubic hair as a sign of love. He refuses because it is a silly game, but also because it is infantalising. He tells them both 'there's something going on out there, I can feel it', but neither Isabelle nor Theo seem to care. Their political awakening comes soon enough though, in the form of a brick thrown through their apartment window. The brick literally shatters their world, but also saves their lives too. Awakening after another of their orgiastic episodes, Isabelle finds a cheque written by her parents and realises that they must have been in the apartment and therefore witnessed their dishabille state and perhaps guessed at their decadent behaviour – the three of them are naked, sleeping side by side in a tent Isabelle erected in the living room. Mortally ashamed, Isabelle decides to kill herself and Theo and Matthew as well, so she switches on the gas and lays down between the two boys and readies herself for death. It is at this point that the window is broken. The intrusion of the street into their self-enclosed fantasy world is thus presented as a life-saving event. The brick breaks the spell of self-indulgence they've all been under and suddenly both Isabelle and Theo realise something is going on outside and that it does concern them, does interest them, and is more important than their fantasy world. The three of them rush first to the balcony to witness the events below and then to the street to join in. But here the happy trio split up because only Isabelle and Theo are willing to take part. Matthew, a self-proclaimed pacifist, turns his back on them. Having urged them both to take note of what is going on outside, Matthew recoils in horror when he sees Theo with a Molotov cocktail in his hands and refuses to join them when they rush hand in hand towards the fray. Bertolucci's last act then is to make May '68 an exclusively French affair, but also wrong-headed and needlessly violent.

Kristin Ross's account of May '68 takes us in precisely the opposite direction to Bertolucci. She is anxious that we see that May '68 was not just a student protest, and that those involved were anything but naive (in the sense of being unaware of history), and perhaps most importantly that it was part of a longer chain of events that stretched far beyond Paris. To begin with, Ross argues for an enlargement of the timeframe in which the events are considered, not just beyond the month of May itself, which as she shows (and Bertolucci's film exemplifies) restricts the events to a limited series of goings-on in the Sorbonne, but back two decades to the start of the Algerian War. This, in turn, enables her to argue that May '68 'was not a great cultural reform, a push toward modernisation, or the dawning sun of a new individualism. It was above all *not* a revolt on the part of the sociological category "youth"' (Ross 2002: 26). It was rather the revolt of a broad cross-section of workers and students of all ages who had grown up with and witnessed the sickening brutality of the Gaullist regime's failed attempt to deny Algeria its independence. 'Algeria defined a fracture in French society, in its identity, by creating a break between the official "humanist" discourse of that society and French practices occurring in Algeria and occasionally within France as well' (Ross 2002: 38). It was impossible to reconcile the ideal of a benevolent welfare state espoused by France's leaders with the truncheon-wielding reality of the hegemonic State, except perhaps in Oedipal terms by casting President de Gaulle in the role of father and relegating the pro-testors to the rank of children. *Anti-Oedipus* is of course directed against this pseudo-psychoanalytic account of the events and indeed Deleuze and Guattari argue that it was precisely the example of Algeria that makes it clear that politics cannot be reduced to an Oedipal struggle. 'It is strange', they write, 'that we had to wait for the dreams of the colonised peoples in order to see that, on the vertices of the pseudo triangle, mummy was dancing with the missionary, daddy was being fucked by the tax collec-tor, while the self was being beaten by the white man' (Deleuze and Guattari 2004a: 106).

What Fanon's work showed us, Deleuze and Guattari go on to suggest, is that every subject is directly coupled to elements of their 'historical sit-uation – the soldier, the cop, the occupier, the collaborator, the radical, the resister, the boss, the boss's wife – who constantly break all triangu-lations, and who prevent the entire situation from falling back on the familial complex and becoming internalised in it' (Deleuze and Guattari

2004a: 107). As Belden Fields writes, the Algerian War was a crucial stimulus for the radicalisation of French Students in the 1960s because it delegitimised the structures of the State. 'The educational system, for instance, came to be viewed as a conduit funnelling young people into military bureaucracies to fight imperialist wars, or into capitalist bureaucracies, whether public or private, to earn a living as a supporting cog in a system of repressive privilege' (Fields 1984: 149). This perceived lack of control over their own destiny, even among the relatively privileged classes to which the majority of students actually belonged, coupled with the oppressive archaism of the educational system itself, and indeed the State structure as a whole, generated among radicalised youth a powerful sense of empathy with all victims of the system. Thus the students saw themselves as being in solidarity with factory workers, despite the fact that their destiny was to be the managers who would one day have to 'manage' these selfsame workers. In other words, in spite of the fact that their class interests were different, the students and the workers were nonetheless able to find a point of common interest in their dispute with the State. The usual divide and conquer tactics the State relies on to stratify the population and ensure that precisely this type of connection between strata doesn't occur failed spectacularly. They failed because the State was unable, at least in the first instance, to present itself as something other than a huge, oppressive monolithic edifice determined to stamp our dissent with an iron fist. Unfortunately, the French Communist Party, still a very strong and widely supported institution, was tarnished by its 'pragmatic' response to the war – the Party line, that the war should be ended by negotiated settlement, was strictly enforced, with the result that the Party too came to be seen as ossified and antiquated and of little relevance to the needs of the present generation (Fields 1984: 151). Deleuze and Guattari clearly shared this view; their frequent anti-reformist remarks should be seen as directed at the French Communist Party.

Ross's second move is to argue for an enlargement of the geographical framework in which the events are considered, not just beyond the Latin Quarter to the outer suburbs of Paris, but beyond France altogether to still another of its former colonies, namely Vietnam, which having rid itself of its French masters in the 1950s was then in the process of expelling the American pretenders. 'In its battle with the United States, with the worldwide political and cultural domination the United States had exerted since the end of World War II, Vietnam made possible a merging of the themes of anti-imperialism and anti-capitalism; the theoretical justification was loosely supplied by Maosim' (Ross 2002: 80). In fact, the events themselves were sparked by an incident – a window of the American Express building on rue Scribe in Paris was broken – that occurred as part of a student protest against the war in Vietnam on March 20, 1968. The irruption of student protest at Nanterre two days later was in part provoked by the heavy handedness of the police response to the anti-Vietnam march. The students at Nanterre rallied themselves under the banner of 'Mouvement du 22 mars', deliberately recalling Castro's 'July 26th Movement' commemorating the attack on Moncada fortress and the start of the insurrection against Batista. 'Vietnam thus both launched the action in the streets as well brought under one umbrella a number of groups – the CVN [Comité Viêt-nam national] was dominated by Trotskyists, the CVB [Comité Viêt-nam de base] by Maoists – as well as previously unaffiliated militants working together' (Ross 2002: 91). For the protestors, students and workers alike, Vietnam made manifest processes that were thought to be merely latent in the West. For one thing, it revealed both the inherent violence of the postmodern capitalist State and the lengths to which it is prepared to go in order to preserve its power. It demonstrated a willingness on the part of the powerful to use violence against the powerless to defend the status quo. Vietnam also revealed the vulnerability of the super state and its susceptibility to a 'revolution from below' (Deleuze 2004: 213). Sartre, for one, was convinced that the true of origin of May '68 was Vietnam because the example of Vietnamese guerrillas winning a war against a vastly superior force, albeit at the cost of an enormous loss of life, extended the domain of the possible for Western intellectuals who otherwise thought of themselves as powerless in the face of the State (Ross 2002: 91).[16]

More concretely, French workers whose livelihoods were threatened by a process we know today as globalisation, the process whereby local markets are forcibly opened to global competitors, also saw themselves as victims of American imperialism. Deleuze and Guattari were keenly aware of the high cost of structural adjustments (to use the purposefully dry language of economists):

> If we look at today's [1972] situation, power necessarily has a global or total vision. What I mean is that every form of repression today, and they are multiple, is easily totalised, systematised from the point of view of power: the racist repression against immigrants, the repression in factories, the repression in schools and teaching, and the repression of youth in general. We mustn't look for the unity of these forms of repression only in reaction to May '68, but more so in a concerted preparation and organisation concerning our immediate future. Capitalism in France is dropping its liberal,

paternalistic mask of full employment; it desperately needs a 'reserve' of unemployed workers. It's from this vantage point that unity can be found in the forms of repression I already mentioned: the limitation of immigration, once it's understood we're leaving the hardest and lowest paying jobs to them; the repression in factories, because now it's all about once again giving the French a taste for hard work; the struggle against youth and the repression in schools and teaching, because police repression must be all the more active now that there is less need for young people on the job market. (Deleuze 2004: 210)

On this point, Ross argues that the geographical boundary of the events of May needs to be widened to encompass Italy, because the political convulsions wrought by the first stages of globalisation were nowhere in Europe felt more keenly.[17] The striking Fiat workers' slogan 'Vietnam is in our factories!' made the connection to American imperialism explicit. This is, then, Ross's third move: she argues for a redefinition of the sociological frame in which the events are considered. May '68 would not have been the event it was if the protest action had been confined to either the students or the workers or even the farmers. It was the fact that these groups, as well as many others, found it possible and necessary to link up with each other that resulted in the extraordinary event we know as May '68. But, and this is Ross's main point, none of these groups – students, workers, farmers, and so on – can be treated as pre-existing, self-contained, homogeneous entities. As for the encounters between these heterogeneous groups, they obviously cannot be treated in the same way that one might regard the actions of states agreeing by treaty to work together for the sake of a common interest. Ross suggests that the process might better be described as 'cultural contamination' and argues that it 'was encounters with people different from themselves – and not the glow of shared identity – that allowed a dream of change to flourish' (Ross 2002: 130). Ross's purpose, however, is not to assert the primacy of the individual, or indeed the primacy of difference, two moves which, as Jameson has shown in his various critiques of Anglo-American cultural studies, lead inexorably to political paralysis. By repudiating both the collective and the same under the utterly misconceived banner of 'anti-totalisation', cultural studies has for all practical intents and purposes divested itself of two of the most basic prerequisites for politics, namely the potential for a common action and a common aim (Jameson 1994). Well aware of the pitfalls of valorising the individual at the expense of the collective, the different at the expense of the same, Ross argues for an approach to the sociological dimension of May '68 that is perfectly attuned to Deleuze and Guattari's work (Ross 2002: 170).

In the long aftermath of May '68, an event which many French intellectuals came to think of as a 'failed revolt', the question of power – what it is, how it functions, who has it and who does not – was the principal concern of the majority of France's leading intellectuals. Along with the interrelated questions concerning the possibility of resistance and (more concretely) the possibility of political action itself, power was the uppermost concern of Louis Althusser, Alain Badiou, Etienne Balibar, Jean Baudrillard, Pierre Bourdieu, Cornelius Castoriadis, Hélène Cixous, Régis Debray, Jacques Derrida, Michel Foucault, Luce Irigaray, Julia Kristeva, Henri Lefebvre, Jean-François Lyotard, Nicos Poulantzas, Jacques Rancière and Paul Virilio. Very far from homogeneous in their political and philosophical allegiances – though most would own to a Left-orientation, providing it was clear that didn't mean they were Marxists (or, in the case of Althusser and Althusserians like Balibar and Rancière, they would own to a Left-orientation providing it was understood that meant they were a very particular type of Marxist) – there is a surprising degree of consistency across the quite diverse body of work produced by these writers in the decade after May '68 concerning the question of power. For instance, they all accept that power is not a simple matter of coercion or repression, the dominance of one group of people over another; that contemporary society cannot be understood in this way as the product or the expression of a powerful ruling elite exercising influence over a powerless majority. Moreover, they all agree that power resides in the ordinary, that tradition, law, language and the way we organise our daily lives is directly and indirectly inflected by the operations of power. They also accept that power requires a degree of complicity on the part of the ruled to function, but disagree on the question of how this achieved. They all agree that the situation in which the planet finds itself at the end of the twentieth century is parlous, to say the least, and they more or less agree on the cause, namely capitalism; what's more, they all agree things are in desperate need of change, but they disagree – often quite vehemently – as to how this change might be achieved. The debate that raged in respect to this last question concerned power directly inasmuch as the central point of contention was whether or not change could be achieved without forcibly taking power through some kind of revolutionary action.

Anti-Oedipus was lobbed into this fray like an intellectual cluster bomb – it had multiple targets, from the primacy of the signifier in linguistics to the dependency on lack in psychoanalysis, but its primary objective was (as Michel Foucault astutely points out in his highly influential preface to the English translation) to caution us against the fascist inside, the desire to seize power for oneself. The principal thesis of *Anti-Oedipus*, around which its many conceptual inventions turn, is that revolution is not primarily or even necessarily a matter of taking power. Insofar as taking power means preserving all the old institutions and ideas in which power is invested it could even be said that revolutions of this type are actually counter-revolutionary in purpose and intent because they change nothing essential. Ultimately for Deleuze and Guattari, accounting for May '68 necessitated a complete rethinking of political concepts like power, power relations, groups, group identity, the event, and so on, and insofar as it takes up this challenge, *Anti-Oedipus* is appropriately described as a May '68 book.

References

Bogue, R. (1989), *Deleuze and Guattari*, London: Routledge.

Deleuze, G. (1995), *Negotiations, 1972–1990*, trans. Martin. Joughin, New York: Columbia University Press.

Deleuze, G. (2004), *Desert Islands and Other Texts 1953–1974*, trans. M Taormina, ed. D. Lapoujade, New York: Semiotext(e).

Deleuze G. and F. Guattari (2001), *Mille Plateaux: Capitalisme et Schizophrénie 2*, Paris: Les Éditions de Minuit.

Deleuze G. and F. Guattari (2002), *L'Anti-Oedipe: Capitalisme et Schizophrénie*, Paris: Les Éditions de Minuit.

Deleuze G. and F. Guattari F (2004a), *Anti-Oedipus*, trans. R. Hurley, M. Seem and H. R. Lane, London and New York: Continuum.

Deleuze G. and F. Guattari (2004b), *A Thousand Plateaus*, trans. Brian Massumi, London and New York: Continuum.

Deleuze, G. and C. Parnet (2002), *Dialogues II*, trans. H. Tomlinson and B. Habberjam, London: Continuum.

Fields, B. (1984), 'French Maoism', in S. Sayres et al. (eds), *The 60s without Apology*, Minneapolis: University of Minnesota Press.

Genosko, G. (2002), *Félix Guattari: An Aberrant Introduction*, London: Continuum.

Genosko, G. (2007), 'The Figure of the Arab in *Three Billion Perverts*', *Deleuze Studies*, 1(1): 60–78.

George, S. (2004), *Another World is Possible If . . .*, London: Verso.

Guattari, F. (1995), *Chaosophy*, ed. S. Lotringer, New York: Semiotext(e).

Guattari, F. (2006), *The Anti-Oedipus Papers*, trans. K. Gotman, ed. S. Nadaud, New York: Semiotext(e).

Hallward, P. (2006), *Out of this World: Deleuze and the Philosophy of Creation*, London: Verso.

Holloway, J. (2005), *Change the World Without Taking Power*, London: Pluto Press.

Jameson, F. (1990), *Late Marxism: Adorno, or, The Persistence of the Dialectic*, London: Verso.

Jameson, F. (1994), *The Seeds of Time*, New York: Columbia.

Nadaud, S. (2006), 'Love Story between an Orchid and a Wasp', in F. Guattari, *The Anti-Oedipus Papers*: 11–22.

Negri, A. (2004), *Negri on Negri: Antonio Negri in Conversation with Anne Dufourmantelle*, trans. M. B. DeBevoise, London: Routledge.

Ross, K. (2002), *May '68 and its Afterlives*, Chicago: Chicago University Press.

Thoburn, N. (2003), *Deleuze, Marx and Politics*, London: Routledge.
Tournier, M. (1988), *The Wind Spirit: An Autobiography*, trans. A. Goldhammer, Boston: Beacon Press.

Notes

1. For an excellent discussion of this apparent contradiction in Deleuze's approach to 'praxis' see Thoburn 2003: 35–7.
2. He was involved in GIP for instance and spoke out against the treatment of Palestinians, the first Gulf War, etc.
3. It is now available on DVD.
4. Of those students, Deleuze said: 'I never told that audience what they meant to me, what they gave me. . . It was like an echo chamber, a feedback loop, in which an idea reappeared after going, as it were, through various filters. It was there I realised how much philosophy needs not only a philosophical understanding, through concepts, but a nonphilosophical understanding, rooted in percepts and affects. You need both' (Deleuze and Parnet 2002: 139).
5. Pinhas also used Deleuze's voice in other ways, combining it with music to produce Deleuze-inspired electronica of a peculiarly haunting variety.
6. Interestingly enough, Guattari described himself as being heavily influenced by Sartre, even going so far as to admit certain concepts like deterritorialisation are simply Sartre's in disguise.
7. As Negri records here, it was Guattari who arranged for Negri's relocation from Italy to France in the early 1980s with the help of Amnesty International. They collaborated on a variety of political projects, including an ultimately forlorn but important attempt to forge an alliance between the Reds and the Greens, and produced a manifesto, *Communists Like Us: New Spaces of Liberaty, New Lines of Alliance* (1985), which foreshadows many of themes Negri would take up in his collaborative work with Michael Hardt, especially *Empire* (2000).
8. For a detailed analysis of this publication see Genosko 2007. The full text of the journal can now be viewed on the web at http://www.criticalsecret.com/n8/quer/4per/pedo/01.htm.
9. Reflecting on the meeting with Lacan to discuss *Anti-Oedipus*, Guattari wrote in his diary that he felt something had broken between them (Guattari 2006: 344).
10. 'May '68 was the largest mass movement in French history, the biggest strike in the history of the French workers' movement (involving some 9 million workers), and the only "general" insurrection the overdeveloped world has known since the Second World War. It was the first general strike that extended beyond the traditional centres of industrial production to include workers in the service industries, the communication and culture industries – the whole sphere of social reproduction. No professional sector, no category of worker was unaffected by the strike; no region, city, or village in France was untouched' (Ross 2002: 4).
11. 'May '68 came as a shock to Gilles and me, as to many others: we didn't know each other, but this book, now, is nevertheless a result of May' (Deleuze 1995: 15).
12. Similarly they rejected as pointless the shrill demand for self-criticism the Maoists made, arguing that it did nothing to engage power as it actually functions. As Deleuze put it, 'in May 1968 the leftists lost a lot of time insisting that professors engage in public self-criticism as agents of bourgeois ideology. It's stupid, and it simply fuels the masochistic impulses of academics' (Guattari 1995: 56).

13. They certainly didn't share the view of commentators like Raymond Aron and (much more recently) Pierre Nora who declared that nothing happened that May. Nor would they go along with the New Philosophers' attempt a decade later to bury the memory of May '68 altogether. See Ross 2002: 67; 171.

14. Thus, I have to disagree with Peter Hallward (2006: 7) when he argues that Deleuze's work has little to offer politically speaking because Deleuze fails to live up to Marx's dictum that philosophy should not simply try to understand society, it should try to change it as well. In my view, he caricatures Deleuze as a contemplative philosopher whose thought somehow resists doing what needs to be done. For Deleuze, theoretical work is in itself a political act because it creates new conditions for thought and there is no more potent formula for change than the changing of ideas and attitudes. In this regard, Deleuze's political thought is compatible with the positions outlined by Holloway (2005) and George (2004).

15. As Ronald Bogue observes, the renown of *Anti-Oedipus* was something of a double-edged sword. Deleuze and Guattari 'became symbols of anti-psychiatry and the spirit of May, and as a result the broader concerns that informed *Anti-Oedipus* were often ignored' (Bogue 1989: 6).

16. On a practical level, too, it was the anti-Vietnam groups, like the CVN and CVB, both of which formed in 1967, which provided the organisational nuclei that helped escalate May '68 from a localised student protest to a nationwide strike.

17. As Nicholas Thoburn (2003) has demonstrated, the workers' movements in Italy were very important to Deleuze and Guattari.

ılar Entities and Molecular Populations
Human History

ınuel DeLanda

We no longer believe in a primordial totality that once existed, or in a final totality that awaits us at some future date. We no longer believe in the dull gray outlines of a dreary, colorless dialectic of evolution, aimed at forming a harmonious whole out of heterogeneous bits by rounding off their rough edges. We believe only in totalities that are peripheral. And if we discover such a totality alongside various separate parts, it is a whole of these particular parts but does not totalise them; it is a unity of all those particular parts but does not unify them; rather it is added to them as a new part fabricated separately.

Gilles Deleuze and Félix Guattari, Anti-Oedipus

A crucial question confronting any serious attempt to think about human history is the nature of the historical actors that are considered legitimate in a given philosophy. One can, of course, include only human persons as actors, either as rational choosers (as in microeconomics) or as phenomenological subjects (as in micro-sociology). But if we wish to go beyond this we need a proper conceptualisation of social wholes. The very first step in this task is, clearly, to devise a means to block micro-reductionism, a step usually achieved by the concept of *emergent properties*, properties of a whole that are more than the sum of the properties of its parts. This means that we cannot conceive of social wholes as mere aggregates of many rational decision makers or many phenomenological experiences. But this leaves open the possibility of macro-reductionism, as when one rejects the rational actors of microeconomics in favour of society as a whole, a society that fully determines the nature of its component parts. Blocking macro-reductionism demands a second concept, the concept of *relations of exteriority* between parts. Unlike wholes in which 'being part of this whole' is a defining characteristic of the parts, that is, wholes in which the parts cannot subsist independently of the relations they have with each other (relations of interiority), we need to conceive wholes that emerge from the interactions between their parts but in which these parts retain a relative autonomy, so that they can be detached from one whole and plugged into another, entering into new interactions.

With these two concepts we can define social wholes, such as inter-personal communities or institutional organisations, that cannot be reduced to the persons that compose them but that, at the same time, do not reduce these persons to the whole, fusing them into a totality in which their individuality is lost. Take, for example, communities as they existed up to two hundred years ago (and in many small towns and ethnic neighbourhoods to this day). In these communities an important emergent property is the degree to which their members are linked together. One way of examining this property is to study networks of relations, counting the number of direct and indirect links per person, and studying their connectivity. A crucial property of these networks is their *density*, an emergent property that may be roughly defined by the degree to which the friends of the friends of any given member (that is, his or her indirect links) know the indirect links of others. Or to put it still more simply, by the degree to which everyone knows everyone else. In a dense network word of mouth travels fast, particularly when the content of the gossip is the violation of a local norm: an unreciprocated favour, an unpaid bet, an unfulfilled promise. This implies that the community as a whole can act as a device for the storage of personal reputations and, via simple behavioural punishments like ridicule or ostracism, as an enforcement mechanism. The property of density, and the capacity to store reputations and enforce norms, are non-reducible properties of the community as a whole, but neither involves thinking of it as a seamless totality in which the members have lost their personal identity. A similar point applies to institutional organisations. Many of these are characterised by the possession of an authority structure in which rights and obligations are distributed asymmetrically in a hierarchical way. But the exercise of authority must be backed by *legitimacy* if enforcement costs are to be kept within boundaries. Legitimacy is an emergent property of the entire organisation even if it depends for its existence on personal beliefs about its source: a legitimising tradition, a set of written regulations, or even for small organisations, the charisma of a leader. The degree to which legitimate authority is irreducible to persons can, of course, vary from case to case. In particular, the more organisational resources are linked to an office or role (as opposed to the incumbent of that role) the more irreducible legitimacy is. Nevertheless, and however centralised and despotic an organisation may be, its members remain ultimately separable from it, their actual degree of autonomy depending on contingent factors concerning social mobility and the existence of opportunities outside the organisation.

It is this type of social whole produced by relations of exteriority, or wholes that do not totalise their parts, that the quotation above refers to (Deleuze and Guattari never use the term 'emergent property', but irreducible properties are implied in many of their analyses). But that quotation also mentions another important characteristic: that the wholes are peripheral or exist alongside their parts. What exactly does this mean? It clearly cannot be a spatial reference, as if communities or organisations existed nearby or to one side of the persons that compose them. It is rather an ontological remark. It means that communities or organisations, to stick to these examples, are every bit as historically individuated as the persons that compose them.

While it is true that the term 'individual' has come to refer to persons (or organisms in the case of animals and plants) it is perfectly coherent to speak of individual communities, individual organisations, individual cities, or individual nation states. In this extended sense the term 'individual' has no preferential affinity for a particular scale (persons or organisms) and refers to any entity that is *singular and unique*. Unlike philosophical approaches that make a strong ontological distinction between levels of existence (such as genus, species, organism), here all entities exist at the same ontological level differing only in scale. The human species, for example, is every bit as historical an individual as the organisms that compose it. Like them, it has a date of birth (the event of speciation) and, at least potentially, a date of death (the event of extinction). In other words, the human species as a whole exists 'alongside' the human organisms that compose it, alongside them in an ontological plane that houses only historically individuated entities.

From the point of view of a materialist philosophy of history this conception of social wholes as concrete individuals constrains the field of valid historical actors. For example, an entity such as 'the Market' would not be an acceptable entity to be incorporated into explanations of historical phenomena: *it is not an individual singularity but a reified generality*. On the other hand, the marketplaces or bazaars that have existed in every urban centre since antiquity, and more recently in every European town since the eleventh century, are indeed individual singularities and can therefore figure as actors in explanations of the rise of Europe and the commercial revolution that characterises the early centuries of the past millennium. Equally valid are the regional trading areas that emerged when the towns that housed local marketplaces were linked together by roads and the trade among them reached a threshold of regularity and volume. Regional markets began to play an important economic role in Europe by the fourteenth century and, as historically constituted wholes composed of local marketplaces, they are valid historical actors. So are the national markets that, starting in England in the eighteenth century, came into being by stitching together, sometimes forcefully, many provincial trading areas themselves composed of many regional markets. By the nineteenth century the railroad and the telegraph made the creation of national markets a simpler task and they emerged in places like France, Germany and the United States, playing an important role in the economic history of these countries. Today we are witnessing the creation of continental markets, made out of pre-existing national markets, but it is too early to tell what kind of impact they will have as historical actors.

Besides being a good example of how to replace reified generalities like 'the Market' with concrete individual singularities, national markets also illustrate another important point. The distinction between micro and macro should never be made absolute, with individual persons playing the role of micro-entity and society as a whole the role of macro-entity. Rather, micro and macro should be made relative to a particular scale, or more exactly, to a particular relation of part to whole. Compared to the regional trading areas they compose, local marketplaces are micro while regional markets are macro. But the latter are micro relative to provincial markets which are, in turn, micro relative to national markets. In other words, in a given country there may be many levels of micro–macro relations between the person and the nation state, kingdom, or empire as a whole. And, unlike the example just mentioned, the part-to-whole relation need not form a neat succession resembling a Russian doll. Starting from individual persons the next macro level bifurcates into at least two different types of individual entities, the already mentioned interpersonal communities and institutional organisations, a divergence that breaks the Russian doll image. Several communities can, in turn, form alliances and become a larger entity, as in those coalitions of communities in the eighteenth and nineteenth centuries that became important historical actors as social justice movements. Organisations can also form larger wholes, either in a more or less decentralised way, exemplified by industrial networks composed of many firms, their suppliers and distributors, or in a centralised way as illustrated by a federal government. The latter is a whole in which many organisations are arranged in a hierarchical way and operate at different scales, some with a jurisdiction extending to the entire country, others with authority only within the boundaries of a province or state, and others operating within the limits of an urban centre and its surrounding region. Such a concrete and singular hierarchical whole composed of organisations is what, ideally, should replace the reified generality referred to by the term 'the State' in historical explanations.

At this point it may be objected that Deleuze and Guattari do in fact include in their historical explanations reified generalities. This need not be a problem since sometimes it is convenient to use familiar terms like 'the Market' or 'the State' when being more precise would get in the way of an argument. A more problematic question concerns that of the relativity of the micro–macro distinction. Deleuze and Guattari sometimes seem to imply that there are indeed only two levels, the micro or molecular, corresponding to the individual person, and the macro or molar, corresponding to society as a whole. But this may also be a convenience when discussing relatively simple social wholes, as when they contrast the supple segmentarity of primitive societies to the rigid segmentarity of early state societies, neither of which contain many intermediate levels. Moreover, other passages show that they did consider the distinction between the molecular and the molar to be applicable at all levels of scale. Take for example the following quotation:

> Every society, and every individual, are thus plied by both segmentarities simultaneously: one molar, the other molecular . . . In short everything is political, but every politics is simultaneously a macropolitics and a micropolitics. Take aggregates of the perception or feeling type: their molar organisation, their rigid segmentarity, does not preclude the existence of an entire world of unconscious micropercepts, unconscious affects, fine segmentations that grasp or experience different things, are distributed and operate differently. (Deleuze and Guattari 1987: 213)

In this quotation they are applying the micro–macro distinction to the individual person's experience, that is, at the level classically referred to as 'micro'. Their discussion of fascism on the following page, on the other hand, shows that the distinction may also be applied at other levels: a governmental hierarchy of organisations is macro while neighbourhood organisations are micro. But what about their explicit denial that the distinction between molecular and molar is a question of scale? In a discussion of the possible errors concerning this distinction they say that 'the two forms are not simply distinguished by size, as a small form and a large form; although it is true that the molecular works in detail and operates in small groups, this does not mean that it is any less coextensive with the entire social field than molar organization' (Deleuze and Guattari 1987: 215). Leaving aside the question of whether a 'social field' is a valid entity in this ontology (a question to which I return below) this quotation should be taken to deny that the distinction between molecular and molar is about *absolute scale*, as opposed to relative scale (relative to a given part-to-whole relation). Otherwise it would be like saying that atoms and organic cells are not distinguished by size (which is false) because in the human body wherever there is a cell there is an atom; that is, atoms and cells are coextensive with the human body (which is true). On the other hand, it is absolutely correct to say that the distinction between molecular and molar involves not just a difference in scale but also a qualitative difference: while some entities, at any given scale, may be captured into larger wholes that assign their parts functions and give them a stable form, those same entities may also exist as *molecular populations* that remain supple and avoid a rigid segmentation into form and function. It is in their discussion of this qualitative difference that Deleuze and Guattari offer some truly new ideas of a theory of social wholes. In particular, they add a crucial insight into the mode of individuation characteristic of molecular populations:

> There is a mode of individuation very different from that of a person, subject, thing, or substance. We reserve the name *haecceity* for it. A season, a winter, a summer, an hour, a date have a perfect individuality lacking nothing, even though this individuality is different from that of a thing or a subject. They are haecceities in the sense that they consist entirely of relations of movement and rest between molecules or particles, capacities to affect and be affected. (Deleuze and Guattari 1987: 261)

This quotation seems to contrast the individuality of persons to that of events, only the latter being true haecceities. But persons, like any other entity, have a micro and a macro side. Persons are not haecceities if what we are considering are populations of perceptions or sensations (as they may exist, for example, in a delirium). In this case it is these micro-components of personal experience that are haecceities while persons are the resulting molar entity. On the other hand, persons can be haecceities when they become part of populations that escape the grip of the social wholes that shape them and give them functions, as when a person leaves his or her community to join a pilgrimage, interact with strangers, and confront a series of eventful situations. But what does it mean to say that haecceities are defined exclusively by *speeds and affects*? The term 'speed' should be taken to refer not only to the rate of change of position with respect to time, but also to the rapidity or slowness with which change of any type takes place: rates of accumulation of power or capital; rates of emigration and immigration; rates of interaction between communities or organisations; rates of technological innovation and so on. For example, an industrial organisation which, from the macro point of view, may be characterised by a stable form and function, may from the micro point of view – that is, as a member of a population of organisations that is not part of a larger whole – be subject to pressures to change by the rapidity with which technology changes, by the slowness with which regulations adapt to these changes, and by the relatively slower or faster responses of its competitors, suppliers and distributors.

The term 'affect', on the other hand, means 'capacity to affect and be affected'. Capacities are different from the properties (formal or functional) that define molar entities although they depend on them. Properties are always given, actualised as present states of a thing, person, or social whole, while capacities may not be presently exercised and are actualised not as states but as events. To take a simple example, a knife is or is not sharp at any one moment; that is one of its properties. But its capacity to cut, though dependent on its being sharp, may never be actualised if the knife spends its life in the kitchen drawer. And when it is actualised it is so as an event which is always double: to cut and to be cut. In other words, a capacity to affect (to cut) must always be coupled to a capacity to be affected (to be cut). In addition, while properties may be exhaustively enumerated, capacities to affect cannot since they depend on innumerable combinations with other capacities to be affected. This means that while properties define the identity of a molar entity, the exercise of its capacities in conjunction with another molar entity may be a source of change and innovation. Thus, while an industrial organisation may have certain defining properties, such as possessing a hierarchical authority structure, these properties give it a variety of capacities to affect defined only in conjunction with social entities having the right capacities to be affected by it. As a member of a population of organisations a given industrial firm may have to exercise its capacity to prevail in a conflict of interest situation with other firms, and may have to improvise and adapt constantly to prevail; it may also have to interact with government agencies, in which case the capacities to be exercised are different, such as being capable of presenting a legitimate face for the purpose of obtaining licenses or certificates; and as the population differentiates (into media, educational, religious organisations) the capacities to be exercised will also vary, pushing the limits of the relatively fixed identity of the firm.

The speeds and affects defining the mode of individuality of the members of a molecular population not caught up into a molar entity are clearly more closely related to becoming than to being. Nevertheless they are also important in an account of how beings, such as emergent social wholes, acquire and maintain their identity, even if rates of change and capacities appear now in a subordinate role. If a given whole has irreducible properties then, for that very reason, it has emergent capacities, some of which are exercised to constrain (or enable) its own component parts. The parts must not only have compatible rates of change, but also the rapidity or slowness with which they change must be coupled to that of other parts. This is exemplified by the existence of homeostatic mechanisms in human bodies and in the control of rates of interaction through schedules and routines in organisations. The capacities of the parts are also subordinate. On the one hand, the very definition of relations of exteriority depends on the distinction between properties and capacities: component parts can retain their relative autonomy because playing a given function in a whole is not a property defining their identity, although it does involve exercising capacities to interact with other component parts. But what capacities are exercised and when is in many cases determined by the whole. Deleuze and Guattari introduced two other concepts to analyse the effect that an emergent molar entity has over its components: *territorialisation* and *coding*.

Territorialisation refers not only to the determination of the spatial boundaries of a whole (as in the territory of a community, city, or nation state) but also to a homogenisation of the roles played by its component parts. The members of a densely connected community, as mentioned earlier, are constrained by the capacity of the community to store reputations and enforce local norms, a constraint that typically results in a reduction of personal differences and in increased conformity. Communities can, nevertheless, still be tolerant of heterogeneity to a certain degree. But when two or more communities engage in ethnic or religious conflict not only will the geographical boundaries of their neighbourhoods or small towns be policed more intensely, so will the behaviour of their members as the distinction between 'us' and 'them' sharpens: any small deviation from the local norms will now be observed and punished and homogenisation of behaviour will increase. Conflict, in other words, tends to increase the degree of territorialisation of communities. Coding refers to the role played by language in fixing the identity of a social whole (or, in the case of animals and plants, to the role played by DNA). In institutional organisations, for example, the legitimacy of an authority structure is in most cases related to linguistically coded rituals and regulations: in organisations in which authority is based on tradition, these will tend to be legitimising narratives contained in some sacred text, while in those governed by a rational-legal form of authority, they will be written rules and standard procedures. A state apparatus, that is, a more or less complex hierarchy of organisations, performs coding operations that affect an entire territory and all the communities and organisations that inhabit it. The more despotic or totalitarian a state apparatus is the more everything becomes coded: dress, food, manners, property, trade. Deleuze and Guattari refer to this operation as 'overcoding' (Deleuze and Guattari 1987: 448).

These two processes yield molar entities, more or less territorialised and coded, out of molecular populations. But other processes, *deterritorialisation* and *decoding*, can perform the opposite operation, giving rigid molar entities a more supple form or even dissolving them into their component parts. A good example of deterritorialisation is the effect that long-distance communication and transportation technologies had on communities. A community of friends linked only by telephone (or more recently by the Internet) does not normally have the property that the friends of my friends are also the friends of your friends. That is, networks of friends or professional colleagues have a much lower density than tightly-knit communities inhabiting the same piece of territory, and this decreases their ability to store reputations and enforce local norms. And as the emergent molar entity looses this capacity to react on its component parts the latter become more molecularised. An illustration of a process of decoding is the effect of the spread of commercial and industrial organisations in Europe starting roughly in the fourteenth century. If a state apparatus can be said to be the main example of a coding (or overcoding) historical actor, these organisations had the opposite effect: to produce a constant flow of money, food, clothes, tools and so on, that circulated against the barriers imposed by government organisations. Precious metals, to take only one example, were heavily coded, particularly in the period labeled 'mercantilism' during which they were thought to constitute the essence of a country's wealth, and yet they routinely managed to leak through national frontiers. The spread of commercial organisations also had the effect of increasing social mobility, first creating and then extending the reach of the new middle classes, and since social mobility decreases the density of community networks, these organisations also had a strong deterritorialising effect.

The picture that emerges from this treatment of the micro–macro problem is one of fully embodied historical actors operating at many different scales while constantly having to perform maintenance operations to preserve their contingently produced identities. So far communities and organisations have been described as having as component parts human beings arranged into networks or authority structures. But for communities and organisations to be fully embodied actors we also need to include their physical infrastructure: the houses, churches, pubs and streets that make up a neighbourhood; the offices and factories in which the staff of an organisation works, including not only the buildings themselves, but also the tools and machines needed to perform its daily tasks. And once we do this, that is, once we locate these historical actors in time and space, and in a world of matter and energy, larger social wholes can be properly conceptualised. A city, for example, is composed of many neighbourhoods, industrial and commercial districts, public areas and government buildings, connected by a more or less extensive network of streets and transportation systems. Cities must also be given an ecological dimension because they must sustain themselves by controlling a stable flow of food and water, raw materials for construction and industry, money and rural immigrants, in and out of its boundaries. Many cities, in turn, can organise an entire geographical region when they become linked together. These may be landlocked regions, dominated by a regional capital and linked by roads, or coastal regions controlled by a maritime metropolis and connected by sea or ocean routes. The faster speed of ships over horses and carriages gave maritime metropolises (Venice, Antwerp, Amsterdam, London, New York) a higher degree of deterritorialisation and decoding up to the advent of the locomotive. The rapidity with which everything from money to news and diseases circulated in these ports, together with their more regular connections to alien civilisations, gave these cities a more supple identity: while landlocked capitals slowly distilled a homogeneous regional culture out of the contributions of immigrant cultural producers from all over a region, most maritime metropolises tended to have a more heterogeneous and hybrid culture.

This form of analysis/synthesis can be carried on further, in a similar manner to the example of national markets above: several regions eventually form a province, and several provinces can be stitched together by war to form larger entities such as a kingdoms, empires, or nation states. Clearly, this analytical and synthetic work needs to be done more carefully than the previous paragraphs suggest, but what matters is that at no point do we reach a level that we may call 'society as a whole', or for that matter, 'the socius' or 'the social field'. Cities, regions, provinces and nation states are all individual singularities – unique and historical, and designated by a proper name – not particular instances of a general category. This matters because in a materialist philosophy of history one must be committed to the mind-independence of physical, chemical and biological entities, as well as to the conception-independence of social wholes at whatever scale. Unlike idealist philosophers who can invent terms that do not refer to anything, materialists must use only terms that refer, at least when dealing with the actual (as opposed to the virtual) dimension of reality. (The virtual dimension, made up of *universal singularities*, is an entirely different subject that has not been dealt with at all in this chapter but that is crucial to explaining why entirely contingent historical entities can nevertheless display regularities.) So what are we to make of entities like the 'feudal social field' or the 'capitalist social field'? Here we must listen to what economic historians have to say even if this means breaking with Deleuze and Guattari. Take for example this quote from Fernand Braudel:

> Finally, if we are prepared to make an *unequivocal distinction between the market economy and capitalism*, might this offer us a way of avoiding the 'all or nothing' which politicians are constantly putting to us, as if it were impossible to retain the market economy without giving the monopolies a free hand, or impossible to get rid of monopolies without nationalizing everything in sight? . . . If people set about looking for them, seriously and honestly, economic solutions could be found which would extend the area of the market and would put at its disposal the economic advantages so far kept to itself by one dominant group in society. (Braudel 1984: 632)

Although Braudel is still using general terms here ('capitalism', 'the market'), the rest of his book makes it clear that he is referring to two different sub-populations of organisations not to reified generalities: commercial organisations engaged in wholesale as opposed to retail; industrial organisations based on economies of scale as opposed to economies of agglomeration; and so on. What is striking about the quote is, of course, the denial that capitalism (that is, big business organisations) ever had anything to do with free trade in markets. Indeed, Braudel's three-volume work is a systematic critique of the idea that capitalism was ever a society-wide system, let alone a worldwide one. He warns us that 'we should not be too quick to assume that capitalism embraces the whole of western society, that it accounts for every stitch in the social fabric' (Braudel 1984: 630). Deleuze and Guattari, on the other hand, remain under the spell of the bankrupt political economy of Marx. This leads them to postulate the existence of molar entities for which there is no historical evidence, such as a capitalist axiomatic of decoded flows. And worse, they base this concept on the least defensible Marxist ideas: 'If Marx demonstrated the functioning of capitalism as an axiomatic, it was above all in the famous chapter on the tendency of the rate of profit to fall' (Deleuze and Guattari 1987: 463). This 'tendency' is, of course, entirely fictitious. It is postulated on the grounds that, if wage labour is inherently a mode of surplus extraction, that is, if every bit of profit that an industrial organisation makes is ultimately a product of labour, and if machines are merely the coagulated labour of the those workers that put its parts together, then as capitalists replace humans with machines there will necessarily be a fall in profits. But has anyone ever produced evidence that a factory run by robots does not produce any profits? Of course not: machines also produce value (and profits) because they are not just a product of labour but, much more importantly, of engineering design and science. And industrial organisation (like Taylorism) is also a source of value, even if it carries hidden costs like the deskilling of a worker population.

Does this mean that the idea of 'an axiomatic of deterritorialised and decoded flows' is useless? No, because we can easily rework it into statements about the deterritorialising and decoding effects of individual singularities such as organisations and cities, particularly maritime metropolises engaged in international trade, without loosing any of Deleuze and Guattari's insight. This may involve correcting some of their historical explanations, as when they deny, contrary to Braudel, that capitalist organisations were first born in cities, that is, that 'it was through the State-form and not the town-form that capitalism triumphed' (Deleuze and Guattari 1987: 434). There should be room, of course, for honest disagreement here. But the crucial point is that, as materialists, we owe our allegiance to the material world, and to the best available historical evidence about the processes that actually occurred in this material world, and not to any individual thinker. If we conceptualise this world as having a flat ontology of individual singularities operating at different scales (in addition to the universal singularities that explain their regularities) then we must restrict the field of valid historical actors, and frame our historical explanations strictly in terms of them. This would be a better way of honouring Deleuze and Guattari's memory and work than any dogmatic attachment to what they actually said.

References

Braudel, F. (1984), *The Perspective of the World*, New York: Harper and Row.
Deleuze, G. and F. Guattari (1977), *Anti-Oedipus*, trans. R. Hurley, M. Seem and H. R. Lane, New York: Viking.
Deleuze G. and F. Guattari (1987), *A Thousand Plateaus*, trans. Brian Massumi, Minneappolis: University of Minnesota Press.

Notes on Contributors

Jeffrey A. Bell is Professor of Philosophy at Southeastern Louisiana University. He is the author of numerous articles and books on Deleuze, including *Deleuze's Hume: Philosophy, Culture and the Scottish Enlightenment* and *Philosophy at the Edge of Chaos: Gilles Deleuze and the Philosophy of Difference*.

Eva Bischoff is Assistant Professor at the North American Studies Program of the Institute for English, American and Celtic Studies at the University of Bonn. She holds an MA from the University of Cologne in modern history, political sciences and philosophy. She is currently completing her dissertation project in which she explores the possibilities and limitations of the theories and methods of postcolonial studies for the analysis of German history.

Ian Buchanan is Professor of Critical and Cultural Theory at Cardiff University and the founding editor of *Deleuze Studies*.

Claire Colebrook teaches English at the University of Edinburgh and has written books on Deleuze, Gender, Irony, Milton, Literary Theory and Post-structuralism. She is currently completing two book-length projects, one on vitalism and one on happiness.

David Deamer is associated with Manchester Metropolitan University where he lectures on cinema and co-ordinates Trauma, a cinema screening and research programme. David is co-founder (with Dr Anna Powell) of the on-line Deleuzian journal *AV* produced by MMU's English Research Institute. David is also a filmmaker with Touch My Face productions which produces academic content for *AV*, documentaries, music videos and short films. He is currently in the process of writing a book on Deleuze's taxonomy of cinema.

Manuel DeLanda is the author of four philosophy books, *War in the Age of Intelligent Machines* (1991), *A Thousand Years of Nonlinear History* (1997), *Intensive Science and Virtual Philosophy* (2002) and *A New Philosophy of Society* (2006), and many philosophical essays published in various journals and collections. He teaches two seminars at University of Pennsylvania, Department of Architecture: 'Philosophy of History: Theories of Self-Organization and Urban Dynamics', and 'Philosophy of Science: Thinking about Structures and Materials'.

Tim Flanagan graduated from the University of Dundee with a thesis on the enduring philosophical significance of the Baroque as set out in the works of Walter Benjamin and Gilles Deleuze. He now works as a tutor in London.

Jay Lampert is Associate Professor of Philosophy at the University of Guelph. He is the author of *Deleuze and Guattari's Philosophy of History* (Continuum, 2006) and *Synthesis and Backward Reference in Husserl's Logical Investigations* (Kluwer, 1995), as well as articles on Hegel, Derrida and other philosophers. Most of his work involves concepts of time, history and memory. He is currently finishing a book called *Simultaneity and Delay*.

Craig Lundy is a PhD candidate at the University of New South Wales in Sydney, Australia. His primary research is in Deleuze and the Philosophy of History. Other research interests include French and German historiography, Nietzsche and Bergson studies. Craig has also spent time as a visiting scholar at the University of Exeter.

Paul Patton is Professor of Philosophy at the University of New South Wales in Sydney, Australia. He is the author of *Deleuze and the Political* (Routledge, 2000) and editor (with John Protevi) of *Between Deleuze and Derrida* (Continuum, 2003). He is currently working on the relationship of Deleuze's conception of philosophy and politics to normative political theory and, with Simone Bignall, editing a volume on *Deleuze and the Postcolonial* (Edinburgh, 2009).

James Williams is Professor of European Philosophy at the University of Dundee. He has written widely on French philosophy. James's latest book is *Gilles Deleuze's Logic of Sense: a Critical Introduction and Guide* (Edinburgh University Press, 2008). His current research is on Deleuze and the philosophy of time, including a forthcoming book also for Edinburgh University Press.

Index